WITCH HUNTS

Witch Hunts

From Salem to Guantanamo Bay

ROBERT RAPLEY

McGill-Queen's University Press

Montreal & Kingston · London · Ithaca

© McGill-Queen's University Press 2007
ISBN 978-0-7735-3186-4

Legal deposit first quarter 2007
Bibliothèque nationale du Québec

Printed in Canada on acid-free paper.

McGill-Queen's University Press acknowledges the support of the Canada
Council for the Arts for our publishing program. We also acknowledge the
financial support of the Government of Canada through the Book
Publishing Industry Development Program (BPIDP) for our publishing
activities.

Library and Archives Canada Cataloguing in Publication

Rapley, Robert, 1926–
    Witch Hunts: from Salem to Guantanamo Bay / Robert Rapley.

Includes bibliographical references and index.
ISBN 978-0-7735-3186-4

    1. Terrorism – Prevention – Political aspects – United States.
    2. Judicial error – History. 3. Trials (Witchcraft) – History. I. Title.

JC571.R365 2007   323.4'9   C2006-904925-4

This book was typeset by Interscript in 10.5/13 Sabon.

To Kate, Alison, Ann, Rob, John, Brenda, and Pat

*My constant joys – without whom I might have started
writing much sooner*

Contents

Introduction

The great witch hunts of the past took place at times of great fear in the West. Fear was a prerequisite for witch hunts. It still is. There are frightening parallels between the hunt for witches in the past and the hunt for terrorists today. The witch has been replaced by the terrorist – with equal dangers to the individual, for the most pronounced characteristic of a witch hunt is that the accused is automatically treated as guilty.

This book first describes three famous witchcraft events of the seventeenth century: Bamberg and Wurzburg in Germany, Loudun in France, and Salem in Massachusetts. It becomes evident that witch hunts have certain characteristics – for example, the accused person is assumed to be guilty without proof, secret accusations are accepted, evidence against the accused is often falsified, torture can be used.

I then turn to modern events that occurred in times of fear: the Dreyfus Affair in France (treason), the Scottsboro Boys in Alabama (gang rape of two white girls by black boys), the Maguire Seven in England (terrorism). They were each about alleged crimes, but they all met the characteristics of and were, in fact, witch hunts. The witch had been replaced by a traitor, a group of rapists, a terrorist cell. Witch hunting is not solely an activity, but also a state of mind that develops when a society is under great stress – and such a state of mind exists today.

The third part of the book concentrates on the United States since 11 September 2001. The antiterrorist PATRIOT Act was passed six weeks later in a climate of fear and anger. There have been rising criticisms against reductions of individual rights and dangerous increases in state powers. Since 9/11 there has been increasing concern over government actions: the treatment of prisoners at Guantanamo Bay in Cuba and Abu Ghraib in Iraq, secret prisons, the torture and deaths of prisoners held by Americans overseas, the handing over of suspects to countries where torture is accepted (rendition). We have seen the Geneva Conventions ignored and flouted. There have also been concerns over military tribunals, the treatment of Muslim illegal immigrants, racial profiling, and the stated attitudes of top government officials, whose conduct in response to 9/11 has been characterized by excessive secrecy and an overemphasis on fear. In these kinds of conditions, witch hunts can occur.

A state of mind exists today in America and in the Western world that makes witch hunts a real and present danger.

Note on Sources

I use case studies in the first two parts of this book to illustrate the characteristics of a witch hunt, stories of the past: Bamberg, Loudun, Salem, Dreyfus, and so on. I have no hope or intention of writing new history. With the exception of the chapter on Loudun, none of the history is my own work. On each of these cases, there is a considerable literature and a mass of records both printed and electronic. All I have done is to write a synopsis of each story – an accurate synopsis – but each based on the work of many fine historians and recorders. I have tried to make the stories that I have used accurate but brief. The range of the stories is wide – in time, geography, and subject. Within each I have quoted from many records to give reality and life to what happened.

If I had been writing new historical studies, I would have provided the source for every fact. But real historians have already done so, allowing me to forego the hundreds of endnotes that this would have occasioned. Instead, I have identified the most important sources that I used so that the reader who wishes to go further can do so. I am grateful to those historians.

The third part of the book is different, being based on current events since 9/11. There, I have relied heavily on the American press for my information. I wanted to recognize publicly my sources, but I also wanted to avoid hundreds of endnotes for particular facts. Instead, in the Bibliography I have listed, for each of my chapters, the articles that I found particularly valuable. Here, I have listed the articles chronologically so that the reader can follow the sequence of events and, in doing so, observe how public opinion has changed on the different issues. I am grateful to the many journalists who wrote these articles and to a free press that has made them possible.

PART ONE

1

Witches and Fear of the Devil

All the wild witches, those most noble ladies,
  For all their broomsticks and their tears,
    Their angry tears, are gone.
                        William Butler Yeats

Yeats was wrong when he wrote these words – the witches have not gone! They are with us every year. For the month leading to 31 October, we are surrounded in every shopping centre by pictures of old women on fiery-orange backgrounds dressed in black, wearing pointy black hats, and riding broomsticks, often accompanied by their cats or dogs. Nobody needs to tell us that such a figure is a witch or that the cat or dog is her familiar, even though we may not be precisely sure what a familiar is.

We know that it is Hallowe'en. "Trick or treat" time. Fun time for the kids, going like small covens from house to house in homemade costumes to ask for candy. These are no evildoers; they chatter away and run from door to door, sussing out like magic those homes where nobody is there to deliver the goods and passing them by without a glance to hit on the next welcoming lights and decorations. Truth be told, there is no longer any "trick or treat" about it – the trick has pretty well disappeared; one gets a "treat" or goes on to the next house. But there used to be a "trick" element, not so long ago. As late as the mid-1900s, the witches and goblins overturned outhouses, soaped windows, performed minor evils on householders whom they did not like or who had failed to deliver – give us a treat or we will play a trick on you, causing you to regret it. No longer. "Trick or treat" is just a formula of words that we all recognize, part of an annual event based on dressing up in costumes and getting gifts of good things to eat.

This describes Hallowe'en for most of us. We have some underlying sense that long past there was more to it, something associated with witches – and with evil. Most of us, in fact, probably know more about witches than we think we do. If we were asked to do so, how would we describe a witch? Well, surely we would evoke the Hallowe'en witch that we are so used to, the old woman in black with the pointy hat and chin, the hooked nose, and warts.

Some 400 years ago, when everybody believed in witches, this was a fairly typical picture of the women who were accused. They were usually old women, village women – as most people lived in villages – often cantankerous old women without men left to protect them, poor widows, wrinkled with old age, with the hooked nose and pointed chin of a person without teeth. In tough times (and those were tough times in Europe, marked by disease, famine, and war), such women would beg a neighbour for bread, meat, milk, clothing, anything, sometimes to be refused, for the housewife was almost as poor as the old woman. Rejected, the cantankerous old besom would often cast behind her curses and vituperations as she hobbled off. No great harm done except to add to her reputation for unpleasantness. But perhaps within a few days an animal would sicken on the farm, a baby would fall sick, a husband or a son would fall and break an arm. Then the curses and threats would be remembered. This was literally trick or treat with a vengeance. The village whispers would begin and spread. The old woman had laid a spell, called upon the Devil to punish the ones who had rejected her. She was a witch, they would say. And others would add experiences that they had had, other examples of evil doing by the same old woman, local and family disasters that she had threatened or foretold. Sometimes the accusations would become formal, a trial would be held, and not infrequently a witch would be burned.

The Hallowe'en witch is stripped of her sense of darkness and evil, a distant reflection of reality. But the village witch was a mixture of what people of those days "knew" about witches and what they thought that they knew. The village witch was witchcraft in its endemic form.[1]

Did these old women really call upon the Devil? Certainly, they were thought to do so; no doubt some did try to practise witchcraft, and perhaps some threatened to use powers knowing that a threat alone might have an effect no matter how empty it might in fact be. Some were women with some knowledge of herbs and healing carried out with hints of secret arts, elements of faith-healing easily mistaken for knowledge and skill with a supernatural connection. Others were totally innocent.

But whatever their connection, witches were deemed serious enough and dangerous enough that between about 1580 and 1650 in Europe, between fifty thousand and eighty thousand human beings were executed as witches by burning or hanging, about three-quarters of them women.

What else do we associate with our Hallowe'en witch? She flies on a fiery-orange background, which is probably a reflection of two ideas: the fire that burned her to death and the fires of Hell, from where she got her powers. She flies on a broomstick. We all know that. Perhaps we don't recognize it as a phallic symbol, but at the same time we may have some idea that she is flying to meet other witches – in fact, flying to a Sabbath where witches met to perform indescribable acts and to worship the Devil.

Our Hallowe'en witches had serious forbears, or at least this was believed by our own forbears. Of course, Sabbaths were held at night. But why do I say "of course" when there isn't really any particular reason why the gatherings should have been at night? Because, instinctively, we know that they were, for witches were involved in evil deeds and evil deeds are performed in darkness and secrecy. "'Tis now the very witching time of night," says Shakespeare. We know what he means.

There was a time when witches roamed, or so everybody thought – and the thought was as frightening as the reality. Just as Christmas Eve is the day before Christmas, Hallowe'en is the day before the feast of All Saints, the hallowed ones. Going way back into European history, the Celts believed that on that night of Hallowe'en, the lines between this world and the next became indistinct, that the dead could come back, rising from their graves, and that those who had been evil could harm cattle, crops, and people. And witches could fly. It was a dark and dangerous night.

Witches could do evil in association with the Devil, it was thought. They could use his power, or he could act for them, or his demons would act on his behalf. Witches, all believed, would make a pact with the Devil: they gave him homage, and he gave them power to cast spells – a sort of reverse trick or treat. There was great fear of the Devil, his demons, and his witches. These were evil personified. The Devil himself, they believed, searched the world, constantly looking for the weaknesses in each man and woman, constantly tempting, constantly seeking out souls to take to eternal Hell. All evil was ascribed to him, the Prince of Liars – and witches were his agents. We can see how, in four hundred years, Hallowe'en has changed into today's trick or treat from a former real world of frightening fear and evil. When we talk of the times of the witch hunts, witches, and witch hunters, this is the world that we go back to – a world of fear. We descend from today's earthly happy holiday for children into Dante's circles of Hell. We go back four hundred years or so to a time of crisis.

Life was at best short in those times, uncertain, as disaster could strike at any moment. Half the children born never lived to be adults, and most of those who died did so in their first five years. The early seventeenth century was a period of natural disasters: the weather was frightful, crop losses were terrible, famine followed. The roads were poor, bridges were infrequent, and canals hardly existed; a famine in one area could not be offset by good crops even from a fortunate area close by. The results of famine were widespread sickness and death. Nor was climate the only source of famine and disaster. Dynastic and religious wars swept across much of Europe at the time, killing, destroying crops, spreading the diseases that followed in the wake of armies.

Throughout the Christian centuries, the church had provided consolation in times of troubles, but in these years between the Black Death and the middle of the seventeenth century, the church reflected the fears of its people and even led them. It concentrated on the dangers of earthly life, the multitude of sins, the temptations of the Devil, of the World, and of the Flesh, the barriers to salvation. The church emphasized fear – fear of the Devil, fear of Hell, fear of the Jews, fear of the infidel, fear of all heretics, and fear of women, who were portrayed as the corrupters of men, the agents of the Devil, and his allies in witchcraft. In the witchcraft cases of the seventeenth century, the focus of fear was the Devil.

It was in this world, full of hardship, full of fears, full of stress, full of danger, that the great witch hunts took place, when dozens, sometimes hundreds, of men and women were hunted in one place, accused, and burned or hanged.

"Sentence first – verdict afterwards." Lewis Carroll wrote these words in *Alice in Wonderland*. They describe the essence of a witch hunt perfectly, for what must have terrified everybody was that in the great witch hunts, if you were accused, you were guilty. Terrible punishment was almost certain. The sentence was in effect passed before there had been a trial or a verdict because guilt was assumed, obliging you to prove yourself innocent – if you could – which was indeed difficult, for (again, as in *Alice in Wonderland*) the accuser, judge, and jury were all the same: "'I'll be judge, I'll be jury,' said cunning old Fury; 'I'll try the whole cause and condemn you to death.'"

There was a logic to the actions that followed an accusation. Since the accused was "known" to be guilty, any evidence favourable to her or him was clearly in error or due to lying – and if the latter, the provider of the evidence was deemed to be an accomplice and was treated as such (this naturally tended to reduce public support for the accused). As for evidence against the accused, sometimes there was not enough, even for these judges. But these accused were witches and thus "guilty" as well as clever enough, with the support of the Devil, to hide their evil deeds. They had to be brought to justice, and in such a climate of fear and guilt, doing so seemed to justify creating false evidence, accepting it, and defending it in the name of a "just" verdict. Since the accused was guilty, torture was permissible to obtain a confession or new accusations against others, for witches were always assumed to know other witches and to have accomplices. There was, moreover, an aura of secrecy to everything, secret accusers, secret accusations, secret testimony – all of which seemed justified to those judges. "How now, you secret, black, and midnight hags!" they might have quoted Shakespeare.

So let us see what great witch hunts were really like, how these characteristics of a witch hunt played out in reality. We shall see witch hunts at their worst, the great witch hunts of Bamberg and Wurzburg between 1626 and 1630.

2

The Bamberg and Wurzburg Witch Hunts, 1626–1630

What has become known as Europe's "witch craze" was at its height between about 1580 and 1650. Most witchcraft trials were local affairs involving only a few local victims, but from time to time the infection became massive in one place or another. These were the great witch hunts.

In Bamberg between 1626 and 1630, about 450 persons were accused of witchcraft: 317 women and 136 men. Of these, at least 278 were condemned to death. At the same time, an equally massive witch hunt was being pursued in Wurzburg just a few miles away. These were horrifying examples of mass witch hunts and of the public hysteria that accompanied such distortions of normal society.[1]

Bamberg and Wurzburg were small territories in what is now Germany. At the time, they were two little states among hundreds in the Holy Roman Empire, each ruled by a king, a duke, or a princeling. These particular two were ruled by prince-bishops who happened to be cousins: Prince-Bishop von Dornheim in Bamberg and Prince-Bishop von Ehrenberg in Wurzburg. From their titles, one can gather that these were Catholic territories, although each contained sizeable Protestant minorities. This would play its part when the accusations of witchcraft began to multiply. But there were other sources of tension in these societies. Germany was being devastated by the Thirty Years' War, with armies and rogue soldiers ravaging towns and countryside. It was also a period of long-term economic stagnation, bad weather, failing crops, and an advancing outbreak of the plague that would kill millions in Europe. It was a terrible time through which to live. This was a society being pummelled into a state of intense fear.

We cannot pin down a single cause or even a group of causes for the start of the witch crazes in Wurzburg and Bamberg. However, there is some evidence that the trigger (rather than the cause) was a failed harvest. When such a natural disaster occurred, particularly on top of other disasters that had already rendered life close to unbearable, people looked for a cause. Since their individual worlds were restricted to the locality in which they lived, they naturally looked for a local cause. A general famine might be blamed on God's anger at man's evildoing, but within a village, the local famine would often be assumed to have a local cause. This could lead to accusations of witchcraft. There is evidence, for instance, that after a severe frost in May 1626 had done enormous damage to the crops in the whole Bamberg area, petitions were raised asking why the sorcerers and witches were destroying even the crops. Surviving judicial documents in Bamberg record one trial in late 1626 where the accused woman confessed to taking part in a conspiracy to freeze and destroy the crops. Other contemporary Wurzburg trials contain similar references to witches being executed for freezing the wine crop. There is more evidence. By 1628 and 1629 some of the principal men of Bamberg were being accused. Two of them, burgomasters, admitted under torture that their evil miracles had caused weather to destroy crops, houses to collapse, and trees to be uprooted. So while we do not know exactly what started things in Bamberg and Wurzburg, the trigger event seems to have been a local weather disaster (within the whole series of European disasters). What we do know is that once things started, the two prince-bishops were convinced that the Devil was at work through his acolytes, the supposed witches, and that they were determined to pursue these women and men to the end.

The prince-bishops have been roundly and justly condemned for their excessive zeal in searching for and eliminating witches. But it is also fair to state that, given their time and place, they were "reforming" bishops, intent on improving the church in their territories. In much of Europe, the priests of the Catholic Church had grown lax in their morals and deficient in their education. A good reforming bishop would tighten up on morals, exercise discipline, institute seminaries to train new priests, and reform and renew ecclesiastical institutions. These two bishops did all of these desirable things in about the same heavy-handed but effective way that they dealt with the invasion of witches. As Walinski-Kiehl argues, they wanted to create "Godly States," Catholic states "where subjects would be devout, conformist and obedient." The elimination of witches and heresy was part of this drive toward the creation of Godly states in their principalities.

Witch hunting in these two territories did not start in 1626 with these two bishops. There had been an outbreak of "witchcraft" between 1616 and 1617, with 86 executions in Bamberg and some 300 in Wurzburg. Perhaps they might have continued if the beginning of the Thirty Years' War in 1618 had not drawn the attention of rulers to even more pressing priorities. But in 1626 and 1627 things started up again. The accusations of witchcraft and the trials seem to have begun in a small way, but they grew and ultimately ran out of control. The two prince-bishops believed that witches were active and operating in conjunction with the Devil; they had to be stamped out, as all heresy had to be stamped out in their territories. They had the means at hand. Torture!

The variety of increasingly terrible tortures that could be applied to a suspected witch are well known and can be found in any encyclopaedia of witchcraft. The purpose of such torture was not to punish the witch but to obtain the names of his or her accomplices; the search for the "truth" was what mattered. And what the minions of the prince-bishops were looking for in Wurzburg and Bamberg were the names of the people whom the witches had seen at the Sabbaths that they had attended.

In both Bamberg and Wurzburg the two men were independent rulers with territories sufficiently small that their power was absolute. But because they were bishops as well as princes, they were the supreme rulers in both the ecclesiastic and the secular fields. They could have torture applied without restriction – and the transformation of individual accusations of witchcraft into a mass hysteria was due to widespread accusations arising from torture.

According to the theories of the witch hunters, all witches, as part of their contract with the Devil, attended Sabbaths. At the Sabbath, witches met together and took part in fearsome acts of lechery and worship of the Devil. What went on at a Sabbath was well known; no doubt it was talked about around the fire at night. The early demonologist Martin Del Rio published a description in 1608:

There, on most occasions, once a foul, disgusting fire has been lit, an evil spirit sits on a throne as president of the assembly. His appearance is terrifying, almost always that of a male goat or a dog. The witches come forward to worship him in different ways. Sometimes they supplicate him

on bended knee; sometimes they stand with their back turned to him ...
They offer candles made of pitch or a child's umbilical cord, and kiss him
on the anal orifice as a sign of homage ... Sometimes they imitate the sacrifice of the Mass, as well as purifying with water and similar Catholic
ceremonies ... After the feast, each evil spirit takes by the hand the disci-
ple of whom he has charge, and so that they may do everything with the
most absurd kind of ritual, each person bends over backwards, joins
hands in a circle, and tosses his head as frenzied fanatics do. Then they
begin to dance ... They sing very obscene songs in his [Satan's] honour ...
They behave ridiculously in every way, and in every way contrary to accepted custom. Then their demon-lovers copulate with them in the most
repulsive fashion.[2]

It was equally well known that since witches went to Sabbaths from
widespread areas, they had to be able to travel great distances at high
speeds. This they did riding a broomstick (the phallic symbolism is
clear) or sometimes an animal. The Sabbath became a central element
of witchcraft trials, particularly so in the case of the mass witch hunts.
   Because witch hunters knew all about Sabbaths and because the
"witches" knew a great deal about these ceremonies from common
knowledge, the former knew what questions to ask and the latter knew
what answers were expected. The hunters in many areas even had their
list of standard questions that in themselves tell us much about the beliefs of the times. For example, in his book *Witchcraft*, Roger Hart tells
us that the justices in Colmar, in Alsace, asked the following questions,
among others:

How long have you been a witch?
Why did you become a witch?
How did you become a witch, and what happened on that occasion?
Whom did you choose to become your incubus?[3]
...
What demons and other humans took part in the Sabbath?
What food did you eat there?
...
Who are your accomplices in evil?
How can you fly through the air?
What tempests have you raised?
Who helped you to produce them?
What plagues of vermin and caterpillars have you created?

So the hunter would ask questions about what went on at the Sabbaths that the witch had supposedly attended. A denial, or the wrong answer, or an insufficient answer, would result in torture. From the question, the accused person would know what was required in response. Over time, a whole theory of Sabbaths developed – a self-perpetuating theory. The more that the accused admitted to having attended Sabbaths, the more the witch hunters became certain of their true existence. More detailed questions elicited more detailed answers. The whole system of demand and response, reinforced by torture, "proved" both the existence of Sabbaths and the existence of witches.

The questions were not limited to what had gone on at the Sabbaths that a particular witch had attended; the names of accomplices and acolytes, also present at the Sabbath, were likewise sought. The way to stamp out all witches was to identify them all. The victim might try to resist giving the answers, particularly names of friends and relatives. But the torture was so great and its increase so inevitable that few could resist. This questioning went on in all witch interrogations, concentrating on friends and adherents. But in the mass witch hunts, the demand became much wider, as the hunters sought to identify anybody and everybody whom the accused had seen at the event. Under torture there was no limit to the demand for names. The only way to stop the torture was to say anything that the inquisitors wanted to hear.

The Bamberg events started with powerless people, and the earliest accusations came in 1626. But at some point accusations (certainly under torture) were made against one or more members of the "establishment" in the city. Normally, an accusation against one of the leading members of the community would receive short shrift. It would be discounted as at least unreliable, having come from a member of the common classes, and probably would be dismissed without serious consideration. Even if it received a hearing, serious investigation would follow before such an accusation was given credence because it would be obvious to the friends and relatives of leading citizens that to accept an accusation against one of them was to open the door to accusations against all of them.

But Bamberg and Wurzburg differed from the norm. By 1628 the witchcraft trials had burgeoned into major events affecting large numbers, with the elites being included as witches. The accusations against important people seem to have been made in 1628 and 1629 – at least the important cases that we know about came from these years – and rather than being restricted by the elites, the accusations spread. In

1626, 15 men and women were accused (throughout the events, the men accused were about one-third of the total). In 1627 the numbers had risen to 85, in 1628 there were 137, and in 1629 they increased to 167, marking the peak of the craze. In 1630 the numbers decreased to 54 and to virtually nothing afterward.[4] So a clear rise, development, and decline over the years can be seen. And the witch hunts developed in this way at least partly because the prince-bishops were convinced that there was an invasion of witchcraft that they had to stamp out; the increasing numbers "proved" that they were right.

What might have added to the intensity of the witch hunts at the upper levels of society was that all the property of an executed witch was forfeit to the bishop's treasury, and the families of the accused, moreover, had to pay extensive fees for the incarceration and execution of their loved ones. This was of little significance when poor villagers were accused, but the income from rich burghers was a very different matter. The prince-bishop of Bamberg did very well out of it, and not only the bishop, for a whole body of associated trades and professions served the witch hunt in these mass cases: jurors, judges, lawyers, court officials, torturers, administrative record keepers, executioners, and even the tradesmen who supplied the wood and built the funeral pyres – all paid for by the victims' families. It is no exaggeration to say that in cases like Bamberg and Wurzburg, there developed during these years a witch-hunting industry. This of course tended to become self-perpetuating unless some outside force intervened to stop the excesses. Another development could result in a measure of retreat – for example, when the witch hunters themselves were accused as their victims brought out their names under torture. This eventually happened in both Bamberg and Wurzburg.

But during the heyday of events in Bamberg, the numbers of accused witches grew. So serious did matters become that the prince-bishop gave the task of stamping it out to one of his subordinates: Suffragan Bishop Friedrich Forner. A group of special lawyers was devoted to his assistance, and special prisons were set up, including a famous building, the Hexenhaus, or Witches' House, specially designed to hold and torture some thirty or forty of those who were accused. There seem to have been smaller equivalents in the smaller towns.

True, the officials who pursued the witch hunt made money out of it, but it should not be assumed that they were impelled by financial gain alone. These men were, in many cases, captured by hatred and fear of the witches and particularly, in Bamberg, by their obsession with the

Sabbath. The bishop's legal adviser was a man named Dr Ernst Vasoldt, who, in searching for witches, took torture to extreme lengths. Vasoldt often demanded of his "clients" one hundred names of accomplices or those seen and met at Sabbaths. Perhaps the first "quality" name was provided in response to such a demand – a demand so wide that it could include anybody. Perhaps a commoner was quite prepared to implicate prominent citizens. And once such men and women were denounced, they would of course denounce others, most likely others from their own class. Suspicion spread like a contagion.

Other elements, too, may have entered into who was named: personal enmities, political rivalries, jealousies, and power struggles may all have played their part. Such elements can be seen in three cases that can be followed in Bamberg: those of Dr Georg Haan, Johannes Junius, and Barthol Braun. We have enough information to see at least the outlines of what happened to them, and in the case of Junius, we have an unusual personal description of his last days.

Dr Haan was vice chancellor of Bamberg, a man of considerable importance. His normal duties would have involved him in questioning accused "witches." But he seems to have been a man of liberal views, at least in the sense that while he may well have accepted that there was a vast demonic attack on Bamberg – as everybody else seems to have done – he appears to have had his doubts about some of the cases. Indeed, he may have concluded that innocents were being swept into the net with the guilty and that excessive torture was resulting in those innocents falsely incriminating themselves and their friends. He seems to have shown some leniency in his treatment of accused witches, and this is possibly what led to his being denounced as a witch himself. This happened in 1628, which would probably have made him one of the first of the elites to be accused. Walinski-Kiehl has suggested that Haan's arrest may have had political overtones in that the witch hunter Vasoldt was jealous of Haan's rapid rise in the Bamberg hierarchy. Jealousy and the elimination of a rival could have been factors. Certainly, the onslaught on Haan was cleverly planned, not a frontal assault but a flanking attack. It was not he who was first accused but his wife and daughter. These were two of the earlier accusations; in fact, they were among the first arrested in 1627. They were soon terrorized into confessing. Haan recognized that a local appeal against their trials would have no success, but he and his son had the right of recourse to a higher authority, the Imperial Court of Appeal in Speyer, which was the court of the emperor. There, they soon obtained an injunction forbidding further proceedings against the mother and daughter. However, they were too late: when they got back to Bamberg, their womenfolk had already been tried and burned.

But worse was to follow. In the agony of their torture, the women had accused father and son, Georg and Adam, as accomplices. They were both arrested. While under torture, Georg Haan gave names. He denounced, among others, five leading burgomasters, who were friends and social equals, accusing each of them of sorcery. He admitted in full his own guilt. Nothing saved him. He was burned at the stake. To be a friend, as the burgomasters had been, or to be a relative in such times was to be at the greatest risk.

As for the son, Adam, he must have known of the agonies to which his father had been subjected during his examination and probably knew from his father's tales what others had suffered. Adam no doubt knew of the total effectiveness of the tortures and decided to forego them. He confessed, admitting like the others that he had met with one of the Devil's agents – in his case, under the guise of one of his servant women – and that he had had an affair with her. Only later did it become evident that she was a demon in disguise. Everything else followed from that: commitment to the Devil, attendance at the Sabbath, agreement to do the Devil's will, and, of course, execution.

An exceptional aspect of this case was that the emperor himself had intervened with an order for the release of the Haans on the grounds that "their arrest was a violation of the law of the Empire not to be tolerated." The prince-bishop ignored his temporal superior. But it is worth noting that as early as 1627 and 1628 what was going on in Bamberg was the subject of complaints to the imperial court and that the emperor took these matters seriously enough that he at least tried to bring about some rational limitation to the damage that was being done. We shall see more evidence of increasing imperial concern and intervention as time progresses. But it must be remembered that these events were taking place in some of the worst years of the Thirty Years' War, when the emperor and most of the hundreds of German states were involved in much greater issues. It was neither difficult nor dangerous for the prince-bishop to ignore his overlord, which he proceeded to do.

It is frightening to see how the innocent so quickly became guilty once the witch hunt was in full progress. In this small cameo, we can see how it went from wife and daughter to son and husband and then out from the family to friends and colleagues – in this case, the burgomasters. One of these, delivered up by Haan under torture, was Johannes Junius. He was a man of honour and reputation who had occupied his position since 1608. Now at fifty-five years of age he was suddenly arrested. He was confronted by Haan, who accused him there and then of having been at a Sabbath; Haan of course had been severely tortured by this time and no doubt was prepared to say anything. We have a partial record of Junius's examination:

On Wednesday, June 28, 1628, was examined without torture Johannes Junius, Burgomaster at Bamberg, on the charge of witch-craft: how and in what fashion he had fallen into that vice. Is fifty-five years old, and was born at Niederwaysich in the Wetterau. Says he is wholly innocent, knows nothing of the crime has never in his life renounced God: says that he is wronged before God and the world, would like to hear of a single human being who has seen him at such gatherings (as the witch-Sabbaths).[5]

Confrontation of Dr. Georg Haan. Tells him to his face he will stake his life on it, that he saw him, Junius, a year and a half ago at a witch-gathering in the electoral council-room where they ate and drank. Accused denies the same wholly.

Confronted with Hopffens Elsse. Tells him likewise that he was on Haupts-moor at a witch-dance; but first the holy wafer was desecrated. Junius denies. Hereupon he was told that his accomplices had confessed against him and was given time for thought.

On Friday, June 30, 1628, the aforesaid Junius was again without torture exhorted to confess, but again confessed nothing, whereupon ... since he would confess nothing, he was put to the torture, and first the Thumb-screws were applied. Says he has never denied God his Saviour nor suffered himself to be otherwise baptized;[6] will again stake his life on it; feels no pain in the thumb-screws.

Leg-screws. Will confess absolutely nothing (and) knows nothing about it. He has never renounced God; will never do such a thing; has never been guilty of this vice; feels likewise no pain.

Is stripped and examined; on his right side is found a bluish mark, like a clover leaf, is thrice pricked therein, but feels no pain and no blood flows out.

Strappado.[7] He has never renounced God; God will not forsake him; if he were such a wretch he would not let himself be so tortured; God must show some token of his innocence. He knows nothing about witchcraft ...

On July 5, the above named Junius is without torture, but with urgent persuasions, exhorted to confess, and at last begins and confesses:

When in the year 1624 his law-suit at Rothweil cost him some six hundred florins, he had gone out, in the month of August, into his orchard at Friedrichsbronnen; and, as he sat there in thought, there had come to him a woman like a grass-maid, who had asked him why he sat there so sorrowful; he had answered that he was not despondent, but she had led him by seductive speeches to yield him to her will ... And thereafter this wench had changed into the form of a goat, which bleated and said, "Now you see with whom you have had to do. You must be mine or I will forthwith break your neck." Thereupon he had been frightened, and trembled all over for fear. Then the transformed spirit had seized him by the throat and demanded that he should renounce God Almighty, whereupon Junius said, "God forbid," and thereupon the spirit vanquished through the power of these words. Yet it came straightway back, brought more people with it, and persistently demanded of him that he renounce God in Heaven and all the heavenly host, by which terrible threatening he was obliged to speak this formula:

"I renounce God in Heaven and his host, and will henceforward recognize the Devil as my God."

After the renunciation he was so far persuaded by those present and by the evil spirit that he suffered himself to be otherwise baptized in the evil spirit's name. The Morhauptin had given him a ducat as dower-gold, which afterward became only a potsherd.

He was then named Krix. His paramour he had to call Vixen. Those present had congratulated him in Beelzebub's name and said that they were now all alike. At this baptism of his there were among others the aforesaid Christiana Morhauptin, the young Geiserlin, Paul Glaser, [and others]. After this they had dispersed.

At this time his paramour had promised to provide him with money, and from time to time to take him to other witch-gatherings ... Whenever he wished to ride forth (to the witch-Sabbath) a black dog had come before his bed, which said to him that he must go with him, whereupon he had seated himself upon the dog and the dog had raised himself in the Devil's name and so had fared forth.

About two years ago he was taken to the electoral council-room ... at a table were seated the Chancellor, the Burgomaster Neydekher, Dr. George Haan, [and many others]. Since his eyes were not good, he could not recognize more persons.

More time for consideration was now given him. On July 7, the aforesaid Junius was again examined, to know what further had occurred to him to confess. He confesses that about two months ago, on the day after an execution was held, he was at a witch-dance at the Black Cross where Beelzebub had shown himself to them all and said expressly to their faces that they must all be burned together on this spot, and had ridiculed and taunted those present ...

His paramour had immediately after his seduction demanded that he should make away with his younger son Hans Georg, and had given him for this purpose a gray powder; this, however, being too hard for him, he had made away with his horse, a brown, instead.

His paramour had also often spurred him on to kill his daughter ... and because he would not do this he had been maltreated with blows by the evil spirit.

Once at the suggestion of his paramour he had taken the holy wafer out of his mouth and given it to her ...

A week before his arrest as he was going to St. Martin's church the Devil met him on the way, in the form of a goat, and told him that he would soon be imprisoned, but that he should not trouble himself – he would soon set him free. Besides this, by his soul's salvation, he knew nothing further; but what he had spoken was the pure truth; on that he would stake his life.

On August 6, 1628, there was read to the aforesaid Junius this his confession, which he then wholly ratified and confirmed, and was willing to stake his life upon it. And afterward he voluntarily confirmed the same before the court.

In this record, under torture, an innocent man was gradually forced to admit his guilt, to tell a story of his bewitchment that was created for him and given to him, and to provide the names of others seen at the Sabbath. But Junius also left another record. There is a touching letter, written in quivering hand and sent to his daughter during his questioning. The dry record of his inquisition is now given life by his own words, and the true horror of the witch hunt is revealed:

Many hundred thousand good-nights, dearly beloved daughter Veronica. Innocent have I come into prison, innocent have I been tortured, innocent must I die. For whoever comes into the witch prison must become a witch or be tortured until he invents something out of his head and – God pity him – bethinks him of something.

I will tell you how it has gone with me. When I was the first time put to the torture, Dr. Braun, Dr. Kotzendorffer, and two strange doctors were there. Then Dr. Braun asks me, "Kinsman, how come you here?" I answer, "Through falsehood, through misfortune." "Hear, you," he says, "you are a witch; will you confess it voluntarily? If not, we'll bring in witnesses and the executioner for you." I said "I am no witch, I have a pure conscience in the matter; if there are a thousand witnesses, I am not anxious, but I'll gladly hear the witnesses."

Now the chancellor's son was set before me ... and afterward Hoppfen Elss. She had seen me dance on Haupts-moor ... I answered: "I have never renounced God, and will never do it ... God graciously keep me from it. I'll rather bear whatever I must." And then came also – God in highest Heaven have mercy – the executioner, and put the thumb-screws on me, both hands bound together, so that the blood ran out at the nails and everywhere, so that for four weeks I could not use my hands, as you can see from the writing ...

Thereafter they first stripped me, bound my hands behind me, and drew me up in the torture. Then I thought heaven and earth were at an end; eight times did they draw me up and let me fall again, so that I suffered terrible agony ... And this happened on Friday, June 30, and with God's help I had to bear the torture ...

When at last the executioner led me back into the prison, he said to me: "Sir, I beg you, for God's sake confess something, whether it be true or not. Invent something, for you cannot endure the torture which you will be put to; and, even if you bear it all, yet you will not escape, not even if you were an earl, but one torture will follow after another until you say you are a witch. Not before that," he said, "will they let you go, as you may see by all their trials, for one is just like another ..."

And so I begged, since I was in wretched plight, to be given one day for thought and a priest. The priest was refused me, but the time for thought was given. Now, my dear child, see in what hazard I stood and still stand. I must say that I am a witch, though I am not – must now renounce God, though I have never done it before. Day and night I was deeply troubled, but at last there came to me a new idea. I would not be anxious, but, since I had been given no priest with whom I could take counsel, I would myself think of something and say it. It were surely better that I just say it with mouth and words, even though I had not really done it; and afterwards I would confess it to the priest, and let those answer for it who compel me to do it ... And so I made my confession, as follows; but it was all a lie. Now follows, dear child, what I confessed in order to escape the great anguish and bitter torture, which it was impossible for me longer to bear.

He then added his own statement of what he had confessed to at the trial, essentially as recorded above, but with some more details:

Then I had to tell what people I had seen (at the witch-Sabbath). I said that I had not recognized them. "You old rascal, I must set the executioner at you. Say – was not the Chancellor there?" So I said yes. "Who besides?" I had not recognized anybody. So he said: "Take one street after another; begin at the market, go out on one street and back on the next." I had to name several persons there. Then came the long street. ["Die lange gasse" – the name of the street.] I knew nobody. Had to name eight persons there. Then the Zinkenwert – one person more. Then over the upper bridge to the Georgthor, on both sides. Knew nobody again. Did I know nobody in the castle – whoever it might be, I should speak without fear. And thus continuously they asked me on all the streets, though I could not and would not say more. So they gave me to the executioner, told him to strip me, shave me all over, and put me to the torture. "The rascal knows one on the market-place, is with him daily, and yet won't name him." By that they meant Dietmeyer: so I had to name him too. Then I had to tell what crimes I had committed. I said nothing ... "Draw the rascal up!" [This is a reference to the torture to which he was being subjected – the strappado.] So I said that I was to kill my children, but I had killed a horse instead. It did not help. I had also taken a sacred wafer, and had desecrated it. When I had said this, they left me in peace.

Now, dear child, here you have all my confession, for which I must die. And they are sheer lies and made-up things, so help me God. For all this I was forced to say through fear of the torture which was threatened beyond what I had already endured. For they never leave off with the torture till one confesses something; be he never so good, he must be a witch. Nobody escapes, though he were an earl ...

Dear child, keep this letter secret so that people do not find it, else I shall be tortured most piteously and the jailers will be beheaded. So strictly is it forbidden ... Dear child, pay this man a dollar ... I have taken several days to write this: my hands are both lame. I am in a sad plight ...

Good night, for your father Johannes Junius will never see you more. July 24, 1628.

On the margin of the letter Junius added: "Dear child, six have confessed against me at once: the Chancellor, his son, Neudecker, Zaner, Hoffmaisters Ursel, and Hoppfen Els – all false, through compulsion, as they have all told me, and begged my forgiveness in God's name before they were executed ... They know nothing but good of me. They were forced to say it, just as I myself was."

This was the witch hunt at its worst! Or perhaps not. Perhaps inhumanity could go even farther. There is a suggestion that since Junius's letter to his daughter was preserved with the other documents of the accusation against him, it was in fact written with the complicity of his jailers, was never really going to be sent to his daughter, and never went. If this is so, then it was deliberately instigated in order to prove to Junius's judges that he was in fact recanting on his confession. Such an act would surely have led to the worst punishments that could be wreaked upon him.

Barthol Braun was the third of the elites for whom some record remains. He was thirty-nine when he was arrested in May 1629, almost a year after Haan and Junius. Like them, he was tortured, and like them, he confessed. He had been a councilman at Bamberg and had himself taken part as a witness in some of the earlier witchcraft trials. There is some indication that he may have been accused as a witch in part because of political rivalry within the city. But what is perhaps more important is that he was a "persecutor" who had suddenly become a "victim." This is different from Haan and Junius. They had not been witch hunters. Now a new situation existed that every other witch hunter could see and fear. They were no longer protected by being on the side of the angels; they could equally be accused of being in league with the Devil. This switch bore within itself the beginning of the end of this major witch hunt. Braun, tortured with leg vices and thumbscrews like those who had gone before – and these were considered mild forms of torture – confessed and was in turn executed.

At the same time as Junius was undergoing his torture, a witch hunt was being pursued in Wurzburg, just a few miles away, marked by the same kind of accusations, tortures, and executions, but whereas in Bamberg the majority of elites were lay people, in Wurzburg many were priests. Another difference in Wurzburg was that for some reason children were accused of witchcraft, tried, and executed. At least forty-one, mostly between the ages of ten and twelve, were accused and burned as witches. Why this is so is again unknown, but what it does reflect is the extraordinary social psychology that developed (and still develops) in mass hunts. William McDougall, in his famous book *Psychology: The Study of Behaviour*, noted long ago that in its behaviour the crowd will sometimes act quite differently from the normal behaviour of the individuals who compose it. The people of Wurzburg, as individuals, would never have condemned young children to death in numbers like this. Yet as a group, they acted in a way that showed a mass psychology that had a nature of its own quite separate from that of its individual members. This is typical of groups of people under great fear and stress – and typical of witch hunts.

The wild thrashing about in search of evildoers that occurs at the height of a mass witch hunt was happening in Wurzburg in the same way as in Bamberg. And just as we have Junius's letter, we have a contemporary document from the other city – but this time written not by one of the accused but by an important functionary. It is a letter written by the chancellor of the prince-bishop of Wurzburg in August 1629 to a friend. It is evident that the chancellor was most uneasy at what was going on and recognized at least some of the dangers and even the errors of the witch hunt policies of his master and his peers:

As to the affair of the witches, which Your Grace thinks brought to an end before this, it has started up afresh, and no words can do justice to it. Ah, the woe and the misery of it – there are still four hundred in the city, high and low, of every rank and sex, nay, even clerics, so strongly accused that they may be arrested at any hour. It is true that, of the people of my Gracious Prince here, some out of all offices and faculties must be executed: clerics, electoral councilors and doctors, city officials, court assessors, several of whom Your Grace knows. There are law students to be arrested. The Prince-Bishop has over forty students who are soon to be pastors; among them thirteen or fourteen are said to be witches. A few days ago a Dean was arrested; two others who were summoned have fled. The notary of our Church consistory, a very learned man, was yesterday arrested and put to the torture. In a word, a third part of the city is surely involved. The richest, most attractive, most prominent, of the clergy are already executed.

A week ago a maiden of nineteen was executed, of whom it is everywhere said that she was the fairest in the whole city, and was held by everybody a girl of singular modesty and purity. She will be followed by seven or eight others of the best and most attractive persons ... And thus many are put to death for renouncing God and being at the witch-dances, against whom nobody has ever otherwise spoken a word ...

To conclude this wretched matter, there are children of three and four years, to the number of three hundred, who are said to have had intercourse with the Devil. I have seen put to death children of seven, promising students of ten, twelve, fourteen, and fifteen. Of the nobles – but I cannot and must not write more of this misery. There are persons of yet higher rank, whom you know, and would marvel to hear of, nay, would scarcely believe it; let justice be done ... P.S. – Though there are many wonderful and terrible things happening, it is beyond doubt that, at a place called the Fraw. Rengberg, the Devil in person, with eight thousand of his followers, held an assembly and celebrated mass before them all, administering to his audience [that is, the witches] turnip-rinds and parings in place of the Holy Eucharist. There took place not only foul but most horrible and hideous blasphemies, whereof I shudder to write. It is also true that they all vowed not to be enrolled in the Book of Life, but all agreed to be inscribed by a notary who is well known to me and my colleagues. We hope, too, that the book in which they are enrolled will yet be found, and there is no little search being made for it.

The confusion of the times, and of ideas about witchcraft, can be read into this document. On the one hand, the good chancellor, on the level of this world, is appalled at how children, innocent young maidens, respected citizens, clerics, respected seminarians, and honourable city rulers can be hauled in and tortured and burned – it makes no sense to him. Yet in his postscript he talks of the extraordinary Sabbath that had taken place as though he believed every word of it. Perhaps he did! Or perhaps he described it in believing terms only because to do anything otherwise was to risk being deemed a witch himself if an enemy read the letter. We do not know. But we do know from his letter that this is what was being said in Wurzburg in 1629 by the witch hunters, and everybody must have been terrified that they might be accused next of having been seen at such a Sabbath.

The witch hunts in the two principalities eventually slowed and then died. A number of events seem to have come together to bring this about. One we have touched upon already (and one can see traces of this in the chancellor's letter): the elites of the two cities were beginning to recognize fully that they might be accused, just as their friends had been. For them, it was all coming too close to home. No doubt there was the increasing feeling not only that things were getting out of hand, but also that people were being accused, tortured, tried, and executed who were almost certainly innocent, not just one or two but large numbers. The views of many of the leading people probably had much in common with those of the chancellor in Wurzburg. But while the climate for change might have existed within each of the territories, it is doubtful whether this would have been enough to bring about an alteration; indeed, even to raise the possibility might well have been in itself cause for an accusation that the doubter was in league with the Devil. So change likely also needed external help. And it appears that plenty of this was developing.

One of the agents of change was a Jesuit. The Jesuits had been strong supporters of these witch hunts, but now they were beginning to have their doubts. One of the Jesuit priests in Wurzburg, Friedrich Spee, had been involved as the confessor in a number of Wurzburg trials. He came to the conclusion that it was not the truth that was sending these people to the pyre but torture. To him, this was a terrible self-revelation, for he had been among the men who had led these innocents to their horrible deaths. He raised his concerns in a book that was initially written anonymously and for a very limited circulation among those who were involved with or who could influence the events that were occurring; even he had cause to fear what would happen if his work became associated with his name. But it was taken to a Protestant town and printed, receiving a much wider circulation than intended and thereby, perhaps, having a much greater effect than it would otherwise have had. Nor was his the only work of this type, although it did become the most famous and had a considerable effect on the general climate of outside opinion about what was going on in the two principalities.

Then there was the emperor. We have seen that he had already come out firmly to the bishop of Bamberg demanding that the laws and procedures of the empire be observed and ordering the release of the Haan family. Ignored though he was in that instance, the matter would not rest there. Increasingly, prominent people, many of them relatives of those already executed, were fleeing to Rome and to the emperor's court in Regensburg. The stories of the atrocities multiplied. The emperor's demands became more imperative and could not be totally ignored. The climate was right for substantial change. This was affected too by the death of Bishop Forner, the fanatical leader of the pack, in 1630. And then, on top of everything else, there was a major change in the course of the Thirty Years' War when the Swedish Protestant king, Gustavus Adolphus, invaded the states of Germany. This was a crisis that overshadowed everything else, capturing the attention of all Germans. Gustavus Adolphus himself threatened to intervene in the excesses of Bamberg. Thus in 1630 there was a marked lessening of accusations and a lowering of tensions; there were far fewer executions, only a fraction of those in 1629. By 1632 the witch hunts were over. The prince-bishop of Wurzburg died in 1631. The prince-bishop of Bamberg died in 1632. Nobody had both the power and the conviction to relight the fires.

What went wrong in Bamberg? Underlying everything that happened was a desperate fear of the power of the Devil, combined with a general belief that this power was being exercised through the witches. Without this fear, the overriding impulse to stamp out the contagion would not have been present. What triggered a fear of the Devil in this case seems to have been a crop failure, a local disaster during a period of disasters. Witches were assumed to be the cause. Fear was a prerequisite because it gave the rulers of Bamberg and Wurzburg the support of the elite, at least initially, to create a witch hunt. A passionate fear is a common accompaniment to witch hunts – both then and now.

Another factor that made these events possible was that the prince-bishops had, at least temporarily, unrestricted powers. Once each decided that the good of the state demanded an overwhelming response against the enemy, there were no limits to the extremes of the actions that he could take. Their excessive actions were abuses of power. We know this because the emperor made it clear to them and demanded that they stop – as ultimately they had to do in response both to him and to Gustavus Adolphus. But for a time, in the turmoil that Germany (or more precisely the empire) was undergoing, they were able to exercise power to an unusual degree and to override normal legal and procedural processes. This is another feature commonly associated with witch hunts – the authorities are able to exercise unusual powers for some period. In this case it happened largely because of the chaos of the period. In others we shall find that public pressure to find and punish somebody will on occasion allow or even require the authorities to exercise special powers, even overriding long established legal protections.

Of course, in this case the authorities were able to bring extraordinary pressure to bear in finding the guilty persons: torture. It was torture that forced self-incrimination and torture that created false accusations against others. In Bamberg and Wurzburg the tortures were horrible and irresistible. But physical torture is not the only way to exercise force against an accused person, and in later cases we shall see a number of variations in the ways that pressure has been used to obtain both false self-incriminations and false accusations against others. In Bamberg and Wurzburg we see how far the authorities were permitted, even encouraged, to go in employing the most horrifying forms of torture when public fear and hatred of the accused persons was beyond bounds.

Finally, in both Bamberg and Wurzburg we see another feature common to all witch hunts. Under normal circumstances, evidence is collected until a specific person is accused of the crime. In witch hunts, this was – and is – reversed. The accusation came first, and then there was the search for evidence to prove the person guilty. We have seen this most clearly depicted in the case of Johannes Junius. He was accused by others under torture. Once arrested, he proclaimed his innocence, strong in the knowledge that the accusations were false. His captors and torturers were convinced that he was guilty because he had been accused. It was their task to force him to admit his guilt, to create an admission full of nonsense, and to accuse others. From the very beginning, there was to be no escape, no possibility of even considering that he might be an innocent man. This was the witch hunt at its worst.

All of these ills were performed by men who in large part believed themselves to be doing good. Anything was justified to stamp out the Devil and the witches because it served the interests of God and the Godly state. In the cases considered below, like those of Dreyfus and the Maguire Seven, parallels were at work; the authorities became similarly perverted in the belief that they were working in the interests of the modern Goodly state.

Fear is the parent of the witch hunt. It was fear that drove Bamberg and Wurzburg. In the natural world, there was fear of the failure of crops, fear of imminent starvation, fear of sickness and death. From the supernatural world, there was fear of witches and of the Devil – fear of evil. These were overwhelming fears that could only be erased by finding and burning those responsible.

We can understand fears of such great dimensions, even though we have not experienced them – the fear of a new worldwide disease, the fear of a nuclear bomb, the fear of a terrorist attack. It is fear at this level that we are talking about. This level of fear drives leaders and governments to centralize powers in order to defeat the evil and to protect society. This degree of fear reduces the rights and protections of individuals in the interest of the common good. In such a climate of fear, witch hunts can take place. It is fear that drives witch hunts!

3

The Characteristics of a Witch Hunt

One characteristic of a witch hunt is always present: to be accused is to be guilty. This is the result of intense fear. We saw this in Bamberg and Wurzburg, and we will see it in each of the cases yet to come. In Bamberg a terrible and threatening crime was committed, or so the populace thought: the destruction of the crops, with all that this implied in starvation, sickness, death. Hatred and anger followed the identification of the source of the evil: the witch. Retribution was demanded: burn the culprit. In such a climate of fear and hatred, with such a demand for instant action, reflection or second thoughts on guilt simply did not happen. A person accused was assumed to be guilty, and nothing but immediate justice would be accepted. Even burnings in error could be accepted as serving the common good. Better that ten innocents should die than that one witch should get away to commit much greater evil.

Do we find it hard to identify with such naive behaviour? Witches, after all, belong to a credulous past.

No, for we can understand such conduct. We have our own witches, witches who stir in us the same reactions of fear, hatred, and anger, compelling our demand for instant justice. Child sexual abusers are one example. Suppose that the staff of a daycare were accused of sexually abusing the children. Would the parents, and the neighbourhood, not immediately call in the authorities, close the school, demand that the accused prove their innocence – if they could?

We know that this is exactly the reaction. Take the McMartin case,
for instance, in the United States. In Manhattan Beach, California, in
1983, a mother who had a child in the McMartin Preschool accused
one of the staff of molesting her son, aged two and a half. There were
no medical signs of this, but the staff member was arrested. The next
day, the local police chief sent a letter to 200 parents telling them of the
arrest and asking them to question their children. The letter indicated
that they should seek information on oral sex, fondling of genitals, buttocks, or chest, and sodomy, possibly committed under the pretense of
"taking the child's temperature." As might be expected, parents were
shocked, scared, horrified, furiously angry. They questioned their young
children. New accusations came in multitudes, some of them becoming
more and more bizarre. Soon the whole of the Los Angeles area knew
what was going on. A consultant for the treatment of abused children
passed 400 children through a series of leading questions; rewards were
offered for reports of instances of abuse at McMartin.

Within months 384 former McMartin students had been diagnosed
as sexually abused, and seven staff members were accused of more than
200 counts of child sexual abuse. Millions of dollars were spent. Two
successive trials were held. The charges were never proved, and the
almost universal conclusion at the end was that there never had been
sexual abuse.[1]

The significance of this case in our context is not the almost certain
miscarriage of justice but that we can see how the public attitudes, from
the time of the first accusations, mirrored the attitudes of a witch hunt.
The fear of child sexual abuse was so overwhelming to the parents, and
to the public, that to be accused was to be guilty.[2]

Child sexual abuse is not the only crime that would raise such reactions. Today, if a Muslim in North America was accused of being a terrorist in hiding who was plotting to carry out an act of terrorism,
would we not assume guilt? Our justified fear of terrorists is so great
that we have passed special laws and procedures to deal with them, just
as there were special procedures to deal with witches. We can understand such fear in our own days. It is the same fear that our forebears
had. Their reaction was to find the witches and expunge them. Ours is
the same. We can understand what a witch hunt was all about.

Think of the consequences that flow from this assumption of guilt. To
put it in the modern context, think of something like the child sexual mo-
lestation case in a daycare setting. The accusation immediately becomes

public. The police say that they have a man in custody. Rumours abound in the workplace and the press. Everybody knows that he would not have been arrested if the police weren't sure. The police hint that there is much more behind it all than they can reveal right now. Angry and frightened parents demand action. Child counsellors questioning the children make new and wider accusations. New arrests and rumours of a network of child molesters and pornographers follow. Other daycare centres in the area fall under suspicion. Suspicion of people in daily contact with small children spreads.

By now, everybody "knows" that the original man accused is guilty. The crime is hateful and frightening. There is no way that the legal system, with all its delays and its maze of tricks, can be allowed to prevent justice being done.

That would be, and is, a typical reaction.

Now let us see what follows. He is guilty, so now we have to find the evidence to prove it. But the evidence is hard to find – this is a crime hidden in secrecy, where the victim is too young to know what was going wrong. What evidence there is, from case workers, doctors, parents, is often anecdotal, or observations are too long after the event for certainty. But since everybody knows that the man is guilty, all evidence against him is accepted and often exaggerated in its validity. If there is favourable evidence, it is discounted and ignored. After all, it follows that if he is guilty, the favourable evidence must be wrong – and perhaps not only wrong. Perhaps the "supporters" of this sexual abuser ought to be looked at a little more closely themselves. Try a threat or two. If they continue to "lie," they might themselves become suspects. Or mention that a charge for smoking marijuana or driving under the influence that was never pursued by the police could still be raised, or that a secret affair might be leaked to the wife if there is no cooperation. Secret accusations might be accepted, made by secret accusers. Jailhouse evidence might be manufactured – or bought. Why not, after all? The man is guilty, and the only way to make the town safe for children is to put him away. In extreme cases, where the crime is great enough and its consequences serious enough, the only way to serve "justice" may be to create false evidence. So be it! The alternative is to see a sexual molester go free. We need a confession! Threats, "tough" treatment, beatings, torture may be necessary to get at the truth. Then there are his friends and acquaintances who have associated with him; they are potential witnesses against him if we can get them to tell the "truth." It may even be necessary (and silently acceptable to the public) to threaten, beat, and torture witnesses. This is typical of what we find in witch hunts, whether the witch be a "witch," a child molester, a terrorist, a traitor, whatever. Witch hunting is not simply an activity: it is a state of mind.

Where there are witches, there are witch hunters. Most often, the witch hunters who carry out these actions are honest men and women. They believe that their duty is to stop a guilty man from going free. It is an honourable cause. The perversions of justice that can arise from good-intentioned evil actions are understandable. And we accept that there are personal benefits as well behind a successful witch hunt. Promotion, public acclaim, success. Why not? They seem, at the time at least, to be well deserved. And since we know that the accused is guilty, let us not waste too much time worrying about whether a few corners had to be cut.

Only in retrospect, often years later, do we finally uncover the truth and realize that justice has been perverted.

THE CHARACTERISTICS OF A WITCH HUNT

Suppose that an event takes place that creates or happens in a climate of great fear, anger, hatred. There is intense pressure on the authorities to act – to find the witches at any cost. We demand instant protection and retribution.

These are the instructions that we write for our witch hunters, for those who will act to protect us. We know how to instruct them because these are the characteristics of a witch hunt.

Thou shalt:

1 Judge an accused person guilty *before* seeking evidence.
2 Apply whatever pressures are necessary on suspects, including beatings and torture, to extract confessions and obtain accusations against others.
3 Accept *any* incriminating evidence, however dubious or vague.
4 Emphasize what you want to hear and ignore testimony or evidence inconvenient to your theory.
5 Create or employ false evidence if necessary to convict.
6 Threaten anyone speaking in favour of a defendant as a suspected accessory.
7 Treat the accused as having no normal rights because he or she is so dangerous.

8 Be prepared to accept secret accusations, to hide the accusations from the accused, and to protect the identity of the accuser.
9 Search and expand the hunt for other witches, acolytes, supporters. Always assume that this witch is only the tip of the iceberg.
10 Justify and excuse all errors by appeals to National Security, the Protection of Society, or The Good of the State.

Of course, we know that not every one of these characteristics will be present in every witch hunt, but there will be a preponderance of them.

We saw many of these characteristics in Bamberg and Wurzburg. But one case is not enough. We shall look at others – different times, different places, different crimes – but in each instance we shall see these characteristics in practice. In each case the witch, or witches, were caught and punished. Only later, often far later, was it finally revealed and accepted that they were innocent. These delays in revealing the truth are also common to witch hunts. The authorities, having erred, fight tooth and nail to avoid admitting error.

We shall see all the characteristics of a witch hunt in the story of a priest who was burned at the stake for causing the demonic possession of a convent of nuns in France. This took place at almost the same time as the Bamberg and Wurzburg witch hunts. The circumstances were quite different, but the characteristics were the same.

We turn, then, to the town of Loudun, the priest Urbain Grandier, and the convent of Ursuline nuns led by the mother superior Sister Jeanne des Anges.

4

The Devil in Loudun

The single most famous witchcraft case in French history – indeed, in European history – took place in Loudun not far from Poitiers and Tours and close to the chateaux of the Loire. A priest, Urbain Grandier, was accused of causing the demonic possession of a convent of Ursuline nuns in the town. At five o'clock in the morning of 18 August 1634, the judges delivered their verdict:

We declare the said Urbain Grandier duly guilty of the crime of sorcery, evil spells, and the possession visited upon some Ursuline nuns of this town of Loudun, and of other laywomen mentioned at the trial, together with other crimes resulting from the above. For redress of these, he has been condemned and is condemned ... his body is to be burned alive ... Prior to proceeding with the execution of the said sentence we order that the said Grandier will be subjected to torture ordinary and extraordinary on the truth about his accomplices.

Issued at Loudun 18 August 1634 and carried out the same day.

So famous did the case become during its life that Grandier's burning attracted from all over France, and beyond, a crowd that some estimated at more than six thousand on that hot August day. So disputed did the trial and verdict become that it was another 250 years before authoritative figures of the Catholic Church in France accepted publicly that Grandier was innocent of witchcraft.[1]

Urbain Grandier arrived in Loudun in the late summer of 1617; he was twenty-seven. He had been educated by the Jesuits in Bordeaux and was a star pupil. His connections with them were sufficiently close that when his father died and left his mother with young children, all dependent upon the young priest, they appointed him parish priest of the Church of Saint-Pierre-du-Marché in Loudun, one of the two rich parishes in the town, and also assigned him another plum post, each with a handsome income, in a town to which he had no previous connection. Today we would say that he was parachuted into the positions. Needless to say, his arrival caused jealousies and resentments among the many local priests who had harboured hopes of getting at least one of these appointments. These grudges would do him much damage – but not until twelve years had passed.

The Jesuits appeared to have chosen well. He was a tall, handsome man, neatly and cleanly dressed in a period when these were not common virtues. But beyond that, he was brilliant, a wonderful preacher, charismatic, very witty. It was not long before he was well established in Loudun society, welcome in the best homes, and successful in his duties as a parish priest.

When he arrived in Loudun, it was a walled city, and at its centre was a powerful castle, the seat of the royal governor, a man named d'Armagnac. It was a town set in a rich and thriving countryside. With its white, walled fortifications and its prosperous population, it should have been a city at ease, but it was not. It was a city divided. Its populace was half Huguenot and half Catholic at a time in France when the adherents of the two religions were bitter enemies, bitter enough that civil wars had been fought and mass killings had taken place. In Loudun the roughly equal numbers within these factions led the members of each side to fear that the other would rise and slaughter them. It would have been bad enough if the two parties had continued to share equal standing, but even this was changing. King Louis XIII was firmly Catholic, and it was becoming clear to many Huguenots in France that their secular advancement would be assisted if they became Catholic themselves. This gradual shift made the Huguenots of Loudun ever more uncertain of their future and the Catholic priests ever more urgent in converting Huguenots to Catholicism.

Religion was not the only division in prosperous Loudun. In recent years, the Crown had become increasingly concerned with the number of powerful walled cities and private castles within the country. Too many revolts had taken place in the past against the king by cities and nobles who could retreat within their formidable walls. Now, at last, the king's government was powerful enough to do something about it. Louis XIII, advised by his first minister, Richelieu, issued orders that the internal fortifications of France were to be pulled down one by one to the point of being ineffective. To many of the people of Loudun, the destruction of their walls and fortifications, already decided upon but not yet actioned, was a terrible and even frightening prospect. Without their walls they would be subject to attack by any wandering band of brigands. Yet, to others, the loss of the walls would be rewarded by the development of a strong central government. So here was an issue that divided the townspeople: strong local government and self-protection versus strong central government and open walls. To be in one party was to support the king and his minister, Richelieu; to be in the other was to be against them. To side too obviously with the losing party was to be left with powerful enemies. This division too was to play its part in Loudun and in the invasion of the devils.

From his first days in Loudun, Grandier was much admired and re-spected by d'Armagnac, the governor. It was a time when every man who aspired to advance needed a patron. D'Armagnac had the king; Grandier had d'Armagnac. The governor, whose duties forced him to spend nearly all his time at the king's side but whose local importance rested in large part upon his fortress and the walled strength of the town, was adamantly against razing the walls. He needed to know who, in the town, was encouraging Richelieu to have the walls destroyed. It was not too long before Grandier was acting in the town as d'Armag-nac's secret eyes and ears. But the governor was not the only person of local importance to admire the priest. He was friendly with nearly every-body else of importance: the de Brou family, one of the most respected in the town; the de Cerisays, whose head was the *bailli*, the second most important man after the governor; the Trincant family, particularly the father, Louis Trincant, who was the *procureur du roi*, the third in line of local importance. And each of these men had large extended fami-lies not only of sons and daughters but of uncles, aunts, cousins, nieces, and nephews. To be a friend of de Brou, de Cerisay, or Trincant was to have status with all these connections. To be an enemy was to have many enemies!

Grandier was an enormous success not only socially, but also in the work of his own parish. Before he arrived it had been moribund under the former priest, who had recently died. But under Urbain Grandier it thrived. Parishioners who had previously drifted away to go to mass in the churches of the Carmelites and Capuchins were drawn back by his preaching and his leadership, somewhat to the resentment of the other priests, for their collections dropped accordingly.

One of the reasons that the Jesuits had chosen him for Loudun was because he might be a positive influence in attracting Huguenots. He certainly became much respected by them and was more pacific to them than many other priests, even developing friends among them. Many of the leading Huguenots were supporters of d'Armagnac, and Grandier would meet with them secretly at the governor's home now and then when d'Armagnac came to Loudun. These contacts, if known about, would be suspicious to many Catholics.

Still, in his early years, he seems to have been able to do no wrong. It was only some twelve years after his arrival, when he lost Trincant's friendship, that the jealousies and envies came to the fore, that his support of d'Armagnac against razing the fortifications brought forward powerful enemies, and that his imprudent relationships with local Huguenots came home to roost in accusations of heretical ideas. Yet he might have been able to overcome all of these had it not been for the demonic "possession" of the nuns. But that was for the future. For now, he had twelve good years.

He had friends, but he created enemies, too. One man who was to play a significant part in Grandier's life and death was his bishop, Henri Chasteignier de la Rocheposay, bishop of Poitiers. La Rocheposay was a proud aristocrat. Did he resent that the Jesuits could appoint a priest within his diocese without taking him into account? We cannot be sure, but he was certainly of a nature to do so. We do know that he had, in 1618, a friendship with a young bishop, another aristocrat, who was exiled from the court. Grandier snubbed the young prelate by insisting on being in a more important position in a local religious procession. He was technically justified, but it must have been galling to the already disgraced young prelate. La Rocheposay no doubt heard of this affront by the upstart priest to his aristocratic and unhappy friend. Perhaps his harsh treatment of Grandier in future years has its origins in this event. There can be little doubt that the snubbed young bishop would not forget Urbain Grandier. How was the priest to know that one day this snubbed bishop would become the king's first minister, Cardinal Richelieu, a man who seldom forgot an insult?

He created other enemies, too, local ones. Witty, charming, and brilliant as he was, these qualities were balanced by faults. He was belligerent in all quarrels. When a priest insulted an aged friend, he was not a peacemaker but destroyed the offender from his pulpit and in the courts. When another priest argued with him over who owned a piece of property, Grandier took him to court as well. He had a violent dislike of the magistrate in charge of the police, a man named Henry, and made a fool of him in public. He did not agree with the approach of the Capuchin and Carmelite priests in the town, who stressed miracles to prove the power of the church and who were bitterly anti-Huguenot; he spoke out against them and ridiculed the statue of the virgin who wept miraculous tears in the church of the Carmelites. More than once he had fist fights with those who opposed him. It was a violent time – men fought more easily and openly. But his greatest weakness was his pride in his own capabilities, and his greatest weapon was his wit. He destroyed his enemies in public by wit and laughter, even from his own pulpit. Such humiliations were never forgotten. And to make the humiliations worse, when he was victorious over his opponents, through whatever means, he made a public issue of it. It was never enough for Grandier to win, he had to make open fools of his defeated enemies.

In those happy and successful days of his first twelve years in Loudun, these enmities and humiliations lay latent, festering in the minds of those who had suffered. They would play their part in Grandier's life and death only after he had brought disaster upon himself.

Grandier's friend Trincant had two daughters. In 1629, after the priest had been in Loudun for twelve years, one of them, Philippe, became pregnant. Grandier was the father. Her dilemma and that of her father can be easily imagined. A priest could not marry. The child would be born illegitimate. Philippe would be forever shamed. A solution was found to her predicament. She was quickly married off to a young and rising lawyer/magistrate of good family, close friends of the Trincants, already allied by earlier intermarriages. Fortunately, the Trincant family was able to cover up the illegitimacy. And if there were those who questioned whether Philippe's husband was the real father, they did it circumspectly. Her father was a powerful magistrate, her husband was about to succeed to this position of authority, and Henry, the tough brutal chief of police, Grandier's enemy, was her cousin. So the baby was baptized as legitimate and recorded as newly born. The presiding priest was a certain Gervais Meschin; later he would make grave accusations against Urbain Grandier.

So Trincant had solved the problem of Philippe and her baby, but he had no way to punish the unfaithful priest. He could not accuse the man openly without disgracing his daughter and his family. He could not take any legal action against him for the same reason. He could not even accuse him to the ecclesiastical authorities through formal channels. To make any public accusation would involve making the facts known. This proud aristocrat, betrayed by his own priest, who was an upstart "immigrant" at that, had no legitimate path by which to mete out the punishment that Grandier so richly deserved. For the rest of Grandier's life, Trincant would seek his revenge.

In the early days of this enmity, Trincant accused the priest of having lived a secret debauched life. He had discovered, he said, that for years Grandier had been seducing women, including his own parishioners. No woman, it was said, was safe from his advances, which he made even in the confessional. Afterward, the priest was refused entry to many of the "best" houses in Loudun. But not everybody believed these accusations. And the magistrate took the position that those in the town who were not with him were against him. From this time on, to be a friend of Grandier was to be an enemy of the whole Trincant cabal.

Then Trincant arranged for these same false accusations to be made against Grandier to his bishop. La Rocheposay, who knew Trincant well, believed him. The consequences for the priest were disastrous. In his episcopal court, La Rocheposay tried Grandier and found him guilty. He forbade him ever to practise as a priest in Loudun. Grandier appeared to be ruined. But he was a fighter and would accept no injustice. And it was an injustice. True, all agreed that he had seduced Philippe; but this was not what he was tried for by the bishop. He had been sentenced on false testimony. So he appealed to the secular courts, claiming that he had been the victim of false accusations, and the court upheld him. Trincant and his fellow creators of lies were disgraced; the witnesses withdrew their false allegations in shame. Armed with this victory, Grandier now appealed to La Rocheposay's superior, the archbishop of Bordeaux, to have the bishop's sentence overturned.

The archbishop held his own investigation and determined that Grandier had been unjustly treated. He overturned the bishop's sentence: the order not to carry out any priestly functions was rescinded. Grandier had won. Privately, the archbishop advised Grandier not to return to Loudun to take back his posts – his bishop, he said, would get him sooner or later. He offered Grandier equivalent posts elsewhere in the archdiocese, but the priest was adamant. And typical of Grandier, he returned to Loudun to take up his restored duties as a priest, on his horse, carrying a branch of laurel, the sign of the returning victor.

The allegations of lechery and seduction had been accepted as false by the secular court and the archbishop, but mud sticks. For many months the delicious gossip and rumours had gone about the town. The very idea that no woman could resist his advances was both shocking and thrilling. There was probably not a dwelling in the town where the rumours about the irresistible, handsome priest had not been discussed and dissected among the women, even in the houses of his friends and supporters, where the accusations were not believed. In the long run, it was this gossip, this aura of seduction, that would lead to the priest's being accused as the author of the demonic possessions that were about to commence.

While Grandier was fighting his battle for exoneration, the ancient walls of Loudun were being torn down at the demand of the king. He had appointed a commissioner, Laubardemont, to oversee the work. This man had been to Loudun before on the king's business, so he already knew the leading people well when he arrived this second time. He had charmed them all the first time. In due course he would be the man who manipulated Grandier's death.

In retrospect, he was a sinister man. In matters to do with Loudun, and in equally unsavoury tasks in other places, Laubardemont was the creature of his master, Richelieu. On the surface he was charming, cultured, agreeable, able. He had already overseen the destruction of walls elsewhere on the king's behalf, and he had the unusual distinction of having pursued successful witch hunts in the southwest of France, in which a significant number of witches had been burned at the stake: he could claim to be something of an expert on the subject.

His charm could be disarming. D'Armagnac relied upon his word, given before the commissioner left the court in Paris, that while the walls of the city would be dismantled, the walls of D'Armagnac's fortress would not be razed. But when he arrived, the commissioner secretly allied himself to the local supporters of Richelieu in the town, who wanted the destruction of everything. They included among their numbers the Trincant family. Only gradually did Grandier and the governor realize that Laubardemont was opposed to them. The eventual result was a defeat for them; both the walls and the governor's fortress were destroyed. D'Armagnac swore never to return to Loudun, where his chateau had been the symbol of his importance and his pride. Both men had stood against the advancing tides of a new age, and together they had failed to prevent the waters from spreading. But Grandier's position was a worse one because he had created powerful enemies at court in trying to delay the cardinal's plans. The destruction of the city walls started in late 1631, continuing through the winter and into the spring of 1632. Gradually, the beautiful white walls and towers were reduced.

Worse was to come. In May 1632 the plague struck Loudun. It was the same disease that had struck Europe in the mid-1300s, the Black Death. From May to September in Loudun that year, between one-fifth and one-quarter of the population died. The city was devastated: the fear and constant stress of those months can only be imagined. These events may have been, in part, the origin of the possessions in the Ursuline convent.

A convent of Ursuline teaching nuns had been opened in Loudun in 1626 – just six years earlier. By the time of the plague, the original eight nuns had grown to seventeen. Its members were almost all young and inexperienced in view of its recent foundation. The daughter of a baron, the mother superior of this new house was Jeanne de Belciel, known as Sister Jeanne des Anges (or Jeanne of the Angels). She was a very clever woman, although too young, at thirty-two, to really be responsible for a convent. Her ambition was to fill her convent with the daughters of the aristocratic families of the neighbourhood. In later years she wrote about her experiences under demonic possession. She admitted that as a young nun she had failed to attend properly to her religious duties, but when her former convent in Poitiers decided to send her and seven other nuns to open a house in Loudun, she became a model nun, at least to all outward appearances. And when they arrived in Loudun, she made it her business to become the indispensable right arm of the mother superior. By the time this nun was called away at the end of the first year, Jeanne des Anges seemed to be the logical person for the nuns to elect in her place. Two of her abilities are already evident: she had a chameleon-like quality of being able to change her character to whatever was necessary for success, and she could manipulate others. She did attract the kind of young women whom she wanted. By chance, she herself was related to Laubardemont, and two of the nuns in the convent were his sisters-in-law. Another nun was related to Richelieu, another to Archbishop de Sourdis – and this was fairly typical of their backgrounds.

Once she had achieved these successes in attracting aristocratic young novices, she became careless again about her own behaviour. She says herself that she spent more time reading than she should have, for she was very proud of the quality of her mind and her learning. She spent too much time at the grille as well. The grille was a lattice work of iron bars where a nun could talk to visiting outsiders, although only with the express permission of the mother superior. But the mother superior could use the grille, and Jeanne did so excessively, not just for the proper business of the convent but for gossip. It was through the grille that she, and then the other nuns, heard tell of the handsome priest (whom they had never seen) who had the reputation of seducing women and whom no woman could resist. All the details of the accusations against him, of his sentencing by the bishop, of its overturn by the archbishop, of the priest's determination to stay in Loudun, crept into the convent – and along with the gossip came temptation, which in time became obsession with the lecherous priest. This obsession with Grandier spread among the nuns very shortly after the beginning of the demonic possessions.

Centuries of experience had shown that the end of a plague brought on loose behaviour and licentiousness. Nuns could not behave this way. But they could have unsolicited dreams, hallucinations. And this, it seems, is what happened. One night in September 1632, when the plague was just over, a young nun woke to find beside her bed the ghostly figure of a priest who was standing in great distress and begging her to pray to God for him because he was unable to pray for himself. She was terrified and assumed that the priest was dead and suffering for his sins. At first she and the other nuns in the building where she was sleeping believed that he was their former confessor who had died in the plague. In the morning she rushed to the mother superior, who was in another building, and told her of the frightening apparition.

The first thing that should have happened in a well-established convent is that the mother superior should have had doubts. Imaginings of various kinds were not that unusual when a group of impressionable and religious young girls were brought together. An experienced mother superior's first reaction should have been to assume that the nun was sick, imagining, or lying. Only when these possibilities had been completely eliminated would a supernatural explanation normally have been entertained. Unfortunately, Jeanne was inexperienced and impressionable. Her instinct was to believe that the strange event had occurred. Indeed, her response went farther than this. Jeanne was not a person who would be comfortable with one of her junior nuns alone having supernatural experiences. By that night, she, too, had suffered a visitation. The whole convent was now drawn into praying for the priest, who, they now concluded, was a victim of the plague.

One person who should have been brought into the picture right away was the new confessor to the convent, Father Jean Mignon, who by pure chance was Trincant's nephew. But, in fact, he and other priests were not brought in until some days later. By then, things had spiralled downward, and he recorded: "they told us that for the whole of the rest of the said month, they have not passed a night in which they have not been subjected to great perturbations, disturbances and terrors. And even though seeing nothing, they often heard voices calling one or another. Others received fist blows, others slaps, others felt themselves involuntarily aroused to laughing uncontrollably."

So by the beginning of October 1632 a large number of the convent population were in a state of hysteria – or were undergoing a supernatural invasion marked by inexplicable events. Father Mignon had by now brought in a number of other priests to help him deal with what was increasingly believed to be a case of demonic possession; the bishop had been informed, and the nuns were under constant care. Then an event occurred that took things to an entirely different level.

Around ten in the evening, Jeanne des Anges was in her bed surrounded by seven or eight nuns, all no doubt praying. By this time the young nun who had started the whole thing had been sidelined and the mother superior had taken over centre stage; during the intervening days she had become the worst afflicted of the nuns. Lying there, without seeing anything, she felt a hand close around hers, and when she opened her hand there were three hawthorn needles in it. To everybody involved, the event was inexplicable and frightening.

The priests recorded the events that followed: "the said prioress, and other nuns, since the reception of the said thorns, experienced strange changes in body and mind of such a kind that they lost all judgement and were agitated by great convulsions which seemed to proceed from extraordinary causes. It was thought that the said thorns carried an evil spell which caused them [the nuns] to be possessed."

Looking back, it is easy to conclude that the mother superior had taken over leadership of events in the convent soon after the young nun reported her experience. This does not necessarily mean that Jeanne des Anges was deliberately acting a part; she may well have believed that the nun had had a valid experience, and, that night perhaps, she may equally well have had some kind of a dream or hallucination herself of the same kind. The increasing hysterical symptoms, which were very probably involuntary, spread to other nuns (who after all were only following their leader), for hysteria of this kind was (and is) contagious, particularly so in confined communities. But another thing happened (and the same will be seen in Salem) once the hysteria had started: it got worse. Perhaps it was the nature of the disease, but in this case there was another factor operating: to hold the attention of others and to overcome any initial doubts that those affected might have developed, things always had to get worse. In this case, they were pushed forward by the event of the hawthorn needles. Everything up to that time could have been involuntary, but the hawthorn needles were chicanery on the part of Jeanne des Anges. Sick she may have been, but she was also manipulating the nuns and the priests by this act, deceiving them by convincing them that real demonic possession was taking place.

In the seventeenth century everybody believed in witches and the Devil. Just as God had his angels, the Devil had his demons. It was possible, they thought, for the Devil and the demons to enter the body of a man or woman and to take over. This was demonic possession. It was not common, but when it happened it was terrifying partly because what happened to the person could be seen and was terrifying in itself and partly because those present feared the power of the Evil One, which was being manifested before their very eyes. In our language of today, we still have traces of belief in possession: "He lost all self-possession," we might say, or "She acted like a woman possessed."

And how did a "woman possessed" act? There were nearly always convulsions and contortions, frequently so violent that they seemed humanly impossible by any natural means. Screaming, shouting, terrible grimaces, violent actions, blasphemy, and commonly, extreme eroticism. And when this happened with nuns, young women who had devoted their lives to God, it was even more unnatural and horrifying. Between the demonic attacks, the women would often return to their natural condition and behaviour without any recollection of what they had done, or more correctly of what had been done to them. Perhaps most frightening of all were the voices of the demons, for they would speak through the possessed person. Each demon would represent a different sin: lust, gluttony, pride, envy, and so on. When a demon took over the body, the possessed person would take on all the physical characteristics that went with its particular sin. When the demon spoke, it would do so in its own voice. And then another demon might take over, and the voice and appearance would change completely. There are well-recorded descriptions of possessions – true reflections of what observers saw. The film *The Exorcist* depicts well some of the extraordinary effects that people saw in cases of "possession." So to understand what was going on, we have to put ourselves in the minds of the priests who were present. They came into the picture when the nuns were already suffering from hysteria. These were not just silly girls acting things out. They were young members of respectable noble families, girls who had been known all their lives, religious young women – the "girl next door" – and well connected. These young women were running, laughing, screaming, convulsing, blaspheming – totally out of character with their past. There was only one possible explanation: they had been bewitched! And as time went on and the convulsions became ever more extraordinary, the doctors would eventually confirm that there could be no natural cause or explanation. The priests decided to exorcize.

These exorcisms were designed to expel the demons from the bodies of the nuns. The procedure was a set of prayers interspersed with questions designed to find out the names of the demons and who had introduced them to the convent. According to current thinking, the demons could not have entered the convent by themselves – somebody had to have introduced them, and the same person had in some way used the hawthorn needles to bring a second wave of demons into the house. So it was important to identify who was acting as the Devil's agent.

On 11 October, after many exorcisms in the previous days, the dam finally broke. The demon was "pressed and pressed again, he at last in great fury said three times that his name was Astaroth," the demon of lust. The exorcists went on, demanding and demanding again to know how the demon had entered, and the demon said that it was a priest. "And commanded several times to say clearly and distinctly who that priest was, replied screaming loud and long, and then hissing out: 'Urbain Grandier.' Pressed to say what was the position of this same Urbain, said: 'The curé of Saint-Pierre.'"

So the invasion of the convent by demons started on 21 September 1632 with a terrifying experience reported by a young nun. By 11 October the young nun was no longer a part of the story. It was Jeanne des Anges, or her devils, who had taken over, and indeed, from this time on, although other nuns were possessed (eight in all), she alone was at the centre of all significant events. There was one other significant change: although the incident had started with the apparition of the nuns' now-dead former confessor, in the intervening period he had disappeared, making no further appearance, to be replaced by Urbain Grandier. And where the original priest was assumed to be a soul in purgatory asking for prayers, his replacement was the handsome, young priest with a reputation for lechery.

By this time, the nuns were obsessed with the priest. From the first time that his name had come into the picture, they had all begun to talk and think about him. Jeanne des Anges herself records: "At that time, the priest of whom I have spoken used demons to excite love for him in me; they gave me desires to see and speak to him. Many of our sisters were of the same sentiments without telling us. On the contrary, we hid from one another as much as we could, and after the demons had thoroughly aroused in us the passion of love for this man, he did not fail to come by night into the house and into our chambers to solicit us to sin." At another point, she talks of his "caresses as insolent as they were immodest by which he pressed her to accord to him that which was not within her liberty to grant." And again, "When I could not see him, I burned for love of him, and when he presented himself to me, and he wanted to seduce me, our good God gave me a great aversion."

She had never seen this man!

In these days from 21 September to 11 October 1632 the whole pattern of the Devils in Loudun was set, and once set it could never be broken. What created the pattern were errors at the beginning that would ultimately have terrible effects. Jeanne des Anges had a history of nervous conditions. She had been under the doctors' care for some months before these events began, and she had been so seriously sick that they feared for her life. So the doctors and the priests erred in not being suspicious when she so quickly held that her convent had been the target of some kind of supernatural intervention by their defunct confessor.

Her own error was that she believed without reservation that the young nun had had a genuine supernatural experience. And now her own character came into play. By the next morning, at the latest, she, too, had had a similar experience – perhaps a nightmare given her already delicate nervous condition. Her next error was not only to believe that she, too, had seen an apparition, but also to tell all the other nuns, although apparently not Father Mignon. And now came the critical error. When she did involve Mignon, he believed her report that supernatural events were taking place and that they had a demonic character. He does not seem to have questioned at any time the events or her wisdom in dealing with them. Perhaps her position as the mother superior made it impossible for him to doubt her or to question her. The priest, well established and well connected in Loudun, agreed that some form of possession was taking place. From now on, anybody who doubted was at risk of being labelled a skeptic and even irreligious.

Jeanne des Anges had also learned a thing or two. This woman, who by her nature often got her way by manipulating others, learned from Mignon's willing acceptance that she could manipulate him. And as he brought in other priests, already prepared to accept demonic invasion because he had forewarned them of what they would be up against, she learned that she could manipulate them, too.

She also quickly learned that the situation would not stand still. The priests who had now started exorcisms had standard questions for which they wanted answers. And answers had to be provided. And each answer led to more questions. If she was to control the events, she always had to be ahead of the exorcists, always had to produce new excitements. Once the exorcists had confirmed their belief that this was a true case of possession, they could never allow anybody else to question it. They would look like fools to everybody, especially to the Huguenots. They had to continue to believe. The nuns could not withdraw: they had to be possessed or their behaviour would make them laughing stocks. The leading citizens of Loudun were committed, too, in many cases, for these were their daughters and nieces convulsing and screaming and laughing uncontrollably in the convent: they had to be possessed, or their families would be shamed. The consequence of being possessed was that the nuns could give in to their greatest temptations. It was all right to give way to their obsessions with the priest because it was not they who were at fault; it was the Devil. And it wasn't even a case of "the Devil made me do it"; it was the Devil doing it.

Some twenty years before, in the town of Aix in Provence, the local convent of Ursuline nuns had suffered a very similar "possession." A local priest, Louis Gaufridy, had been accused of being responsible and burned at the stake as a witch. It was a very famous case. So it was not long before the Loudun exorcists recognized a pattern: a priest, an Ursuline convent, demonic possession. Surely, this was Aix all over again! It was still only twenty-one years since Gaufridy had been executed. The priests present at Loudun, now in the prime of their careers, had been students in seminaries or newly ordained when the event took place. Everybody knew about it because the principal exorcist there had written a book that everybody in their world read. The parallel was obvious to them. Grandier was accused – and clearly, Grandier had to be guilty.

But if it was obvious to them that a repetition of Aix was occurring, this conclusion had not yet been drawn outside the convent. True, word had already crept out and was spreading in the town that there was demonic possession in the convent, which was frightening. It became official when the exorcists advised the royal authorities in the town that the nuns were possessed. The exorcists represented the religious authorities, and their task, among others, was to identify who was causing the possessions, but it would be the responsibility of the royal authorities to arrest the culprit, try him, execute him − so they had to be introduced at an early stage. Thus it was that when the exorcisms took place on 11 October 1632, the *bailli* de Cerisay and his lieutenant were present. In his minutes de Cerisay gives us the first physical description of one of the possessed nuns: "Mme de Belciel [Jeanne des Anges's civil name] began to make violent actions and movements accompanied by sounds like the grunting of a pig, then thrusting herself down in the bed began to grind her teeth, and made other faces like a person devoid of her senses." He was clearly amazed that the mother superior could have lost her self-possession to such a degree and that she could be overtaken by a power that was so far beyond her control. He was concerned that things had been allowed to go this far without his being called in earlier, and his concern increased when his friend Grandier's name was given during the exorcism as the man responsible for introducing the demons into the convent. Then Mignon took him aside and told him that this case "was somewhat similar to the story of Gaufridy who had been put to death by virtue of the sentence of the Parlement of Aix, having been convicted of magic." De Cerisay realized immediately that Grandier was at great risk.

He was skeptical about how the exorcisms were being held because he felt that the questions being put to the mother superior were designed to lead to a preconceived answer. From this time on, he fought to have priests brought in to perform the exorcisms who were objective. He doubted Mignon's competence, he doubted Mignon's objectivity in view of his relationship with Trincant, and he doubted the reality of the possessions, considering them to be as likely to be caused by sickness as by demons.

This was the beginning of months of struggle between the exorcists and the civil authorities, between church and state, and the issue was who had the right to see that the exorcisms were being properly conducted when the consequences were so grave. While the *bailli* fought ceaselessly for sound and objective exorcisms, the local church authorities resisted what they saw as incursions from the civil authorities. It is enough to say that in the long run, de Cerisay lost, as did Grandier.

There was another aspect of the exorcisms that should have caused concern. They should have been conducted in quiet seclusion. In fact, within a few days of the first revelations about Grandier, local notables were present at the exorcisms – and, of course, other local notables demanded equal treatment, so the numbers grew. Soon the nuns were no longer the centre of the theatrics; they became merely the props to the play. As in any other play, the audience became part of the process, and the audience had to be pleased. In time, the exorcisms would become so famous and so startling that they would be made public, open to everybody at no cost and in numbers reaching up to twenty-five hundred. But this was still in the future.

Grandier learned of the accusations that the demons were making against him. He seems at first to have been so confident in his innocence that he did not take them too seriously, but as the exorcisms went on and more accusations were made, he became concerned. Eventually, on 22 October 1632, he went to Bishop de la Rocheposay to try to have the exorcists changed. He never saw the bishop, only one of his senior priests. He got the message that the bishop would do nothing for him. From now on the exorcists had control, and they started from the "knowledge" that Grandier was accused – and thus guilty. All their efforts henceforth would be directed to finding evidence against him.

From this time on, the afflictions in the convent increased. More and more of the nuns were suffering from convulsions, screaming and cursing, and denying God, with thoughts of Grandier constantly in their minds. De Cerisay and his supporters in the civil authorities wanted them separated and placed in the homes of worthy people, where the doctors and the priests could go about their duties in a sober fashion. Nothing was done. De Cerisay and his lieutenants themselves approached the bishop, their language becoming stronger with time. They said that it was "all cheating" and that these "so called miracles" were being performed only "in order to convert the Protestants." Grandier, they said, had never seen the nuns, nor had they seen him, and if he had power over the demons, he would already have employed them against his enemies. La Rocheposay did nothing.

Then, as so often happened in the Grandier affair, the case took a sudden new turn. Archbishop de Sourdis happened to visit a local abbey. Grandier rushed to him and told him all that had happened. Naturally, the prelate told the beleaguered priest, "I told you so," but he did

promise to look into the matter. He carried through. He sent his doctor
to the convent. The devils were quiescent while he was there, and the
nuns told him that they were no longer possessed. De Sourdis acted
forcefully by issuing an order. If new possessions arose, new exorcists
were to be named, and the afflicted were to be sequestered, purged, and
judged whether they were sick. Threats and discipline were then to be applied, and only after all this had been done was their condition to be
considered supernatural. Moreover, he required that additional tests
be applied to prove possession before it could be assumed.

A relative quiet returned to the convent. The exorcists were dis-
banded, and only Mignon was left to attend to the spiritual needs of the
nuns. As far as the town was concerned, it was as though nothing had
ever happened – or at least as though nothing real had happened. But of
course, the townspeople were aware of all that had gone on and knew
that all had so suddenly stopped. No new nuns were joining the house.
Families were withdrawing their young daughters who might have become nuns, and those who had nun daughters in the house now often
withheld the dowries that they had promised. The good reputation of
the convent was in tatters, and the nuns had become a laughing stock.
They were fortunate to have Mignon as their confessor, for it was he
who kept them going in these hard days, making sure that they had at
least the essentials of life.

And there perhaps it might have ended if Laubardemont had not re-
entered the picture. As the king's commissioner, he had been overseeing
the destruction of the walls but was back in Paris during all these happenings. Now, some eight months later, he returned to Loudun on the
king's business. He met with Trincant and with his friends and powerful Catholic allies in the town. He dined with them, was brought up-
to-date with all that had gone on. He knew that the events in Loudun
had not been taken seriously at court; they had been more a matter of
humour than concern. But now he was assured by Trincant and the others, men whom he respected and whom he knew to be friends of the
cardinal, that the possessions had been real. He should go and see his
kinswomen himself, they told him: the mother superior (who was related to him) and his two sisters-in-law. All good Catholics in the town,
he was told, had been shamed by the intervention of the archbishop,
who knew nothing of what was really going on. Go see his own relatives. The good name of his own family and that of his wife were bound
up in this, they told him. So he went.

The next day at the convent, he met his relatives, who told him in graphic terms all that had happened to them. The disturbances were still continuing, they said, and although Father Mignon was doing his best, the demons had not gone. They complained bitterly that Grandier had truly cast a spell on the convent. They pointed out that de Sourdis's order had, in effect, said that they were sick or charlatans and that this brought shame not only on them, but also on their relatives. Laubardemont took these thoughts back with him to his friends in the town. They must have been pleased to see that he was at least half convinced. Laubardemont was the key to getting a serious review of the possessions, to getting the good names of the nuns retrieved, to getting an evil man punished, to retrieving the Catholic cause in Loudun. Laubardemont had the ear of the cardinal, and the cardinal had the ear of the king.

The commissioner returned to Paris shortly after and brought the matter to his master, the cardinal. He described the intense concerns of Richelieu's friends and supporters in Loudun. Since he already had an established reputation as a witch hunter from his earlier days, his opinions would carry weight at court. And there was more, for as an experienced king's commissioner, he had a wider view to convey on matters of state. He was able to add his own opinion that the priest in Loudun was helping to aggravate Catholic-Huguenot tensions in a city already divided. Apart from any considerations of witchcraft, Grandier was a danger to the tranquillity of the state, which had just gone through a third Huguenot war and needed no disturbances. Almost certainly entrusted to him by Trincant in the greatest confidentiality, Laubardemont carried with him a secret for the ear of the cardinal alone: the disgrace of Philippe Trincant's seduction by the priest and the fact that no punishment was possible, all attempts having been brought to naught. This alone would sway the cardinal, whose sense of morality was very high. In short order, Richelieu took the matter to the king, a virtuous and moral man. The result was a royal order: Grandier was to be arrested by Laubardemont, the possessions were to be investigated and recorded, he would arrange and conduct Grandier's trial, and he was to reach a final sentence without regard to any opposition, appeals, or objections whatsoever. The wording of this order was ominous. There had been no trial, no investigation of the facts, no opportunity for defence on the part of Grandier. He was guilty! And in the investigation that Laubardemont was to conduct, the instructions were that the priest was to be found guilty. And anybody who raised opposition, appeals, or objections was to be ignored. The witch hunt was in full cry now: Grandier was accused and found guilty, and now the exorcists and Laubardemont were authorized – indeed, ordered – to find the evidence that would prove guilt.

On 6 December 1633 the commissioner arrested Urbain Grandier in Loudun. That same day, accompanied by the priest's principal enemies in the city, he went to Grandier's home to search it thoroughly. They discovered documents that would appear at his trial and one that would not. They later claimed that they had found a book of magic, but it never appeared; indeed, they continued to search for it among his friends until his death. This missing book is significant. Gaufridy in Aix was supposed to have had a book of magic given to him by his priest uncle, so Grandier had to have one, also from his priest uncle. If they could not find it, they concluded, it was not because it did not exist but because it was hidden by accomplices. This was truly in the spirit of a witch hunt! They believed absolutely what they wanted to believe. This went beyond finding questionable evidence but using it anyway, beyond being too easily prepared to believe false evidence, beyond deliberately creating false evidence: it went as far as believing false evidence that did not even exist.

But one document was found: a treatise arguing that priests should be allowed to marry, supposedly written by Grandier. This was serious stuff. It went totally against the tenets of the church and indicated a deep Huguenot influence, for their ministers could marry. In essence it argued that a priest could have such deep sexual needs that it was better for him to marry than to sin. This was heresy! On top of that, it was assumed – and always has been since then – that the document was written to persuade a woman that sexual relations with a priest, going as far as marriage, were permissible. Laubardemont and his friends were quick to assert that the woman was a particular friend of Grandier named Madeleine de Brou – and soon her name was being bruited abroad as Grandier's acolyte in witchery. The search for accomplices was on, as it nearly always is in witch hunt cases. Other names would soon join hers.

Grandier would ultimately be imprisoned in the top portion of a house in Loudun that happened to belong to Mignon. The windows were walled in, the chimney was barred, everything was built to avoid his escape; there was a popular fear that because of his special relationship to the Devil, the demons would come to help him.

Laubardemont began to hear evidence, treating it in a manner that was heavily biased against the accused man. All the charges that had been made against him to the bishop and that had later been struck down were raised again and recorded as though nothing had ever happened to disprove them. All the old accusers who had been shamed for false testimony came forward once again as bold as brass. In fact, false evidence was not only accepted, but encouraged. Anybody who testified against him was given a respectful hearing. Anybody who tried to testify in his favour was treated with discourtesy and disbelief; often such testimony was not even recorded. And underlying all the overbearing conduct of the commissioner and his staff was the constant unstated threat that those who favoured the "guilty" man might well themselves be denounced as his followers and agents of the Devil. This was no light threat. At witchcraft trials it was always assumed that the guilty person had sought out acolytes and persuaded them to join in the worship of the Devil. As we have seen, the accused "witch" was routinely tortured to reveal names – as Grandier would be.

And the bishop, too, still smarting from the archbishop's earlier reversal of his decisions on Grandier, could take satisfaction in his recovered clout. Now that the king had directed a complete investigation, La Rocheposay could take back control of the exorcists in his own diocese. The possessions began again, as did the exorcisms under exorcists appointed by the bishop. The sensible orders of the archbishop were treated as though they had never existed. La Rocheposay's position was clear and would remain so until the end: Grandier was guilty!

Now, for the first time, the priest was brought into the presence of the nuns to see if they would recognize him. He proposed that, since they had never seen him, somebody else should be presented in his place to see if they addressed the imposter as Grandier himself. But Laubardemont had no intention of dancing to the priest's tune. Grandier was taken before the nuns, who had already been told that he was coming. Not surprisingly, they recognized him as the man who had been invading their convent night after night and seeking their seduction. Laubardemont recorded that they had recognized him. This was important; he now had the evidence of the whole convent of nuns that Grandier was a sorcerer.

A new and frightening danger now entered. The two leaders of the newly arrived replacement exorcists began to teach and preach that the Devil, under exorcism, could be forced to tell the truth. The power of the Catholic Church over the Devil was so great, they said, that even though he was the Prince of Liars, he could be made to speak the truth when all of the power of the church was exercised against him. This was a most dangerous theory – dangerous not only to Grandier but dangerous to the people of Loudun. The theory said that any accusation made during the exorcisms not only could be believed, but *had* to be believed. And by now the exorcisms were public, and accusations were being made by the nuns against not only Grandier, but also Madeleine de Brou, de Cerisay and his wife, and other friends of the priest. Two priests, for example, were accused by the demons in one of the possessed women of trying to rape her. They managed to escape the accusation, but it was obvious that a widespread witch hunt could easily be starting. Shades of Bamberg! This was a serious enough possibility that the *bailli* and a number of other leading citizens felt it necessary to send a letter to the king saying that "something very prejudicial to the public and tranquillity of your faithful subjects is being committed in that some of the exorcists are abusing their office and the authority of the church by asking questions in the exorcisms which tend to the defamation of the best families in the said town." The king did not respond, but fortunately de Cerisay's status was sufficient to stop more wild accusations from being made. But the exorcists still held their ground: every accusation against Grandier made under exorcism was valid evidence against him.

One of the revelations under exorcism came from Jeanne des Anges's demons: that Grandier carried the Devil's marks "in two places in the most secret parts of his body, in the two buttocks close to his anus, and in the two testicles." The Devil's marks were supposed to be insensitive places on a witch's body that had been touched by the Devil to mark the witch as an adherent. One of Trincant's relatives, a surgeon, was tasked with testing for the marks. The procedure was standard: a long sharp needle with one end rounded was employed, and "He had Grandier stripped naked, eyes bound, and shaved everywhere and probed and pierced right to the bone in many parts of his body." Grandier could not help screaming with the pain so that people in the street could hear him. The insensitive points were found. Grandier's friends argued that the surgeon reversed the needle and used the round end at these points. As far as Laubardemont was concerned the tests were valid. The Devil's marks had been found.

Some days later an even more solid proof came to hand. Jeanne des Anges vomited forth a pact between the priest and the Devil. It was done before a great crowd because her demon had forecast that it would happen on this day. It read:

My Lord and Master, I acknowledge you as my God and I promise to serve you as long as I live and from this time I renounce all others including Jesus Christ and Mary and all the Saints in heaven and the catholic and apostolic Roman Church and all its benefits and prayers which might be offered in my favor. I promise to adore you and to pay homage to you at least three times a day and to do all the evil that I can and to draw to evil as many persons as I can, and with all my heart I renounce my anointing and baptism and all the merits of Jesus Christ and ...

I give you my body, my soul and my life, as holding it from you, having given it over forever and irrevocably.

Signed by Urbain Grandier with his blood.

At the very least, Jeanne des Anges was a partner with one or more of the exorcists in creating this "miracle." It is quite probable that she acted alone. In later days of the inquiry, she would bring forth more items like these; they played well with the crowd and with the exorcists. By 23 June 1634, when the bishop came to Loudun, three additional "pacts" that had been delivered up by the demons in the past weeks were presented to him.

On this same day, Grandier was confronted publicly by the eight nuns who were the worst afflicted. In front of hundreds of people, the possessed nuns filled the church with screams and yells and crude language, led by Jeanne des Anges. They rushed at him and threatened him so severely that he had to be rescued. Before he was taken away, Grandier asked the exorcists to order these demons to break his neck or at least to make a visible mark on his forehead if he had committed the crime of which he was accused. After all, he implied, they had said that under exorcism the Devil had to do what he was told to do. La Rocheposay refused, saying in effect that the demons might already have made a pact with Grandier not to harm him. This directly contradicted the the exorcists' statement that the church could force the devils to do anything under exorcism, but nobody paid this any attention.

The exorcisms, by now, were wonderful theatre for the masses, and all free. There were the devils' voices, changing from one to another as they were being exorcized. In the case of one nun "several voices were heard disputing with each other at the same time." And then there were the convulsions: an eyewitness wrote that "they struck their chests and backs with their heads, as if their necks had broken, and with inconceivable rapidity ... Their faces became so frightful one could not bear to look at them; their eyes remained open without winking. Their tongues issued suddenly from their mouths, horribly swollen, black, hard, and covered with pimples ... They threw themselves back till their heads touched their feet, and walked in this position with wonderful rapidity, and for a long time. They uttered cries so horrible and loud that nothing like it was ever heard before." Another eyewitness reported that: "Asmodée made her face swell up and in an instant it was so frightful, that without exaggeration, it was three times its normal size, and above all, her eyes instantaneously became as large as those of a horse; she held this posture for more than a quarter of an hour, and then suddenly, in an instant, returned to her natural state, which was that of a beautiful young woman." As these are eyewitness reports, it is hardly surprising that observers truly believed that the women were possessed by the Devil.

Another quite extraordinary feature was the eroticism evidenced in the words and actions of these young nuns, who, after the exorcisms, would return to their natural state and would remember nothing of what had happened. During the exorcisms, one nun, who was in fact Richelieu's relative, "fell to the ground blaspheming, in convulsions, lifting her petticoats ... displaying her private parts without any shame and uttering filthy words." To these events the doctors added their professional opinion that the convulsions were beyond nature, that they were indeed supernatural, and that the nuns were not merely sick. It is not surprising at all that Grandier was viewed by most people as a malevolent sorcerer. Something beyond the normal human understanding of the time – and, indeed, beyond much of our own lay understanding – was taking place. The error of this conclusion was not that extraordinary events were taking place but that the line was drawn from them to Grandier.

Grandier himself held to the end that Mignon was directing the nuns on behalf of Trincant. The Trincant family's personal hatreds were involved in this case, without question. There were personal issues in Bamberg and Wurzburg, too. And they will be seen again in Salem. So it is true that Mignon may have been manipulating events against the family enemy, but in addition Jeanne des Anges was manipulating everybody about her, including Mignon and the other exorcists – who thought that they were in charge. What cannot be known is how much of her manipulation was deliberate, how much was sickness, and how much was due to the fact that the exorcists had persuaded her that she was possessed, thereby relieving her of any responsibility for her acts.

At Grandier's trial there were thirteen experienced judges and seventy-two witnesses. All the evidence that had been collected was presented. The evidence of the nuns and their possessions and exorcisms formed the core of the case, but there was much more that seemed to prove Grandier's guilt. One young woman came forward and testified that Grandier had taken her to a Sabbath. This was important because it proved beyond doubt that Grandier was an agent of the Devil. She also accused Grandier of having had carnal relations with her. By now she had replaced Grandier's friend Madeleine de Brou, who in the meantime had been proved innocent of any wrongdoing or immorality by the court, at great cost to her accusers. Laubardemont and his staff had tried hard to make Madeleine the centre point of the accusations against the priest but had been unsuccessful – largely because she was of a good family who could bring substantial pressure against the commissioner. So this new young woman was introduced because she fulfilled the need to have a parallel to the Gaufridy case! It does not appear that she was taken too seriously because she does not appear again after his death, but her evidence was held against him. There were the Devil's marks and the pacts with the Devil, and, of course, the enormous mass of people who had seen the public exorcisms were in large part in no doubt that there had been real possessions.

One piece of testimony was not presented. It concerned an event that had taken place some eight months earlier. There was an incident between Laubardemont and Jeanne des Anges:

After having made her deposition, while [Laubardemont was] receiving that of another nun, [the mother superior] dressed in her chemise, her head bare, with a rope around her neck and a candle in one hand, stood in the pouring rain in the courtyard for a period of two hours ... When the door of the parlour was opened ... she threw herself on her knees in front of Sieur Laubardemont, declaring to him that she had come to admit the sin she had committed in accusing an innocent Grandier. Then when she withdrew, she tied the rope to a tree in the garden and would have strangled herself had the other nuns not run to her aid.

Two other nuns who had accused Grandier also confessed to
Laubardemont that their accusations were false. His response was that
Grandier's ability even to make the nuns state that they were guilty
and that he was innocent proved his collusion with the Devil. This
type of response was (and is) not uncommon in witch hunts. The accusers allege that the accused person, or group of people, are so clever
and so manipulative that confessions in their favour should be taken
as false testimony or, at the very least, as unreliable testimony.

The verdict of death was delivered very early in the morning of 18 August 1634. There was, in those days, no lengthy process of appeals; the
condemned man was tortured and burned the same day.

First thing in the morning, the priest was shaved of all hair on his
body; it was feared at the time that demons could hide in a person's
hair and be carried and passed to others like a contagious disease. In
rags, he was taken to where the magistrates (and selected guests) were
assembled. The exorcists sprinkled the area and especially the condemned man with holy water, accompanied by special prayers to
protect all present from invasion by the demons. Then Grandier's sentence of torture and death was read out publicly. He pleaded with the
judges for compassion, fearing that in the agony to come he would lose
hope in God's mercy. His pleas were unsuccessful. The judges took over
now, demanding that he name his accomplices (just as they had done in
Bamberg), and then Laubardemont approached him and held a whispered conversation using promises, threats, even tears in a further attempt to have the prisoner admit to his crimes and to accuse others.
Grandier refused. He asked for a priest to whom he could confess his
sins before dying, but they refused to allow him the priest he wished,
fearing that one who was sympathetic to him would be less likely to
solicit an admission of guilt or to persuade Grandier to name names.
Then he was turned over to the torturer. Laubardemont was present
and in charge. The torture was hideous, but the condemned man would
admit to nothing that they wanted. And the torture continued; it had
to, for the priest-exorcists who were present believed that the eternal
soul of this man and many others depended upon his confessing and
asking for forgiveness for all the evil that he had done. But he continued
to declare his innocence of the crime of sorcery and of any responsibility for the possessions.

Eventually, they gave up because they feared that he would die before his execution. He was allowed time alone to recover a little. Once
more Laubardemont pressed him to confess all his evil. In those days

the authorities allowed no lessening of punishment (in this case, gar-
roting before the fire was lit at the stake) without an admission of
guilt. Grandier continued to refuse. Then he was taken through the
streets in a tumbrel, stopping at appointed places to have his sentence
read to all and to speak aloud a statement that was given to him. To
the very end, he stated that he was not guilty of the sins of which he
was accused but that he accepted all the things that were being done
to him as a just punishment from God for the sins he really had committed. He went to his execution bravely. The fire was lit in anger and
fury by one of the exorcists (against all proper process), so enraged
was he by the continued refusal of the condemned man to admit his guilt.
It blazed in the square before the Church of Sainte-Croix in front of
Trincant's house, viewed by the whole Trincant family.

The possessions should have come to an end, in theory, with Grandier's
death, but they did not. Far from it, the exorcisms of the nuns and of
secular women continued far into the future. Jeanne des Anges, always
the worst of the afflicted, continued to suffer from demonic possession
until the end of 1638, more than four years after Grandier's execution;
throughout this whole period, she was being exorcized. There were always some people who never believed in the validity of the possessions,
but most did. Many of the unbelievers were Huguenots, but there were
also Catholics, and the continuation of the possessions and the exorcisms was one of the factors supporting this disbelief. In her lifetime,
Jeanne des Anges became famous and much respected as having been a
worthy opponent of the Devil who ultimately overcame him. Not until
1693 was a major book published by a Huguenot minister that ultimately
led to widespread questions and doubts about the justice of Grandier's
trial and execution.

The exorcists, who certainly bore much of the responsibility for this
injustice, thought of themselves as honourable men performing a dis-
tressing task. They saw it as their duty to protect society through the
elimination of the witches and of the great dangers that they posed.
Their intent was to fight an invasion by the Devil and his adherents, to
save souls, and to gain heretic converts. These Catholic priests seemed
to have been handed a wonderful, perhaps God-given, opportunity to
prove to the Huguenots that God had given to his Catholic Church
power over the Devil. The result, they hoped, would be conversions to
the true faith. And to them this was no small matter. Heretics – as the
priests believed the Huguenots to be – would be condemned to eternal

damnation. To a Catholic priest of the time, converting a man or a woman was not simply a worldly success; it meant saving the person for the whole of eternity, and in this endeavour almost anything was justified. True, if they were successful they would gain great personal honour and advancement. But to most of the thirty exorcists who became involved over the life of the "possessions," this was not what drove them.

We often think of witch hunts as mass affairs, as in Bamberg, Wurzburg, and Salem. Here, however, is the case of an individual's treatment that clearly had all the characteristics of a witch hunt. One-person witch hunts are just as real and just as frightening, just as dangerous to society as classic mass cases. Only one man was at the centre. But the whole community of Loudun became at risk from the excesses of the witch hunters. When they proclaimed that whatever the Devil said under exorcism must be taken as the truth, nobody was safe. One-person witch hunts can have enormous repercussions. If Grandier had broken down under torture and given the names of innocent men and women, Loudun would have become another Bamberg.

Grandier was an unusual example of a prominent "witch" partly because he was male but mainly because he was a priest: few priests appeared as culprits in witchcraft trials. Fortunately for us, his case became famous in his lifetime. The enormous crowds at the public exorcisms and at his burning resulted in many contemporary memoirs and documents that have been preserved and passed down. In later times, down to our own days, it has been the subject of a very extensive literature that provides a valuable history of the terrors of a witch hunt. We are fortunate that this perfect example of a one-person witch hunt is so well recorded.

There are people who say that there are only mass witch hunts and that one-person cases are only miscarriages of justice. But this is incorrect. Grandier certainly saw himself as the victim of a witch hunt led by Father Mignon, and he said so. Clearly, the twelve judges were in no doubt that they had been searching for and trying a witch. We have only to read the verdict passed upon Grandier: "We declare the said Urbain Grandier duly guilty of the crime of sorcery, evil spells, and the possession visited upon some Ursuline nuns of this town of Loudun." Nor undoubtedly did Grandier have any doubt when he was at the stake.

What makes a witch hunt is that the case fulfils the characteristics of a witch hunt that we defined earlier. Grandier was accused, and once accused, he was guilty. Everything followed from this assertion. So there was the assumption and finding of guilt; then there was a long search for evidence that would prove the unsupported assumption. From that point on, any evidence against the priest was accepted without question by the exorcists and by his enemies; any evidence or support in his favour was ignored. Under Laubardemont, witnesses in Grandier's favour were ignored and often threatened. All the false evidence of the past was accepted as though the courts had never found in his favour. Retractions by the nuns of their earlier accusations were ignored and put down as the influences of the Devil. Torture was applied in terrible forms to force confessions from the priest and to gain new accusations against his presumed acolytes. And overriding everything was an order from the king himself stating that anybody who stood in the way of a conviction was to be ignored or punished if necessary. First the verdict, then the trial!

Later, we shall see two other examples of one-man witch hunts: the Dreyfus case in France about a century ago and the Maher Arar case in our own time.

5

The Arbitrary Terror of a Witch Hunt

"Thou shalt not be afraid for any terror by night: nor the arrow that flies by day. For the pestilence that walketh in the darkness: nor for the sickness that destroyeth in the noon-day," says Psalm 90. It is a promise that God will protect the faithful man and woman. It is a promise against the worst fears of every man and woman: the sudden, totally unexpected arrival of sickness and death by day or night; the instant, arbitrary, obliteration of the self that strikes without cause or warning.

This is the same terror that strikes in a witch hunt. As we saw in Bamberg and Wurzburg, innocent and arbitrary accusations, like a virus, carried with them a disease that struck without warning, causing terrifying torture and death as it spread through the new victims' accusations to yet other victims. No man or woman was safe. There grew to be a frightening fear of neighbour, a distrust of old friends, even close family; every man and woman was indeed an island. We shall see the same thing in the next case: Salem Village.

The accusations in Bamberg were highly arbitrary, unexpected, dissociated with reality. It all started with a trigger incident that in itself was totally unconnected with a witch hunt: crop failure. This was not the cause of the witch hunt, but it was the precursor. Then somebody (we don't know who) said that a witch must be the cause. Anybody could be accused. Throughout all that followed, everybody, in like fashion, became potentially accused and potentially a victim. Nobody in Bamberg (or in Salem, yet to come) was safe, whether of high or low standing.

It was the same in Loudun. It is the same today.

One of the most frightening things about a witch hunt is that any-body can be drawn in, accused, and assumed guilty. At first sight, in Grandier's case, for example, we might easily assume that he was the obvious person to be accused. This is far from the truth, in fact. He had no connection with the nuns, had never been seen by them, had nothing to do with them. Anybody could have been accused in those early exor-cisms of Jeanne des Anges.

Just as there had been in Bamberg, there was a trigger incident in Loudun: the plague, which had nothing at all to do with Grandier. It was the plague that brought about the hallucinations: the young nun who unwittingly started it all imagined the spectre of the convent con-fessor, who had died in the plague – no connection with Grandier at all. The handsome priest with the libertine reputation came into the picture only when Jeanne des Anges, clearly obsessed with the things that she had heard about him, brought out his name under exorcism. Somebody was going to be blamed for the invasion of the demons, but only once Grandier's name had been spoken, was he accused – and guilty.

But anybody else's name could have been brought out of the nuns' disturbed minds. It could, for example, just as easily have been Father Mignon, the new confessor turned exorcist; in fact, during the day *pre-ceding* the night on which the nun had her hallucinations about the dead priest, one record says: "she was totally preoccupied with im-proper thoughts, and had a violent desire that Sieur Mignon [Father Mignon], her director [her confessor], should fall into a great sin; fur-ther, she felt an extreme chagrin at having declared to him her secret thoughts," presumably in the confessional. So Mignon's name could just as easily have been put forward in place of Grandier's in an erotic hallucination. If Grandier had not been available as a lightning rod, somebody else would have been selected. And no doubt, in a convent so easily disturbed by erotic thoughts, many other names could have been chosen. It was purely arbitrary that the name was Grandier's. The first accusation in a witch hunt is always purely arbitrary. Once accused, then and only then was Grandier guilty and only then did all the char-acteristics of a witch hunt come into play, including the arbitrary – and, in this case, unsuccessful – search for accomplices.

The plague in Loudun was truly "the pestilence that walketh in the darkness" and "the sickness that destroyeth in the noon-day." It cre-ated a climate of fear that in turn created the "possessions" and the ar-bitrary accusation that followed. The full classic witch hunt involving masses of people never developed in Loudun. But this was only because Grandier would not accuse innocent friends to escape his torture and because when innocents were accused by the demons under exorcism, opposition to the hunt on the part of some men of authority in the town was powerful enough to limit the excesses. Nevertheless, the threat of everything going out of control as it had in Bamberg was serious enough for the *bailli* and his supporters to write to the king and express precisely this concern.

Witch hunts can strike down you or me. For "witch" substitute the word "terrorist." Or terrorist supporter. Or suspected supporter. If the attributes of a "witch" can be applied to you (and we will see that they can), then you could become the victim of a witch hunt. What identifies a witch hunt is that the characteristics of a witch hunt are involved. As the saying goes: "If it walks like a duck, swims like a duck, and quacks like a duck, then it probably is a duck." If it meets the characteristics of a witch hunt, then it is a witch hunt.

6

The Salem Witches

The events, and all the dread that they brought about, took place in the area of the Village of Salem in Massachusetts in 1692. They started in quite a small way with four girls making accusations of witchcraft against three women. There had been other cases in the recent past, not dissimilar, that had come and gone. But this one took on a life of its own. The contagion spread quickly, first within Salem Village itself, then to other surrounding townships. In this thinly populated rural area, some 200 people would be accused of witchcraft, 19 would be executed as witches, and one old man of over eighty would be pressed to death under heavy stones. First the local rural government became involved, then the local municipality of Salem Town, and as the fear increased and the consequences grew ever larger, the Colony of Massachusetts and its governor took the lead in controlling the events and in running the witch hunt and the witch trials. Then, almost as suddenly as things had started, they were closed down, once more by the governor. There were no more executions, no more accusations, and eventually, no more prisoners in the jails awaiting trial or execution. Everything from the first public accusations to the last execution took some seven months – seven months of "Consternation," as a local minister later put it.[1]

There were early indications of the storm that would arise, and after it had passed, it took time for life to settle back to normal, but between late February and September 1692 the tempest swept everything before it, more like a tornado in its effect, tossing lives into turmoil, spreading fear, and hatred, and death, leaving nobody unterrified or untouched.

Some five years after the events of the Salem witch trials, the Reverend John Hale, the Puritan minister of one of the neighbouring parishes, wrote what was in effect an eyewitness account. He starts:

It is known to all men, that it pleased God some few years ago, to suffer Satan to raise much trouble amongst us ... the beginning of which was very small, and looked on at first as an ordinary case which had fallen out before at several times in other places, and would be quickly over. Only one or two persons belonging to Salem Village about five miles from the Town being suspected were Examined, etc. But in the progress of the matter, a multitude of other persons both in this and other Neighbour Towns, were Accused, Examined, Imprisoned, and came to their Trials, at Salem, the County Town, where about Twenty of them Suffered as Witches; and many others in danger of the same Tragical End: and still the number of the Accused increased unto many Scores; amongst whom were many Persons of unquestionable Credit, never under any grounds of suspicion of that or any other Scandalous Evil. This brought a general Consternation upon all sorts of People, doubting what would be the issue of such a dreadful Judgment of God upon the Country; but the Lord was pleased suddenly to put a stop to those proceedings ... But it left in the minds of men a sad remembrance of that sorrowful time.

Salem Village was a rural area of Massachusetts, not far from Boston, an area settled in 1626 by Puritans who had fled there to create godly communities.[2] The village was so named, but it was not a village as such but a scattered settlement of farms. It bordered Salem Town, a port of importance – a fact that had, over time, created tensions in Salem Village. The farmers who were closest to the town were pulled toward involvement in commercial interests connected with the port, with ships, with trade, and with the wider international world. Those who lived farther from the sea had less interest in the world outside. They looked more toward the interior and to the Indian wars, to the raids and settlement burnings that forced their own young men to go to the defence of the frontier. Herein lay a problem. It was natural, for instance, that those who were concerned with the town would want to see taxes going toward matters concerning trade and town growth, while those whose concerns were primarily rural would want taxes used for matters of more local interest. Increasingly, there was a faction in the village that pushed for separation from the town and that searched for more independence of action. This showed itself within the church as well. The local church in the village had in effect been subordinate to the church in Salem Town, and there had been a consequent movement among villagers to become independent, to have their own church structure and their own minister. This, too, was a cause of friction, for the independence of Salem Village as a church community had tax repercussions that flowed from how much the minister was to be paid and how the church itself was to be supported.

At the time of the first "witch attacks" in 1692, the minister was a man named Samuel Parris. He had arrived three years before, in 1689, and he came into a divided and fractious community. A previous incumbent, for instance, the Reverend George Burroughs, had left Salem Village to get away from the disputes, infighting, and constant criticisms within the community. His predecessor, too, had left in part because of the disagreements and petulant behaviour. Burroughs would be hanged as a witch and as the leader of the witches – but this was still to come. Of immediate importance is that the community in Salem Village was divided into factions when events began and that it had been for some years.

It was into this potential quagmire that Samuel Parris stepped. He had been born in London in 1653 and had moved to Barbados to pursue the sugar trade, but bad harvests had driven him from there to Boston in 1680. In 1688 he decided to switch careers and become a minister, and later that same year, he was negotiating with the village. This was during the final push for independence of the Salem Village church from Salem Town, and Parris, married with a child, a servant, and slave dependants, wanted to be ensured of both religious and financial independence. He demanded and got the minister's house and two acres of land, together with a supply of wood for each winter. This issue of the minister's house was just a further point of contention and division within the community, for his demand was that he should own it, not just occupy it, and there were those in the community who objected to the terms of his contract. These seemingly trivial issues were important to this rural community in creating factions and supporters or opponents of the minister.

But at the start, things went well for him. Membership in the Puritan Church community was restricted to people who were committed to a full religious life of Christian living. Parris set high standards for entry; he began to build and expand his godly community and seems in his first year to have served it well. The second and third years did not go as successfully: he signed on fewer people, and his pay and emoluments began to fall into arrears. By the winter of 1691 to 1692 all the old factions were at work once more, and he personally, no doubt, had real concerns about what the future would bring. This was where things stood when the witch craze broke out – within the Parris household.

We do not have an exact date for the beginning, but it probably started in January, possibly even in late December of the previous year. It only became public at the end of February 1692. The December or January onset can be guessed at fairly easily because we know that in the formal warrant issued against a supposed witch, Sarah Good, on 29 February, she was called to account "for suspicion of Witchcraft by her Committed, and thereby much Injury donne to Eliz parris, Abigail Williams Anna putnam and Elizabeth Hubert all of Salem Village afores'd Sundry times within this two months and Lately also don, at Salem Village Contrary to the peace of our Sover'n L'd and Lady W'm & mary King & Queen of Engld &c."[3]

The two dates are important because the record of the sufferings of the girls is only known as of February 1692 – before this time we know that they were afflicted, but we do not know in what way or, perhaps more important, to what degree. Why is this significant?

Nobody now believes that witchcraft was really practised on an enormous scale in Salem Village; it was, in the beginning, all in the minds of these girls. They were almost certainly sick – or loosely speaking, hysterical – and beyond that there was deliberate fraud on their part from time to time; we shall see evidence of this. Probably early in January, possibly even in December (the Reverend John Hale said "In the latter end of the year 1691"), Parris's nine-year-old daughter, Elizabeth, and her eleven-year-old cousin, Abigail Williams, who was an orphan and servant in the Parris house, began to act strangely. But at first it is very likely that the affliction was not far advanced.

We do not know precisely how it all began. Different people have put forward different theories: that the two children were playing at witchcraft; that they were trying to divine who they would be married to; that they had read a book on a supposed case of witchcraft that had taken place a few years before near Boston – we know that Parris had this book, *Memorable Providences* by Cotton Mather, in his personal library. Of course, if they knew of this case, they would have known quite a good deal about the symptoms and actions of an afflicted person. Whatever the beginnings were, the children were almost certainly up to something that they should not have been. They may just have been playing, and the first signs of something wrong may have been quite simple, as they had been with the nuns at Loudun. But the signs were obviously taken seriously, and probably, being taken seriously, the children took them further. Their problem, no doubt, was that once adults began to believe them, the children had to continue; there was no possibility of going back.

We do not know the progression of events in those two months. The girls may have gone into their fits and their accusations right from the beginning. But more probably, it started small. In their later accusations, they complained frequently that they were pinched, and that pins were stuck in them, and that they were bitten. And to prove the last of these, they showed the signs of tooth marks. To prove that they had been pinned, they showed the pins. These were likely their early complaints, accompanied by shouts and screams, quite possibly blasphemies, athough these may have come later. All this was taking place in the Parris household. And it was violent enough and progressed quickly enough that although he was a man who had travelled, was educated, and had seen something of the world, Parris became convinced that in his daughter Elizabeth and in Abigail Williams, he had a frightening case taking place.

At the ages of these children, if it was suggested to them that they were bewitched, it probably had its effect, just as the Loudun nuns believed themselves to be possessed when they were told they were. Certainly, by late February, whatever had gone before, they were exhibiting the typical symptoms of hysteria – so many of the characteristics are similar to those we saw in Loudun. And at the same time, they were capable of working together to support the accusations of witchcraft against others that they were by then making. Something like this must have happened because by the time the afflictions and their consequences had become public at the end of February, people believed the girls. And also by the end of February, it had already spread beyond their household to two other girls who lived close by, Ann Putnam and Elizabeth Hubbard. Throughout it all, one gets the impression that the prime mover was Abigail Williams.

In response to all this, Parris called in doctors to give judgment whether these were natural or supernatural events. We know this because the Reverend Hale, who was called in early to help, tells us that "he [Parris] made his application to Physitians, yet still they [the girls] grew worse: And at length one Physitian gave his opinion, that they were under an Evil Hand. This the Neighbours quickly took up, and concluded they were bewitched." And it was probably the fits that made the case, just as they did in Loudun. Hale describes their sufferings as he saw them at the end of February: unseen persons "did pinch, prick, and grievously torment them ... These Children were bitten and pinched by invisible agents; their arms, necks, and backs turned this way and that way, and returned back again, so as it was impossible for them to do of themselves, and beyond the power of any Epileptick Fits, or natural Disease to effect. Sometimes they were taken dumb, their mouths stopped, their throats choked, their limbs wracked and tormented so as might move an heart of stone." Of course, by this time the girls may have been well beyond any self-directed appearances, at least in some of their actions. And at the same time they were at least partially self-possessed because, as we shall see, they acted in concert and dissembled together. They were probably both suffering from hysteria and practising chicanery at the same time. But to those present, it all seemed the work of the Devil.

These events of course did not stay ungossiped in this rural area, where everybody knew everyone else. And in a time and place where witchcraft was almost universally believed in, the conclusion to which everybody came was that there was a witch in the neighbourhood who was the cause of the possession of these girls. By now, too, in late February, the number of possessed had grown. Besides Elizabeth Parris and Abigail Williams, there were by this date six others ranging in age from eleven to twenty and one mature woman of thirty-six. Although these girls and young women were always at the centre of the events, more adults both male and female would also be afflicted as events developed, including Ann Putnam senior, who became one of the most seriously affected. Ann Putnam junior was one of the earliest afflicted.

Thus we come to 25 February 1692, when the first solid accusations of witchcraft were made. Just as there was a deal of common knowledge about witches among the ordinary people, there were supposed protections against their attacks. One of these was the witch cake. Supposedly to be made of various specific ingredients like rye meal, in this case urine from the girls was added to it, and the whole was baked and fed to a dog, probably on the assumption that the dog was a witch's familiar and that in some way the witch would be uncovered. It was the aunt of one of the afflicted girls who decided upon this secret action and who persuaded Parris's slave maid, Tituba, to bake the cake. The cake had no beneficial effect upon the girls; rather, it threw them into great pains and fits: "After this, the Afflicted persons cryed out of the Indian Woman, named Tituba, that she did pinch, prick, and grievously torment them, and that they saw her here and there, where no body else could. Yea they could tell where she was, and what she did, when out of their humane sight."

Tituba, when questioned, admitted to baking the cake but denied having any knowledge or involvement in witchcraft, admitting only that her mistress in Barbados had taught her how to discover a witch. The immediate action within the community was to institute days of fasting and prayers, for Parris had been advised by his minister friends to do this and see what developed.

So at this time there was a widespread belief that somebody was practising witchcraft upon the girls, and the girls in their words and actions were believed to be bewitched, but there was still hope that prayer and fasting would overcome the Devil. This, rather than exorcism, was the proper practice in Puritan society. In this case it did no good. Within a few days the contagion had spread. The first accusation of being a witch, levelled against Tituba (which, as far as one can judge, was not taken too seriously), had spread. As Hale recalled it, "In a short time after other persons who were of age to be witnesses, were molested by Satan, and in their fits cryed out upon Tituba and Goody O(sborne) and S(arah) G(ood) that they or Specters in their Shapes did grievously torment them."

This accusation against Osborne and Good marked the shift from a controllable situation to the beginnings of a full-blown witch hunt. Sarah Good and Sarah Osborne were women of the village. Good was an indigent, cantankerous woman with a poor reputation – turbulent, spiteful, malicious, and generally disliked. Sarah Osborne also had something of an unpopular reputation, although unlike Good, she was financially quite well-to-do. Neither was much of a churchgoer, which counted heavily against them in this community. Both of these women resembled the common picture of a witch: old, bad-tempered, popularly disliked, and occasioning disapproval. The girls had chosen well: it was not difficult for people in the community to believe that these two women were the cause of the witchcraft and its effect upon the girls and young women. And they had chosen well in another way: they did not accuse the two women of coming directly upon them and causing their pains and fits. It was their "spectres" who appeared. They were not there physically themselves when they caused harm, but it was the "shape" of them that came and did harm. The implication was well understood: the Devil had borrowed their spirit, or spectre, and used it to do his work. From the beginning of the Salem witch trials, this business of the spectres was to haunt events, for it always explained why the women could be in one place and their spectres in another, doing evil, thus freeing the afflicted accusers of ever having to explain how this "bi-location" was possible.

On the other hand, this "spectral evidence" was to cause much theological discussion among the ministers in the next few months. When it came time to try the accused witches, as it very quickly did, the secular judges looked to the ministers of local Massachusetts to advise them whether this evidence of spectres should be accepted in a court. The theological questions were not unlike those that arose in Loudun. Could the Devil use the spectres of other people to carry out his work, and if so, could he do it without their permission, or did they have to be in league with him? Was it the Devil who was acting? Or was it the accused person? And if it was the Devil, could anything he said or did be believed? The ministers were divided, but in that spring and summer, those who believed that spectral evidence should be accepted as valid won the day. Later, there came about a common belief among them that they had gone too far and that spectral evidence was unreliable; by then it was too late for all those who had been executed. So at the time that the accusations were being made against Sarah Good and Sarah Osborne, people believed that their spectres really were attacking the girls. Once the women were accused of being witches, evidence against them was accepted without serious questioning, whereas in other circumstances it would have been laughed out of court.

The accusations of the girls were taken so seriously that "some of their Village Neighbours complained to the Magistrates at Salem, desiring they would come and examine the afflicted and accused together; the which they did." And quickly. Four men of Salem Village came forward on 29 February and laid complaints against each of the women "for suspition of Witchcraft by her Committed, and thereby much Injury donne to Eliz parris, Abigail Williams Anna putnam and Elizabeth Hubert all of Salem Village afores'd Sundry times within this two moneths." Sarah Good appeared the next day, 1 March, at the local inn, the home of one of the leading persons, and was questioned by two appointed men, John Hathorne and Jonathan Corwin. Even at this early point in the proceedings, the women Sarah Good and Sarah Osborne were assumed to be guilty and treated as such.

The questioners, Hathorne and Corwin, demanded admissions of guilt at length, and Sarah Good denied them and scorned the proceedings and the accusers. But what the record does not give any picture of is the atmosphere within the room where all this was going on. It was crowded with local people (so much so that within the next few days everything had to be removed to the meeting house to accommodate the numbers), and the girls were there. When Good was told to look upon them "presently they were all tormented." And this was no silent matter, they were shouting and screaming, possibly blaspheming, for the records said that this was one of their symptoms, falling into horrifying fits, in obvious pain. It was at this point on 1 March that Sarah Good, being repeatedly asked who was responsible and "who was it then that tormented the children," replied "it was osburn." She had confirmed what all suspected, that Sarah Good and Sarah Osborne had been acting as witches together.

That same day, Sarah Osborne was also questioned to see whether there was any case against her, for the purpose of these inquiries was to see whether they should be imprisoned and later tried for witchcraft:

Sarah Osburne upon Examination denied the matter of fact (viz) that she ever understood or used any Witchcraft, or hurt any of the aboves'd children.

The children above named being all personally present accused her face to face which being don, they ware all hurt, afflicted and tortured very much: which being over and thay out of theire fitts thay sayd that said Sarah Osburne did then Come to them and hurt them, Sarah Osburn being then keept at a distance personally from them. S. Osburne was asked why she then hurt them, she denied it: it being Asked of her how she could soe pinch & hurt them and yet she be at that distance personally from them she Answered she did not then hurt them nor never did. She was Asked who then did it, or who she Imployed to doe it, she Answered she did not know that the divell goes aboute in her likeness to doe any hurt. Sarah Osburn being told that Sarah Good one of her Companions had upon Examination accused her, she nottwithstanding denied the same.

It seems clear today that the children, in making these accusations together, were acting in concert. Even if it was possible to argue that they were already suffering from hysteria, they were certainly supporting and aiding each other in their actions. Was there a leader? We do not know, but probably one was taking the lead and the others following. It

must have been heady days for them. Women and their opinions were
not that much respected at the time, and female children even less so,
yet here we see a group of them so much in control of the crowd (and
even the authorities in law, medicine, and religion) that everything they
said and did was taken as gospel. It is likely that they did not fully realize at this date that they were no longer just playing at getting two old
women into some trouble – and hardly likely that they fully realized
and accepted that executions would rest upon and follow on their
words. Their problem, assuming they recognized that they had a problem, was that once committed they could not withdraw. They had to expand their accusations to others in order to prove their own innocence.
And in their youth, they must have been very conscious of the power
that they had now been handed. Heady stuff!

Was Sarah Good's accusation that the real witch was Osborne
enough in the eyes of the questioners to pursue them both to trial?
Probably. One accused witch accusing another was powerful material. That she denied her own guilt was only what one would expect
if she was guilty. But in this case it was Tituba, questioned on the
same day, who really confirmed what all knew in their hearts. She
denied practising witchcraft but said that the Devil had approached
her "to bid me serve him." Then she turned the questioning from herself to others, saying that she had seen "four women sometimes hurt
the children."

"Who were they?"
"Goode Osburn and Sarah Good and I doe not know who the other were."

And she introduced a new "character" into the story later in the
questioning:

"What attendants hath Sarah Good?"
"A yellow bird and she would have given me one."
"What meate did she give it?"
"It did suck her between her fingers."

Not only had she accused Goody Osborne and Sarah Good, but she had
also introduced their familiars, given to them by the Devil. Everybody
knew that witches had familiars. She gave one to Sarah Osborne, too,
after a later question:

"What hath Sarah Osburn?"

"Yesterday, shee had a thing with a head like a woman with 2 legges, and wings. Abigail Williams that lives with her Uncle Parris said that she did see the same creature, and it turned into the shape of Goode [Goody] Osburn."

Tituba's answers wove back and forth between denials of her involvement and details of witches and familiars, all to the accompaniment of accusations from the girls and their loud torments. There were other witnesses who came before the meeting and accused all three women in turn. But what Tituba additionally confirmed was that there was a conspiracy of witches that even went beyond Good and Osborne to include at least two other women and a man, but she did not know who they were. Her confirmation of a major attack by the Devil upon the community was of the greatest significance to the future of the case. This is what everybody feared and what many expected. This was now no isolated ungodly commerce between two despised old woman and a slave; their conduct was only the tip of the iceberg. There was much more to be discovered, new names, new accusations. The ministers in New England were already concerned that the morals and standards of the two previous generations had fallen. Here was proof. The Devil had seen the weakness and chosen to attack here. The godly community was being assaulted by the Devil, and the only way to overcome and defeat him was to identify and wipe out every one of his acolytes. Search! Find! Destroy! The witch hunt was on. And the girls would provide the witches.

The conclusion of the day did not take long. All three women were sent to jail to await further examination and trial. For the moment it is enough to say that Sarah Osborne died in prison, from what specific cause we do not know. Tituba, for some reason, was never given up to punishment, which is strange considering the part that she played and the information that she brought forward. It has been suggested that her status as a slave might have saved her: a slave was property, not lightly to be destroyed. This may have played some part, but there must surely have been a conclusion somewhere that she was not a witch or at least not a guilty witch in local terms – she was merely someone who practised what might be expected of a slave from the islands.

The state of the village can well be imagined: three women identified; others mentioned but not known; the whole neighbourhood, including the surrounding villages, with but one theme for gossip; ministers from surrounding parishes arriving to assist in combating the Devil. The afflicted girls showed no signs of getting better – and were probably growing worse, having discovered what most impressed their audiences. The topic of every conversation would be the witches, especially those who had been seen by Tituba but whose names were not known. Every neighbour would be suspect. Every strange incident of the past would be dissected to see who might have been responsible; every old woman would have her life reviewed in gossip conversation. And there was at least one man involved, too, according to Tituba. No doubt, the most feared and suspected were those who were most disliked and whose tempers – and, in the circumstances, whose reprisals – were most dreaded. Over the next days the pressure built up, the tension and the fear increased, the suspicions grew.

Events came to a head on 11 March when Ann Putnam junior accused another woman, Martha Corey. Young Ann's was a surprising accusation, and perhaps it was a measure of the overexcitement and passion of the time that the accusation was so readily accepted. Martha Corey, unlike those first accused, had a sound reputation in the community (despite a mulatto child in her past) and above all was a member of the church congregation in good standing. This was much more than just being somebody who went to church. It meant that she had passed intense scrutiny and had high standards of moral and religious life, for it was believed that only those who were fully accepted into the church in this way were elected by God to be saved on death. Under normal circumstances it would have been almost unbelievable that such an accusation would be accepted and acted upon. Much later, people would question whether Martha Corey and other church members could possibly have been guilty, but in the disarray of the time it was interpreted that the Devil was so active, so powerful, so determined to take over New England for his kingdom that he had even managed to insert his witches into the church.

There was, however, sufficient doubt in this case that two men of sound reputation were sent to Martha Corey to question her. They devised a means of testing her reliability. It was her spectre who had appeared to Ann Putnam junior. So they went to the young girl to ask what the spectre was wearing so that they could see whether Martha Corey was in fact dressed in the same manner. Young Ann was too clever by half to fall into their trap. The spectre, she declared, had blinded her so that she did not know what Corey was wearing. The men went on to Martha Corey, who denied any involvement; indeed, she faced them quite calmly when they said that according to the accusations, she had dishonoured God and the church. She expressed certainty in her own innocence and in her belief in and adherence to the word of God. It seems clear that she was convinced that her life would speak for her and that this injustice would pass her by. It was not to be. Within two or three days, Abigail Williams made further accusations against her, accompanied by screams and fits. Under the pains of her fits, she accused Martha Corey of nourishing a familiar, a little yellow bird. (Tituba's revelation had again come home to roost.) Mercy Lewis supported Abigail's contention that Corey was a witch and made specific accusations against her. In short order, the extraordinary appearances and contortions and accusations of the girls had won the day. Certainty was assured when Ann Putnam, the mother, was tormented by Martha's spectre. A formal complaint was laid against Corey.

So by now the initial limited results of accusations against two cantankerous old women and a slave had jumped a major boundary and spread to a respectable churchgoer. The contagion was spreading and would soon threaten everyone. Everything that happened in the future rested upon the foundation of these few days between 25 February and 11 March. The result would be a witch hunt that has remained famous and known worldwide from then until now.

Instructions were now issued that Martha Corey, too, was to be questioned formally. This was set for 21 March. This time the session was moved from the inn to the meeting house because of the crowds. But two days earlier the contagion had already spread farther, as supported by the eyewitness record of the minister Deodat Lawson, who had been asked to come to Salem Village to observe what was going on. He was a former minister in the parish and knew the people involved and was known by them. He came to help his friends. But some measure of the suspicions of those days can be gathered from his secondary reason for coming: "But especially my concern was augmented, when it was reported, at an examination of a person suspected for witchcraft, that my wife and daughter, who had died three years before, were sent out of the world under the malicious operations of the infernal powers." The accusations were now taking on terrible proportions, and people both believed and were frightened by them, even the educated leaders.

Lawson recorded his experiences of that day:

On the Nineteenth day of March last I went to Salem Village, and lodged at Nathaniel Ingersols [the inn] near to the Minister Mr. P[arris]'s house, and

presently after I came into my Lodging Capt. Walcuts Daughter Mary came
to Lieut. Ingersols and spake to me, but, suddenly after as she stood by the
door, was bitten, so that she cried out of her Wrist, and looking on it with a
Candle, we saw apparently the marks of Teeth both upper and lower set,
on each side of her wrist.

In the beginning of the Evening, I went to give Mr. P[arris] a visit. When I
was there, his Kins-woman, Abigail Williams, (about 12 years of age) had a
grievous fit; she was at first hurryed with Violence to and fro in the room,
(though Mrs. Ingersol endeavoured to hold her) sometimes makeing as if she
would fly, stretching up her arms as high as she could, and crying "Whish,
Whish, Whish!" several times; Presently after she said there was Goodw. N.
and said, "Do you not see her? Why there she stands!" And the said Goodw.
N. offered her The Book, but she was resolved she would not take it, saying
Often, "I wont, I wont, I wont, take it, I do not know what Book it is: I am
sure it is none of Gods Book, it is the Divels Book, for ought I know." After
that, she run to the Fire, and begun to throw Fire Brands, about the house;
and run against the Back, as if she would run up Chimney, and, as they said,
she had attempted to go into the Fire in other Fits.

The next day, in church, while Lawson was giving his sermon, Abigail
Williams rose up and cried out, arguing with him about what he was saying. It was extraordinary that a young girl of twelve should be allowed to
do this and that it would be accepted, yet it was. It was taken for granted
that she was not speaking for herself but under some form of possession
by the Devil.

But let us return to the previous day. Abigail accused Goodwife N.
(or her spectre, which only Abigail could see) of offering her what was
assumed to be the Devil's book to sign. From now on the Devil's book
would frequently become involved in accusations. Signing the book
made the person an acolyte of the Devil, a witch, and what Goodwife
N. was doing, according to Abigail, was inviting her to become a witch.
And who was Goodwife N.? She was Rebecca Nurse. A more unlikely
witch would have been hard to find, yet the accusation was believed.
She was the wife of a well-to-do farmer, a deeply religious woman,
pious, a leader in charity. Abigail accused her on 19 March. Within the
next few days, during and after the examination of Martha Corey, the
two of them were accused by the afflicted of appearing singly and together torturing Ann Putnam's mother. In Lawson's presence Abigail
railed against the spectre of Rebecca Nurse: "Goody N. Be gone! Be
gone! Be gone! are you not ashamed, a Woman of your Profession, to

afflict a poor Creature so? what hurt did I ever do you in my life! you have but two years to live, and then the Devil will torment your Soul, for this your Name is blotted out of Gods Book, and it shall never be put in Gods Book again, be gone for shame, are you not afraid of that which is coming upon you?" As the result of her "tormenting" Ann Putnam senior, a complaint was laid against Rebecca Nurse, and she in turn was examined by Hathorne and Corwin on 24 March. Things were moving fast, and the number of afflicted was increasing day by day. And we must remember that if the number of afflicted had grown, the number of accusations had grown with them. The speed at which things moved is horrifying, even at this distance.

Given the number of afflicted at Martha Corey's examination and the hostility and disbelief in her innocence shown to her by Hathorne and Corwin, it is understandable that she stood little chance of defending herself. The accusations, the fits, the pains, the shouts and screams of the afflicted who were present far outweighed her protestations of innocence and denials of commerce with the Devil. Those present could even see her guilt with their own eyes. One observer, Deodat Lawson, recorded:

It was observed several times, that if she did but bite her Under lip in time of Examination the persons afflicted were bitten on their armes and wrists and produced the Marks before the Magistrates, Ministers and others. And being watched for that, if she did but Pinch her Fingers, or Graspe one hand hard in another, they were Pinched and produced the Marks before the Magistrates, and Spectators. After that, it was observed, that if she did but lean her Breast against the Seat, in the Meeting House, (being the Barr at which she stood) they were afflicted. Particularly Mrs. Pope complained of grievous torment in her Bowels as if they were torn out. She vehemently accused said C[orey] as the instrument, and first threw her Muff at her; but that flying not home, she got off her Shoe, and hit Goodwife C[orey] on the head with it. After these postures were watched, if said C[orey] did but stir her feet, they were afflicted in their Feet, and stamped fearfully. The afflicted persons asked her why she did not go to the company of Witches which were before the Meeting house mustering? Did she not hear the Drum beat? They accused her of having Familiarity with the Devil, in the time of Examination, in the shape of a Black man whispering in her ear; they affirmed, that her Yellow-Bird sucked betwixt her Fingers in the Assembly; and order being given to see if there were any sign, the Girl that saw it said, it was too late now; she had removed a Pin, and put it on her head; which was found there sticking upright.

This description gives us some impression of the confusion, noise, and general atmosphere that was being accepted in a formal legal examination by two magistrates (who would later, it turned out, be among the judges of the witches at their trials). One can also see the childish nature of the pranks being played by the afflicted upon the crowd: whatever Martha Corey did was repeated by the children as in a game; if she stirred her feet, they stamped theirs. Martha Corey was sent to jail to await trial as a witch.

Three days later, on 24 March, it was Rebecca Nurse's turn. Hathorne and Corwin treated her, initially at least, with more open minds, such was her good name. The form of questioning to start with was more respectful and less hostile. But now there were interventions and accusations from the floor. One man said that since she had been in his house, he had twice suffered seizures of some sort. Then the afflicted took over, overriding Hathorne's questioning:

Thomas Putman's Wife, Abigail Williams and Thomas Putmans daughter accused her that she appeared to them, and afflicted them in their fitts: but some of the other said, that they had seen her, but knew not that ever she had hurt them; amongst which was Mary Walcut, who was presently after she had so declared bitten, and cryed out of her in the meeting-house; producing the Marks of teeth on her wrist ... her Motions did produce like effects as to Biteing, Pinching, Bruising, Tormenting, at their Breasts, by her Leaning, and when, bended Back, were as if their Backs was broken. The afflicted persons said, the Black Man whispered to her in the Assembly, and therefore she could not hear what the Magistrates said unto her. They said also that she did then ride by the Meeting-house, behind the Black Man. Thomas Putman's wife had a grievous Fit, in the time of Examination, to the very great Impairing of her strength, and wasting of her spirits, insomuch as she could hardly move hand, or foot, when she was carried out. Others also were there grievously afflicted, so that there was once such an hideous scrietch and noise, (which I heard as I walked, at a little distance from the Meeting house) as did amaze me, and some that were within told me the whole assembly was struck with consternation, and they were afraid, that those that sate next to them, were under the influence of Witchcraft. This woman also was that day committed to Salem Prison.

Another person was committed on that same day: Sarah Good's daughter, Dorcas. She was four or five years old. Two of the afflicted girls accused her of having tormented them and showed small sets of teeth marks as proof. She was sent to join her mother in jail (she spent months there, and when released she never recovered her normal life or disposition). Dorcas Good was the first, and worst, example of the accusations against one person being extended to other members of a family. It was not safe to be related to an accused witch; contagion was suspected and, in reality, assumed. A sermon delivered by Parris three days later only made matters worse. The involvement of Martha Corey and Rebecca Nurse worried some people because they had been full members of the church. How could it be that members who had been assumed to be among the elect could possibly be witches. Surely, this went against all Calvinist belief in election by God? But he told them, as their minister, that this could be, and he gave theological support for his argument. It would turn out to be a significant argument to put forward, for from that time on, accusations could be made against anybody, no matter how good they appeared to be in moral or religious life. Within this community, with his advice and blessing, any accusation could be valid. And further, he argued that spectre evidence was valid. The person herself did not have to appear, only her spectre – and of course this could be seen only by the afflicted, by those persons who made the accusations. The field was now wide open!

In retrospect, it seems strange that nobody recognized that Parris was no longer an independent minister preaching to his flock. His daughter was involved directly. Some of the other accusers, particularly the Putnam family, were his strongest supporters. He was in fact protecting the accusers and had a personal interest in doing so.

Over the next few weeks the number of people accused of witchcraft grew. On 28 March Elizabeth Proctor was denounced. The Proctors, John and Elizabeth, were members of the church, well respected, and prosperous by local standards. She had been married to him for eighteen years and was pregnant with his seventeenth child. It was difficult for people to believe that this woman of such solidity in the community could be guilty of this terrible crime. But the afflicted continued with their accusations, even though they seemed less certain of themselves under questioning. However, when the formal examination took place on 11 April, they were far more solid in their denunciations. They accused her (or, to be more precise, her spectre) of biting, pinching, choking, of trying to coerce them to sign the book, and of having seen her and other named witches at large gatherings of their kind. The witches' Sabbath had now been brought in and in future was to appear more and more often and in greater detail. Another woman of good standing was examined with Elizabeth Proctor; her name was Sarah Cloyce, Rebecca Nurse's sister. The same accusations were made against her: she, too, had appeared at the Sabbath, along with Sarah Good. Denials by these two godly women held no sway. Both Elizabeth Proctor and Sarah Cloyce were sent to jail for trial.

This examination differed from earlier ones in one respect. The chief examiner was no longer Hathorne but the deputy governor of the Colony, Thomas Danforth. The witch hunt was no longer a local matter.

It was during Elizabeth Proctor's examination that her husband, John, was accused. In some ways he was a natural target, for from the beginning he had made it plain to all that he had little faith in the afflicted or their accusations. He had spoken out against them to a number of people. Indeed, one of the afflicted was in his own household: Mary Warren was his servant. His response to her behaviour is well conveyed in his own reported words: "If they were let alone so we should all be devils and witches quickly. They should rather be had to the whipping post but he would fetch his jade home and thrash the devil out of her ... And also added that when she was first taken with fits he kept her close to the wheel and threatened to thrash her, and then she had no more fits till the next day he was gone forth, and then she must have her fits again firsooth:"

Such an unbelieving and contemptuous attitude was dangerous to the afflicted, but by now they knew their power. It is most probable that this was what led Ann Putnam and Abigail Williams to claim that he was a wizard. They were supported by an interjection from a member of the audience to this theatre, a man named Benjamin Gould. He had taken no part in earlier examinations of accused people, but now he came forward and said that "he had seen Goodman Corey and his wife, Proctor and his wife, Goody Cloyce, Goody Nurse, and Goody Griggs in his chamber." It was of course their spectres whom he was claiming had appeared to him. This testimony now linked all the accused as one band in concert. Such interjections by persons not afflicted, or not seriously afflicted, became quite common as examinations progressed, so gradually, it was not only the accusations and fits of the girls that were condemning their neighbours, but also the supporting information put before the magistrates by independent observers – although what led the witnesses in their minds to make such affirmations is difficult to understand.

Easier to explain is another form of evidence that was occurring with some frequency during the examinations: evidence of *maleficium*, or acts done in the past by the supposed witch that were evil in intent and performed through the power given by the Devil to the witch. Thus an accusation would be made by the young women, for example, and this would be followed by evidence of village residents who in casting their minds back remembered an occurrence where the accused witch had caused harm. When a number of these events were brought forward in evidence by a number of different people against one witch, it added heavily to the denunciations.

By 2 June seventy people had been accused. By now the contagion had spread well beyond the original limits. At least sixteen of the surrounding parishes now had accused persons. It is not difficult to imagine the fear that this must have spread throughout these rural communities. There was the fear of the witches, of course – which is obviously what underpinned the whole edifice. But there must also have been a terrible fear on the part of many of being accused. Rumours would abound everywhere, nothing else would be talked about, and the gossip and suspicions must have spread through every neighbourhood. Surely, if the Proctors and Rebecca Nurse were accused and in prison, nobody could have felt safe from ill-founded innuendos. Probably, some felt that the safest way to save themselves was to be on the side of the angels, accusers rather than accused. Perhaps this is why Giles Corey testified against his wife Martha. If so, it did him little good. A cantakerous man in his early eighties with an undesirable reputation from the past, he, too, was in turn accused. The young girls went into their fits, and he was jailed like the others.

Another who was accused was Bridget Bishop. She was unfortunate enough to already have a reputation from the past of being a witch, having appeared before the magistrates way back in 1680. After she was accused, she was examined in her turn by the magistrates. A man came forward in support of the accusations and brought up cases of *maleficium* going back for years. She had made money disappear from his pocket, caused potholes in the road, prevented him from lifting a bag of corn. He was not alone in such charges against her: others came forward, both men and women. Bridget proclaimed her innocence and denied that she had harmed young girls in any way or done the evil of which she was accused, but it did her no good. She, too, was jailed. She would be the first to die by hanging.

April rolled into May, and then June began. The jails were full in the surrounding areas, the conditions horrible. In the meantime, the governor, Sir William Phipps, arrived from England on 14 May to discover that his colony was stricken with witchcraft, in addition to all its other problems. He moved quickly, issuing an order on 27 May: "Upon consideration that there are many criminal offenders now in custody, some whereof have lain long, and many inconveniences attending the thronging of the jails this hot season of the year, there being no judicatories or courts of justice yet established: Ordered, that a Special Commission of Oyer and Terminer be made out to William Stoughton, John Richards, Nathaniel Saltonstall, Wait Winthrop, Bartholomew Gedney, Samuel Sewall, John Hathorne, Jonathan Corwin and Peter Sergeant, Esquires, assigning them to be justices, or any five of them."

He was setting up a special court to deal with all the jailed accused. The list of judges was certainly not beneficial to those who were to defend themselves – and defend themselves they had to because they were not allowed lawyers. We know that Samuel Sewall, Jonathan Corwin, and John Hathorne were already convinced that a great witch invasion was taking place, and they had already sent to jail a substantial number of those to be tried. Further, Winthrop, Sargeant, Gedney, and Stoughton had all attended at least one examination. Nevertheless, they appeared to be a well-picked group, all men of experience, some with substantial experience as magistrates, and a number had previous experience of witchcraft trials. The only one who seems to have been reluctant was Nathaniel Saltonstall, so much so that he would resign after the first death sentence was passed.

Once appointed, the trials were hastened forward. The whole of the province was in a turmoil, and action had to be taken swiftly and courageously to bring about justice, to defeat the contagion, and to show the populace that they were being protected. They chose as their first suspect Bridget Bishop, who had a past record of involvement as a witch and who could be judged quickly and cleanly.

In the record of her first hearing on 19 April, the first line reads: "As soon as she came near all fell into fits." Shortly after, it states: "Eliz. Hubbard Ann Putman, Abigail Williams & Mercy Lewes affirmed she had hurt them," and later, "They say you bewitcht your first husband to death." Then the record shows that "The afflicted persons charge her, with having hurt them many wayes and by tempting them to sine to the devils Booke at which charge she seemed to be very angrie and shaking her head at them saying it was false they are all greatly tormented (as I conceive) by the shaking of her head." On 2 June 1692 Bridget Bishop was on trial on the following grounds:

causing the fits of the girls, murder, and trying to get them to become acolytes of the Devil by signing his book.

Deliverance Hobbs, also an accused and in prison with Bridget Bishop, stated that the accused had tried to get her to sign the Devil's book – this was "jailhouse testimony" (not uncommon in witch hunts then or now). This was among the first confessions of guilt; in the coming months they would become more common. The reason for these confessions was to become obvious: the accused persons who admitted guilt were saved from the death sentence, as was Deliverance Hobbs. But their testimony was accepted as valid, as hers was. Another witness, provided startling evidence: "This Deponent doth veryly beleive that the said Bridget Bishop was Instrumentall to his Daughter Prisillas Death: about two years agoe, the Child was alikely Thriveing Child. And suddenly Screaked out and soe continued in an unsuall Manner for about a fortnight & soe dyed in that lamentable manner."

Another man provided further spectral evidence, also dating back fourteen years. This would have been shortly before the first time that Bridget Bishop had been questioned for witchcraft, so these may have been old complaints being revived. He too finished up by accusing her of having caused his child to sicken and then die. A further deponent was the Reverend John Hale, who had earlier been brought in to see the afflicted girls before the whole affair grew out of hand. He began by going back five or six years and recalling that at the time, "the said Bishop did entertaine people in her house at unseasonable houres in the night to keep drinking and playing at shovel-board whereby discord did arise in other families & young people were in danger to bee corrupted." He recalled another parishioner, a woman named Christian Trask, who had objected to the goings-on, had conducted consequent dealings with Bridget, and had subsequently suffered from fits, "but since I have seen the fitts of those bewitched at Salem Village I call to mind some of hers to be much like some of theirs." He continued: "The said Trask when recovered as I understood it did manifest strong suspicion that shee had been bewitched by the s'd Bishop's wife [Bridget]." Later, she died. Hale came to the view that her wounds – her cut windpipe, another wound in her throat, and her cut jugular vein – could not have been caused by the short pair of scissors that were beside her "without some extraordinary work of the devill or witchcraft."

No doubt, this evidence provided by John Hale had great effect. He was a respected Puritan minister from an adjacent parish and experienced in his dealings with a community of believers. Moreover, he had known Bridget Bishop in the past, and he had been in on the afflictions almost from the beginning. Of course, the judges would lay great weight on his assertions.

His evidence gives us an interesting insight into the beliefs of these people at the time. Gaming and other loose living were indications of a general immorality on the part of the person involved. Acts of alleged *maleficium* were proof of witchcraft. Spectral evidence was further proof. Once witchcraft was alleged, even murder could be assumed as the responsibility of the accused, without any material evidence at all. The immense and fearful power of the witch was taken for granted.

Others followed with stories of a common thread: some argument or disagreement with the woman was followed by a child falling ill and having fits, by "creatures strangely dying," by spectral visits. One said that on that very day, 2 June 1692, "I saw the Apperishtion of Bridgit Bishop. and Immediatly appeared to [two] little children and said that they ware Thomas Greens two twins and tould Bridget Bishop to hir face that she had murthered them in setting them into fits wher of they dyed."

The accusing girls had much to answer for, but so had the other deponents. It seems clear that once a woman was accused of witchcraft, everybody looked back over the years for any evil event that had happened and that could be coupled with her. Again, this was typical of witch-hunt mentality: it was believed that the person involved was so connected to evil that anything evil that happened must in turn be connected to them. In such a climate, false evidence, unsupported allegations, and any testimony against the witch were all accepted without serious questioning.

The end was swift. On 8 June a death warrant was issued against Bridget Bishop, which said "That upon fryday next being the Tenth day of this instant month of June between the houres of Eight and twelve in the afternoon of the same day You safely conduct the s'd Bridgett Bishop als Olliver from their Maj'ties Gaol in Salem afores'd to the place of Execution and there cause her to be hanged by the neck untill she be dead." On that Friday, she was taken to Gallows Hill near Salem Village and hanged. Soon afterward Nathaniel Saltonstall, one of the appointed judges, resigned from the list of magistrates appointed to the court; he was not comfortable with all that had happened.

The next trial did not, in fact, take place until 29 and 30 June. In the intervening period, over a dozen of the province's leading ministers gave a document to Governor Phipps. Its contents show that there was some unease about the whole business of the witchcraft invasion and about the accompanying allegations and accusations. They clearly believed in the reality of the witchcraft, but they also had doubts about some of the proceedings leading to the trials. They were critical of some of the examinations that had taken place, particularly of the chaotic interjections and actions of the afflicted during the examinations of the accused, which they felt were prejudicial to the defendants. They were also doubtful about whether the look of an accused upon the afflicted or a movement of her body that resulted in fits and reactions could be taken as valid evidence of anything (an interesting point because it almost implies that they were suspicious that the girls and the other afflicted might be play-acting). And they noted with disapproval that if the witch touched the afflicted and the fits died away, it was considered proof of the witch's power.

But of greatest concern and the source of greatest confusion among the ministers was the spectral evidence. Some held that it should be accepted as valid: if a spectre appeared, it was the same as the witch herself appearing. According to this line of argument, when the Devil "borrowed" the witch's spectre, it was with her agreement. Others felt that her agreement was not necessary and that the Devil could act on his own, in which case a spectral appearance could in no way be used as a proof of activity as a witch.

Something must have been troubling the ministers when they raised this last issue. Running underneath the uncertainties with which they were dealing was an unstated concern. Some of the accused, largely women who met the stereotype of a witch, caused no great doubts. But how could one explain that members of the elect, God-fearing church-goers of unimpeachable reputation, were being accused as witches. Were they really witches? Or was something going wrong?

The result of all this was a confused document that raised issues but that provided no really solid advice beyond encouragement to the judges to carry on with their necessary work but to be cautious. It was too early in the whole affair to take a stand one way or another. Nobody, including the ministers, had any doubts that the Devil was attacking, signing on acolytes with the intention of making the province his own. There were perhaps some concerns about the veracity of some of the afflicted's conduct, concerns that were implied rather than stated. But the real concern was that the innocent should not be dragged in with the guilty. So be careful, they said. This was really not much help given the excitement and fear at the sight of dozens of men and women in jail awaiting trial, the new and terrifying revelations arising every day, and the contagion spreading into all the surrounding parishes.

By the time of Bridget Bishop's trial, there were 70 people accused. The numbers would grow fast, as would the expansion of afflictions and accusations during the coming summer. In the records of the Salem witchcraft trials, 140 people are listed as accused of witchcraft in 1692. These are names that we know about without any doubt. There may have been others; the figure of a total of about 200 is sometimes mentioned. But even 140 people in scattered rural parishes is an enormous number: there were 26 in Salem Village, 12 in Salem Town, 42 in Andover, which was a neighbouring parish, and scattered outbreaks in twenty-two other close parishes.

It is not the accused alone whom we need to consider. For example, in his essay "New Directions," John Demos says, "There is at least minimal information about 165 people accused as witches during the entire period of the Salem outbreak … 42 males and 120 females," but he also adds that "Thirty-four persons experienced fits of one sort or another during the Salem trials and qualify thereby as accusers" and that "Eighty-four persons came forward as witnesses at one time or another during the Salem trials." If the afflicted, the accused, and the witnesses are added together, a total of 283 people were directly involved, quite apart from judges, jailers, and other functionaries. If we consider the scattered rural nature of the many townships affected, there can hardly have been a single family that did not have some involved member, a mother or father, brother or sister, uncle or aunt, grandfather or grandmother, or cousin. There may have been much bigger cases in Europe, but no case had as great an effect on the whole population and caused more local fear.

There is one clear example of how the contagion spread. In Andover a certain John Ballard's wife had fallen ill some months before. She suffered from great pains and pressure (and, in fact, would die some time later). In July Ballard was advised by his neighbours to look to the afflicted girls of Salem Village for help in determining who was responsible for his wife's sufferings.

The girls from Salem convinced those present that the woman's sickness was indeed the result of witchcraft, "Whereupon," one of the newly accused women said, "we were all seized, as prisoners, by a warrant from the Justice of the peace and forthwith carried to Salem. And, by reason of that sudden surprizal, we knowing ourselves altogether innocent of the crime, we were all exceedingly astonished and amazed, and consternated and affrighted even out of our reason."

We left Salem Village at the hanging of Bridget Bishop on 10 June, and we left the last specific mention of the newly accused in the village on 11 April, when Elizabeth Proctor, Sarah Cloyce, and John Proctor were examined and imprisoned – all of whom had been members of good standing in the community up until this time. Between these two dates, many more were accused, questioned, and imprisoned. Susannah Martin, for instance, had appeared in court for assaulting her husband, and she had appeared in court again against relatives over the subject of a disputed estate. She was a contentious neighbour and had been charged in the 1660s with witchcraft based on suggestions that she had killed an illegitimate child when she was single. Presumably, she was found innocent on that occasion. But once accused, the label as a witch stayed with her. She may have used this to intimidate her neighbours – an aspect of witchcraft that we have not met before but that is known to have happened from time to time. Another of the accused, a certain Dorcas Hoar, had an established reputation as a fortune-teller, and in Puritan New England this was closely associated with using the powers of the Devil. There had even been an earlier inquiry into whether she had caused her husband's death, for she had certainly predicted it. When she was accused by the afflicted, the extension to witchcraft was easy to accept. With such backgrounds, there was no shortage of witnesses ready to come forward and accuse these persons of *maleficium*.

But if some of the accused looked, and perhaps acted, as the village people expected witches to act, others clearly did not. Rebecca Nurse and Sarah Cloyce we have already met – women who were to all possible appearances far from what one would expect of a witch. Now there were others accused, examined, and imprisoned. Mary Bradbury (of Salisbury) was much respected, and her minister spoke of her in the highest of terms, praising her practice of the gospel and her works of charity. Other men of high standing supported this picture. Sarah Buckley, in turn, was very limited in worldly possessions but respected for her Godly life. Then there were the rich, for in this crisis not only the poor were at risk. These accused rich people were of good standing in the community – although, no doubt, in their lives they had vexed others in their climb within the local society. John Alden of Boston, for example, was a prosperous sea captain. He was unusual to this case because when the afflicted accused him, they (like the nuns with Grandier) had never seen him, and when one of the afflicted was asked to pick him out from a group of men, she at first identified the wrong man. Somebody had put the afflicted girls up to it.

Perhaps the most extraordinary case, however, was that of George Burroughs. He would be accused as the leader of the whole witch affair. Further, in the accusations against him, the whole theory of Sabbaths and of witches flying to meetings and celebrating under his leadership reached full development. There had been mention before of groups of these (mainly) women meeting in this way, but now it became rounded out and detailed. And this is somewhat indicative of how this whole witch hunt developed. At first it was relatively simple, with the girls having fits and complaining of choking, pinching, and pricking with pins. But the fits seem to have become worse over time; the girls no doubt grew to know what had most effect, and perhaps, since they were likely both sick and deliberately performing at the same time, the fits escaped their control. But with Burroughs, they took another major step, this time into the world of Sabbaths, which now became a central point of their accusations. Curiously, they described a few details of the meetings, but they do not seem to have got into the more sexual aspects that were supposed to be involved in Sabbaths. Was this because some of the main accusers – Abigail Williams, Ann Putnam – were too young to be up on these matters, or was it because in this Puritan society such descriptions would have been unacceptable? We do not know. What we can say is that with Burroughs things took a turn for the worse.

George Burroughs had been the minister in Salem Village for a while, having departed in 1683 in a highly disputatious atmosphere. No doubt, this left some very angry and offended people in the part of the community that had opposed him. Still, his departure was some years past, and he was some good distance away in Casco, Maine. His name first came up on 20 April. Ann Putnam junior was suffering terribly from a new spectre who was oppressing her. The spectre revealed his name, George Burroughs. He said that he had got many others to sign the book. The next day her father wrote to the magistrates to tell them that his daughter had revealed the leader of the whole conspiracy. Ann Putnam junior would have been a child of about two when George Burroughs left Salem Village, so here is another instance where some adult must have put this idea into her head. A witch hunt was always a great occasion to settle old scores. The shock of the accusations was tremendous throughout the whole province. In this society the ministers were the leaders of the Godly, the protectors and expounders of God's word. If ministers had been lured into the Devil's service, what hope was there for belief in anybody's innocence?

Once Ann Putnam started accusing Burroughs, many others joined in, either as afflicted persons making the accusations or as witnesses supporting the accusations and adding more. He was examined by the magistrates on 9 May. There had already been suggestions in earlier examinations that there was an unknown leader of the witches; Burroughs was now elected to the position, with many accusations against him. And terrible accusations they were. The Putnams said that he had been very harsh on his first wife when he had been in Salem Village, to the degree that they had felt it necessary to remonstrate with him. A Casco witness and another from Falmouth in Maine confirmed that he had been equally harsh to his wife up there. These were not damning accusations in themselves but would certainly place any Puritan minister in a bad light and prepare the minds of many to accept more serious ones later. What made the accusations worse was that these were not the same wives; these first two had died. They were saying that he was a wife abuser! Five of the afflicted girls claimed that the abuse had finished up with murder. Here is part of what Ann Putnam junior said:

on the 5'th of may 1692 at evening I saw the apperishtion of Mr George Burroughs who greviously tortored me and urged me to writ in his book which I refused then he tould me that his Two first wives would appeare to me presently and tell me a grat many lyes but I should not beleve them: then immediatly appeared to me the forme of Two women in winding sheats and napkins about their heads: att which I was gratly affrighted: and they turned their faces towards Mr. Burroughs and looked very red and angury and tould him that he had been a cruell man to them. and that their blood did crie for vengance against him: and also tould him that they should be cloathed with white Robes in heaven, when he should be cast into hell: and immediatly he vanished away: and as soon as he was gon the Two women turned their faces towards me and looked as pail as a white wall: and tould me that they ware mr Burroughs Two first wives and that he had murthered them ...

(Nice child to have around the neighbourhood.) Then there were the accusations that Burroughs not only was the leader of the witches, but also presided at their meetings, which, when described, were obviously simplified Sabbaths:

Mary Warren Testifyeth that when she was in prison in Salem about a fortnight agone Mr George Burroughs, Goody Nurse Goody procter, Goody

parker, Goody pudeator, Abigail Soames, Goodman procter, Goody Darling
& others unknowne came to this depon't & Mr Burroughs had a trumpett
& sounded it, & they would have had this depon't to have gone up with
them to a feast at Mr parrisses & Goody Nurse & Goody procter told her
this depon't they were Deacons & would have had her eat some of their
sweet bread & wine & she asking them what wine that was one of them
said it was blood & better then our wine but this depon't refused to eat or
drink with them & they then dreadfully afflicted her at that tyme.

Mary Warren had been earlier accused as a witch and was in prison, as
was Abigail Hobbs; both gave similar evidence against Burroughs, no
doubt with the hope of saving their lives. It is worth noting that Warren
testified not only against George Burroughs, but also against other
women who were in prison with her as witches; and there were many
other examples of the accused turning on each other in the hope of saving themselves. This was "jailhouse" testimony – always dangerous.

Another kind of evidence produced against Burroughs was quite singular to the Salem affair. It was believed that a witch could be given
strength far beyond the natural. One witness testified that Burroughs
"told mee that he had put his fingers into the Bung of a Barrell of
Malasses and lifted it up, and carryed it Round him and sett it downe
againe." This testimony was confirmed by another who vouched that
"he Saw Mr George Burroughs lift and hold Out a gunn of Six foot
barrell or thereabouts putting the forefinger of his right hand into the
Muzle of s'd gunn and So held it Out at Armes End Only with that fin-
ger and further this deponent Testifieth that at the Same time he Saw
the Said Burroughs take up a full barrell of Malasses w'th but two fingers." He obviously had prodigious strength, and here it was taken to
be supernatural – and evil.

Others came forward to accuse him of using the "evil eye" and of
causing strange happenings and apparitions, and indeed, nothing was
too far-fetched to bring against the poor man. Spectral appearances,
torturing the afflicted, recruitment of witches – all were combined with
murder and Devil worship to make this man, this minister, the worst of
all and the prize of the witch hunters.

And so spring melded into summer, and the jails were full all around
the area; the local ones were so crowded that additional and then yet
more accommodation had to be found. Conditions grew worse as the
crowding grew and the heat of summer increased in the dark fetid cells.
Sarah Osborne had died in prison. Others did, too, in these months;

three are known about, although there may have been as many as thirteen others. Property of the accused was seized in some cases, and most certainly some people must have benefited thereby. Whether this was behind some of the accusations is impossible to say, but this certainly happened in Bamberg and Wurzburg, and it would seem to fit the characters of some of the accusers here.

As the summer wore on, a surprising thing happened: more and more of the accused confessed to the crimes with which they had been charged. Not that confessions during witch hunts were unknown, but usually they came about as the result of torture. In this case, while the interrogations were harsh and bullying, there was little physical torture, with one or two exceptions. But in this case most of the confessions, and there were many, came from men and women who had not been coerced in such a fashion. What clearly did happen was that they were told that if they confessed, they might hope for mercy. In the case of Dorcas Hoar, for example, she confessed to four clergymen, and they asked the judges to delay her death until she had time to "perfect her repentance." She was the first of the people who had been condemned to death to have her sentence deferred. And she lived. So did many others who were accused but subsequently never came to trial.

The peculiar thing about these confessions is that those who confessed to being witches gained their lives, whereas those who refused to confess, among them some saintly people, were the ones who were executed. This was a total reversal of what might have been expected.

A few escaped death in other ways. In occasional cases, some, knowing that they were about to be accused or had been accused, managed to slip away from the area before they could be found and arrested. As well, a total of five escaped from one or other of the jails.

Not until 29 and 30 June did the next trial take place. The prisoners were Rebecca Nurse, Susannah Martin, Sarah Wildes, Sarah Good, and Elizabeth Howe.

A strange turn of events occurred with Rebecca Nurse: she was not left without supporters. Speaking out for another's innocence in the climate of that summer was a perilous act, yet this did not stop a significant number of her neighbours from taking this dangerous step. A petition testifying to her good name was signed by thirty-nine people. The jury, perhaps influenced by the support of her family and friends, found her innocent. The afflicted "made an hideous out-cry."

The magistrates were not happy with the result of this trial, and they now raised a question with the jury. While Rebecca Nurse had been giving her testimony, Deliverance Hobbs and her daughter had come into the courtroom. They had already confessed to signing the Devil's book. Rebecca reacted to them with the words: "What! Do these persons give in Evidence against me now? They used to come among us." The judges, in effect, asked that the jury take time to consider what these words meant, and the jury no doubt read their meaning. They asked and received permission to take time to consider. The question was whether Rebecca, in using the words "They used to come among us," referred to their coming among a group of witches that included Rebecca Nurse or to their coming among the group of the suspects in the prison. The prisoner argued that she only meant that "they were Prisoners with us" and that, as accused persons, they should not be allowed to testify against her. Upon reconsideration, the jury found her guilty. Her church on the following Sunday excommunicated her, formally making her no longer one of the congregation. She and the others on trial with her were all executed as one group on 19 July, all firmly proclaiming their innocence.

Another trial took place between 2 and 6 August. This time it was the turn of George Jacobs Sr, Martha Carrier, George Burroughs, John and Elizabeth Proctor, and John Willard. Once more all were condemned, and all except Elizabeth Proctor died together. She was permitted to live because she was pregnant. This execution in particular drew great crowds because George Burroughs, the presumed leader of the whole witch invasion, was to be hanged. The prisoners, as was usual, were allowed to make a last public speech, and he spoke well, proclaiming his innocence to the last and praying. It was far from what might have been expected from a guilty man.

In fact, people were beginning to be struck by the behaviour of some of the condemned on their last day. Here they were, about to die and meet their Maker, and if they had any hope of eternal life, it could only be attained by confessing that they had been guilty and showing remorse. But far from this, people like Rebecca Nurse and George Burroughs in their last moments were speaking and acting as though they were truly innocent.

The next group suffered on 9 September. There were six: Martha Corey, Mary Easty, Alice Parker, Ann Pudeator, Dorcas Hoar, and Mary Bradbury. Mary Easty joined Rebecca Nurse and George Burroughs in becoming a household historical name.

Mary Easty was the sister of Sarah Cloyce and Rebecca Nurse; all were accused of witchcraft, and only Sarah survived. Mary refused to admit guilt. Like her sisters, she was a pious churchgoer with a solid reputation. She and her husband lived with their seven children on a large and prosperous farm. Also like her sisters, she was accused and put in jail, but unlike them, after she had been there for two months, she was released for reasons that have not come down to us in the existing records. She believed, as did her family, that her release would be the end of it, but not so. The afflicted girls were determined to have her and became so violent in their fits and accusations that she was again arrested. She proclaimed her innocence throughout: "I will say it, if it was my last time, I am clear of this sin." She was executed on 22 September, but before this took place, she wrote and submitted a petition that, unusually, concentrated not on her own case alone but begged mercy and justice for all the innocents:

The humbl petition of Mary Eastick unto his Excellencyes Sir Wm Phipps and to the honourd Judge and Bench now Sitting in Judiacature in Salem and the Reverend ministers humbly sheweth. That wheras your poor and humble Petition[er] being condemned to die Doe humbly begg of you to take it into your Judicious and pious considerations that your poor and humble petitioner knowing my own Innocencye Blised [Blessed] be the Lord for it and seeing plainly the wiles and subttlity of my accusers by my selfe can not but Judg charitably of Others that are going the same way my selfe if the Lord stepps not mightily in ... the Lord above knows my Innocencye then and likewise does now as att the great day will be known to men and Angells ... I petition your honours not for my own life for I know I must die and my appointed time is sett but the Lord he knowes it is that if be possible no more Innocent blood may be shed which undoubtidly cannot be Avoyd[e]d In the way and course you goe in.[4]

Then she proposed to them that "your honours would be plesed to examine theis Aflicted persons strictly and keepe them apart some time," and she suggested that they should also requestion some of the confessed witches because she believed them innocent. She finished: "[The] Lord above who is the searcher of all hearts knowes that as I shall answer it att the Tribunall Seat that I know not the least thinge of witchcraft therfore I cannot I dare not belye my own soule I beg your honers not to deny this my humble petition from a poor dying Innocent person and I Question not but the Lord will give a blesing to yor endevers." She died with three others who had been tried with her. Dorcas Hoar saved herself by confessing to witchcraft.

Mary Easty's petition was to become important. It was seen by many to be totally inconsistent with guilt and with association with the Devil. After her, others were tried and condemned, but they were not hanged, for commonsense at last began to intervene.

Three days before she died, there had been another execution, of a kind. Old Giles Corey, Martha Corey's husband, was, as we have seen, a difficult and cantankerous old fellow with a disreputable past. Under the justice system of that time and place, a person was obliged to plead guilty or not guilty. This implied acquiescence in the justice system. If the accused refused to plead, he could be "persuaded" by a process called "peine forte et dure," an increasing weight of stones being placed on his body until he either died or gave in. But Giles Corey, contrary as ever, refused to "put himself upon the country." He was pressed to death on 19 September.

No one aspect of the witch hunt of 1692 brought things to an end: over the summer a number of matters had raised doubts in the minds of the more objective and thoughtful people. Some, from the very beginning, must have questioned in their own minds whether these young girls should be so readily and completely believed. As their accusations grew wider and wilder over the spring and summer months, with contradictions and clear falsehoods now and then, the number of doubters grew, probably further increasing as it became evident that nobody was safe from accusation. The contagion had spread to a point where it was now a threat to everybody.

Particularly worrying were the death scenes associated with people with strongly religious backgrounds who died not only proclaiming their innocence but showing all the behaviour and appearance of innocence, particularly George Burroughs, Rebecca Nurse, and Mary Easty. Serious doubts arose about whether at least some of those who had died had been condemned in error. Beyond the behaviour was the fact that in some cases, like that of Rebecca Nurse, the condemned had been supported in their own arguments of innocence by petitions from the wider community. Observers were quick enough to see that in the middle of this witch crisis, any person who signed such a petition stood in grave danger of being accused as an accomplice, yet so strong was their opinion that they were prepared to take these risks. Further, as the summer progressed, so, too, did concern that an increasing number of churchgoers were being named. This went against the whole thought of Puritan theology: when the numbers were small, it had seemed possible, but as they grew, this very growth caused thinking people to question the accusations.

Another factor was the number of confessions taking place. On the one hand, when an accused confessed, it seemed to confirm that there really was a serious invasion of witches. But even as the numbers of confessions steadily grew, they were being thrown into doubt by increasing cases of subsequent retraction. Moreover, what was one to make of the fact that in general those who confessed were being saved from death, while those who proclaimed their innocence were being put to death? And further still, some of the confessed began to relate numbers of witches in the country that were increasingly doubtful, even up to 500. This sort of thing seemed closer to imagination than to reality. To these "facts" supplied by the confessions was added another increasing set of figures, for the initial references to small groups of witches gathering together had also grown: one "witch" reported seeing 25 together at a Sabbath in mid July, another upped the number to 77 a week later, it was 120 a third of the way through August, and the number had reached 200 by the end of the month, presided over either by George Burroughs or by the Devil himself.

Spectral evidence had been a concern from the beginning, but the concern only increased as the summer passed. Tied to this, to an increasing degree, was a concern about the procedures of the court itself. It became evident that the judges had a strong, perhaps overwhelming, predisposition to assume the guilt of the accused and to completely disregard any evidence in their favour. Further, their readiness to accept the screams and fits of the afflicted and to permit them in the course of the trials was far from conducive to a proper court atmosphere. Moreover, the accused had no right to the assistance of legal counsel; this was not allowed in witchcraft cases. But it was becoming obvious with such numbers involved that this was undercutting a vital part of the system of justice that had developed over centuries. How could justice be assured in these cases when such a right had been unavailable to those accused? By October, ministers, magistrates, and most respected men and women had lost confidence in the court and its judges.

Events came to a head when one of the most respected and learned of the Puritan ministers, Increase Mather, father of Cotton Mather, was asked by fellow ministers to write a document that would establish for the magistrates what could be accepted as valid evidence and what could not. His response was his work titled *Cases of Conscience Concerning Evil Spirits Personating Men, Witchcraft, Infallible Proofs of Guilt in Such as Are Accused with This Crime*. He presented this to his fellow clergymen on 3 October 1692. He did not really settle all the issues that had been raised, but he was of such standing in the society of the time that the very fact that he associated himself with the questions gave important support to those who by now were increasingly concerned that something had gone far wrong. In the conclusion to his paper, he contended that the magistrates should be as demanding in their judgment of evidence in witchcraft trials as they would be with any other capital crime and that they should err on the side of mercy, with these words: "It were better that ten suspected witches should escape, than that one innocent person should be condemned."

The real significance of Increase Mather's document was that it was a statement from a highly influential man that reflected the views now held by many others. One of those most affected was the governor of the colony. In the face of the increasingly consolidated public opinion that was developing against the trials, Governor Phipps, on 29 October 1692, brought an end to the Court of Oyer and Terminer. Those of importance in the community, including Increase Mather, had carefully avoided any direct criticism of the magistrates, but it was obvious to all that their procedures were no longer acceptable and had been in error.

Over the coming months, the outstanding cases were reviewed: gradually, those who had been imprisoned were released; those who had been condemned to death but not executed were issued pardons. The summer storm was over!

Salem was a case that fits most people's idea of a classic witch hunt – large numbers of witches involved, widespread fear, a body of inquisitors all too ready to find guilt and to punish it with death. Not surprisingly, it shows many similarities to the Bamberg and Wurzburg events, even though separated by space, time, and religion. There was the precursor of a witch hunt that we have seen before: the deep fear of an invasion of evil, in this case by the Devil. There was intense public pressure to find *all* the witches and to find them *now*, even if normal and proper investigative processes had to be bypassed. As soon as the accusations were made, the accused were considered guilty and treated as such, no matter how fine the reputations of some of them may have been. There was false evidence, provided by the girls, that was accepted by the inquisitors without any normal doubts being raised in their minds. The persons accused were placed in the position of having to prove themselves innocent, but doing so was impossible against authoritative and prejudiced judges. The judges and inquisitors heard and emphasized what they wanted to hear and ignored things that were inconvenient to their theory. There was at this time little testimony in favour of the accused, but even the little that did emerge was ignored; petitions signed by a surprising number of people in support of accused persons, like Rebecca Nurse, were ignored. Or again, when Abigail Williams declared that she had been blinded by Martha Corey's spectre and could not see what she had worn, this did not make the inquisitors question in their minds whether the girl was pulling the wool over their eyes as well as her own; they assumed that she was telling the truth and that Martha's assertions of innocence should be given no weight despite the goodness of her life. And it is worth noting that the initial accusations were made against social misfits – Sarah Good, Sarah Osborne, and the slave woman. Would the accusers have been so readily believed if the first accusations had been made against Martha Corey? These are all symptoms associated with witchcraft trials. Nor should we overlook that the principal judge never gave up on his insistence that he had been right all along in what he had done and in how he had done it. This kind of persistence on the part of the authorities against accepting that errors had been made is something common to witch-hunt trials, then and now.

In early 1693, twelve of the jurymen publicly apologized for the errors in their judgments, some months too late to do much good. And not until 1711 did a special committee recommended compensation for many of those unjustly executed and for others condemned but not executed. Some claims by relatives dragged on for years: the Burroughs family were still looking for additional compensation in 1750. In most cases attainder was reversed early on, after innocence became obvious, but some names were missed in error. Most of these were corrected in 1957, only a little more than three hundred years late. A few were still missed, and the attainder still stands against them. The law does not act precipitately.

7

Hysteria Set Loose

From his brimstone bed at break of day
A walking the Devil is gone,
To visit his snug little farm the earth,
And see how his stock goes on.
                    Samuel Taylor Coleridge

To the people of Salem (and to the people of Bamberg), the Devil did indeed seem to be visiting his snug little farm on earth. And how frightening it was, in fact. But as the visitation progressed, it was not the Devil who most came to be feared but his sudden choice of victims, directed by the girls. Many a man or woman woke happy and carefree in the morning to be struck with disaster before night – accused without cause or warning and without any protection.

This arbitrary choice of victims was (and is) one of the most terrifying things about a witch hunt. It would strike anybody, high or low, and once struck, once accused, there was no defence against it. If you were accused, you were, in the eyes of all, the Devil's agent.

Witch hunts did not die with the 1600s; they continue in our own times. Now the witch has become a terrorist perhaps or some other evil in our society. Terrorists are real, as we well know. But what happens when you are accused as a terrorist and are innocent? And when your family or friends are accused with you? Bamberg tells us. Salem tells us. In times of great turmoil, there will always be witch hunters, always fearful accusers, and always witches – for witch hunting is a state of mind. You do not need to have a witch, only somebody whom everybody fears.

The mass of people become hysterical during a witch hunt and believe anything until the disease runs its course. Think of Bamberg. Think of Salem. In Salem, at the height of the crisis, the girls could say anything, any nonsense at all, and it was believed. Women of sound reputation and lives of great virtue could be brought low by silly girls and hysterical women because the mass of people, including leading members of the government, the law, and the church, believed them. Extraordinary! Yet this is what happens in a witch hunt, and not just in the mass witch hunts. It happened with Grandier, too: the exorcists declared that whatever the Demons said under exorcism must be taken as the truth. Looked at in the cold light of day, this went against everything the church said about the Devil – they called him "The Prince of Liars." But the mass of these same Catholics succumbed to the hysteria of the times.

Obviously, mass hysteria can exist without witch hunts. But if we are to gain any benefit from the past, we must recognize its threat to us in times of great fear and crisis. In our next case – the Dreyfus Affair – the witch has become a traitor to his country when his country is in great danger. Watch how the witch hunters used hysteria against him.

PART TWO

8

The Dreyfus Affair

In the huge open space in front of the École Militaire, the soldiers were drawn up company by company, lining the whole parade ground, dressed in their parade uniforms; officers on horseback, swords drawn, were in front of their battalions. They had been waiting on parade since early this morning of 5 January 1895; this was the way of armies, had been since time immemorial. But this was no ordinary parade of pomp and pride. This was a display designed to begin the lifetime punishment of a traitor, to disgrace him, degrade him, expel him, to vomit him forth. This was the commencement of just retribution for the treachery of an officer of the General Staff, found guilty by court martial of the crime of selling military secrets to the hated Germans.[1]

As the hour approached, there was not a sound on the great parade square beyond the jingle of harnesses or the stamping of hooves. Outside the gates, the large public crowd hushed as the last seconds ticked off. Five horsemen appeared: a general, two officers, and two dragoons. In the centre of the parade ground, their horses caracoled, as though to emphasize the terrifying significance of this event. Then as the clock struck, the general drew his sword; the drums rolled, playing a slow funereal beat that underscored the solemnity of all that would happen. An officer appeared, a slight man of medium height, in dress uniform – the prisoner. Dwarfed by four big artillerymen, he was marched into the centre of the square and brought to a halt in front of an enormously tall and powerful man, specially chosen to tower over him. The small group, still to the beat of drums, then marched over to where the general sat on his horse. As they came to a halt, the drums stopped. Not a sound could be heard, except for the hooves of the general's horse as it shifted on the cobbles of the square. Another officer came forward. In a voice that filled the parade ground, he read the terrible judgment of the court martial. As soon as he was finished, the helmeted giant stepped forward once again, faced the criminal, towered over him, and then item by item, slowly, with majestic grandeur, tore from the prisoner's kepi the badges and gold braid, every insignia and decoration, and from his tunic each button, every mark of rank and military adornment, and from his trousers the bright braid that marked him as an officer of the General Staff. The prisoner was by now but a shuffler in old clothes. As the last step in this part of the degradation, the traitor's sword was drawn from its scabbard by the giant and broken in two over his knee. For a professional soldier, there could be no disgrace greater than this public expulsion. The crowd outside the gates accompanied this humiliation with hisses and shouts, boos and defamations: "Death to the Jew," "Death to Judas." Still the prisoner showed unseemly pride, standing, as best he could, at attention. But nothing in his bearing could defeat the purpose of the ceremony. Before all men, all soldiers, that special breed of men, every act within the ceremony was designed to express disgust at the dishonour done by the prisoner to his country, the army, discipline, duty, heroism, his fellow soldiers. The drums began to beat again, and now the living corpse was paraded slowly about each side of the square in front of the ranks. He should have been silent, shamed, but wasn't. As he progressed past company by company, he shouted repeatedly in a voice that did not carry far but that could yet be heard: "Innocent, Innocent. Long live France."

Nobody believed him. There was no doubt of Dreyfus's guilt. He had been convicted by a court of brother officers of selling military secrets to the German military attaché at the German Embassy. There was proof! This was well known, for it was not the kind of thing about which the French Army made mistakes. Nor was his guilt all that surprising once one thought about it. Dreyfus was not a real Frenchman anyway but an Alsatian in origin, and Alsace had been annexed by Germany after the 1870 war. Although Dreyfus's father and mother had left Alsace for France with their young children after that event, the family business was still based there, as were close family. An Alsatian traitor was still a traitor, but it was less shocking than if he had been a true Frenchman. Besides, he wasn't even a true Alsatian, come to that. He was a Jew!

Dreyfus was hustled from his disgrace to prison in Paris to be exiled for life in a French penal colony. At first, he was hopeful that his wife and children would be allowed to join him before too long; this was not uncommon for criminals exiled to the penal colonies in South America. He was sadly deceived. The authorities planned that he would never again see his wife and children. There was no question, he found, of being treated like an "ordinary" criminal. He was to be the sole prisoner on the island. He was at first allowed a small area to move about outside during the day, but at night he was chained to his bed. His guards left him completely alone; he made his own fires, cooked, cleaned, cut wood for himself, everything. Apart from almost inedible food supplies, it was as though he was cast adrift on an island totally alone. He had little or nothing to read. He had all the time in the world to despair. He existed in his stone hut, four metres square, on the barren rock of Devil's Island, its windows barred, its lamp lit day and night so that the warders could observe him every moment; they were not allowed to speak to him, except with orders. For weeks, months, years, this terrible punishment went on. From time to time throughout this eternity, heavily censored letters reached him from his wife, but never were they allowed to hint to him what was happening in France. Five years he endured, by which time he was a physical wreck; he had even forgotten how to hold a conversation.

During those years since he was first found guilty by the court martial, there had been at first only a very few who doubted his guilt and were brave enough to say so. Then the questioning became more widespread. In France the Dreyfus Affair became a moral issue and then a political one, all unbeknownst to the man himself on far-off Devil's Island. Careers were broken in his name, and governments rose and fell as a result of his case. The church, the state, and the army were threatened by the least suggestion of his innocence, and they fought a hard, bitter, and unscrupulous battle to prevent any suggestion of his innocence or review of his guilt. The Dreyfus Affair split France and changed its political structure forever.

An innocent man, unquestionably innocent, had been put to a living death as a hated and reviled traitor to his country.

Alfred Dreyfus was born in Alsace in 1859. His family lived in Mulhouse, an important industrial town, which is where he spent his early years. The Dreyfus family was Jewish and had originally arrived in Mulhouse generations earlier. Over time, the family had become

well-to-do industrialists, owning a number of factories in Alsace and
other parts of France. They were comfortably off and had intermarried
into other prosperous bourgeois Jewish families. Like most other French
Jews, they considered their distinction to be a religious one rather
than racial. In their eyes, as in those of many other Frenchmen, they
were French.

The Franco-Prussian War of 1870 changed the life of young Alfred
Dreyfus. At the age of eleven he stood looking out the window of the
family house in Mulhouse as the Prussian Army marched into the
captured city. Within a few short weeks, the mighty French Army in an
almost unbelievable turn of fortune had been totally defeated by Germans. One of the results of the defeat was that the rich French province
of Alsace was annexed to Germany, with the citizens of Alsace becoming German citizens. All France could do for them was to offer continued French citizenship to any who wished to leave the lost province.
Most of the Dreyfus clan stayed; with their factories to run and their future dependent on them, they had little choice. Alfred's father and his
family left Alsace and went to France; it made good sense to have a foot
in both camps.

In France, these expatriate Alsatians were as French as anybody else.
But those who remained in Alsace were in a more ambiguous situation.
To the French, they were members of one of their two lost provinces, Alsace and Lorraine, which the whole of France was determined to recover
one day. At the same time, they were now German citizens, and because
Alsace had always been a border province with some parts more French
or German than others, those who stayed were, in one sense, regarded by
the French as French and, in another, suspect as Germans.

This Alsatian connection played no part in the life of Alfred Dreyfus
as he was growing up in Paris, any more than his Jewishness did. He
was just a normal, young French boy, very clever, hard working at his
studies, of an average height and a rather slight build, and somewhat
myopic, which caused him to wear glasses all the time.

Why he chose the army as a career is uncertain, for there was no
particular military background to his family. But it was his choice. He
quickly stood out as an officer of great potential, and his excellent eval-
uations ultimately led to an appointment as a probationary officer of
the General Staff – an open road to high rank. The French Army, re-
formed, updated, darling of the Republic, hope for future revenge
against Germany and recovery of the lost provinces, was a calling
almost religious in nature; Alfred Dreyfus appeared to have a great

future. It was an outstanding appointment for a Jewish officer, for there had been few of them on the General Staff in earlier years; at the time of his probationary training, he was the only one.

The General Staff had four main divisions, and officers under training worked six months in each of them. Any officer got a wide experience this way and became known to, and judged by, a considerable number of senior officers. Alfred's marks, and the comments of his superiors in their reports, were generally favourable. Here and there were indications that anti-Semitic prejudices affected the assessments of his performance, but on the whole, he was well rated. Where there were adverse judgments and opinions of him, they were not so much professional as personal and certainly not likely to affect significantly his career as an officer with a future. He was a bit of a cold fish. He had an analytical mind and was good at leading subordinates and at organizing, but he showed little warmth toward others, appearing unemotional, too mechanical and logical, arrogant even; in any professional discussion he was usually right and said so. He kept to himself more than most of his peers and didn't mix socially more than he had to. Later, after disaster struck, he would write to his wife: "My somewhat haughty reserve, my freedom of speech and judgment, my lack of indulgence are at present causing me the greatest harm." He was never one of the crowd; when trouble came, he was not part of a camaraderie that would surround and support him.

In 1890, at the age of thirty, he married a young woman from a good Jewish family; his home life with her and their two young children was idyllic. They both recognized it as such. Life and the future looked good for Dreyfus and his family in late 1894. He had by this time been circulated through all four sections of the General Staff successfully. When disaster struck in October, it came without the least possibility of expectation. It was almost unbelievable.

One small part of the General Staff was devoted to military intelligence. It operated under the title of the Statistical Section but was in fact the military intelligence agency. Its activities were largely directed against the Germans and the Italians, France's immediate neighbours and potential enemies. Far down the chain of "spies" was a woman who cleaned the offices in the German Embassy, one of which was occupied by the German military attaché, a colonel named Schwartzkoppen. The cleaning woman's duties included emptying the wastepaper baskets. Her duties as an intelligence agent involved delivering the contents every few days to her superior, a Commandant (Major) Henry in the five-man intelligence section. This was how, on 26 September 1894, the Dreyfus Affair began.

Henry was a large, florid man who had risen from the ranks. His loyalty to the army and to his superiors was unequaled. His regular duties included searching the undigested contents of the German's wastepaper basket for carelessly discarded secrets. This day's batch contained a letter that was presumably written to the German military attaché. Although it did not show Schwartzkoppen's name, it came from his wastepaper basket, and he was known from past lesser finds to be careless with his papers. This letter was written on flimsy paper in ink and was addressed only to "Monsieur." Although the writer said that he had no real news, the letter did in fact contain some important information, which was listed under five headings. The first was a technical note on a particular piece of French artillery, and the second had to do with a change in French plans in the event of a mobilization of the French Army. This was followed by some details of a change in artillery formations. The fourth item concerned the French colony of Madagascar, and the final one had to do with a manual on field artillery. This item was very hard to obtain, and the author said that he could get a copy but only for a very few days. The notes ended with "I am just off on manoeuvres."

This letter became universally known as the "bordereau," the name commonly used for an itemized list on an official form. Its discovery caused immediate concern in the small intelligence agency. It seemed beyond question that within the French Army there was an audacious spy who was actively passing secrets to the Germans. From the contents of the bordereau, it was evident that the author must have access to a wide range of information that was secret and that could be known only to a few. Any one item of information might be known to a limited number of people, but very few could have access to all five of them. This was evidence of treachery of the most damaging kind.

The bordereau was shown immediately to the head of the intelligence section, Colonel Sandherr. He in turn showed it to his superior, General Gonse, who was deputy chief of the General Staff, and from him it quickly went progressively up the line until it reached the minister for war, General Mercier. The speed of its transmission is a measure of the immediate concern that it aroused. From the beginning, it was agreed that the author of the bordereau must be an officer with such a substantial knowledge of the work of the General Staff that he must be a member of it. This dangerous spy had to be found and unmasked quickly before more damage could be done. The French Army, fully recovered from the 1870 disaster, rearmed with the latest weapons, its pride and élan regained, could not afford to have its secrets given to the "enemy." The very thought of a French officer connected to the General Staff being a traitor was both horrifying and totally repellent.

The bordereau was photographed and copies were circulated to the heads of the various departments of the War Ministry in the reasonable hope that since the officer seemed to come from this restricted circle, the handwriting would be recognized. This approach had no immediate success and appeared to be a dead end until one senior officer suggested that the internal evidence in the bordereau could give a lead to the traitor. Within the ministry there were four bureaus. Only someone who had knowledge from all of them could have written the bordereau. The only officers who were likely to have knowledge of the work of all four bureaus at the level of the information was, it appeared, a probationer of the General Staff, who would have passed six months in each bureau during his training. The suggestion was made that the intelligence section should be looking for an artillery officer who was a probationer of the General Staff. They were close but mistaken, as time would show.

Only three officers seemed to fit this pattern, and one of them was Captain Alfred Dreyfus. When samples of handwriting from his work were compared to that of the bordereau, the investigators were struck by the similarity: the slope was the same, the t's were crossed in the same way, and the i's were irregular and similar in both documents – it seemed to them not a question of similarity but one of identity. The word was immediately passed up the line again through the same chain as before; the relief that real progress was at last being made was considerable.

That same evening, the minister for war was told of the progress. Later that evening, another officer, Commandant du Paty de Clam, was called upon to assist with his special knowledge. Du Paty de Clam was serving on the General Staff, but he was called upon at this time because he had something of a reputation as a handwriting expert. By the next day, Sunday, 7 October, he gave as his opinion that although there were some differences between the two handwritings in the samples that he had been given, the similarities were such that an official expert should be called upon. Thus, in very short order, the whole of the chain of command above Dreyfus were directly and personally involved right to the very top, with Henry and du Paty de Clam on the "frontline" to feed them facts and to protect their interests and the interests of the army.

By this time, General Mercier, the minister of war, had three "facts" to consider, all of which had come to him through this chain of command. First was the advice that, from internal evidence of the document, the bordereau could have come only from one of a small number of General Staff probationers. Second was the ever more certain belief that the handwriting in the bordereau was that of Captain Dreyfus, one of these probationers. Third was the opinion, now being expressed, that Dreyfus was an unpopular officer – sufficiently unpopular that a number of his brother officers believed that if there was a traitor among them, Dreyfus best fitted the part.

If he had been accepted as one of the "club," a member in good standing, his brother officers might have asked more questions and searched harder for alternatives and would at least have entered the search with minds open to a mistake having been made. As it was, at the first serious suggestion of his guilt, the barriers of doubt were lowered. Personal lack of popularity might even have played a lesser part if Dreyfus had not been both Jewish and Alsatian. But with his father now dead, a large part of his personal fortune was still in Alsace, involved in factories under the direction of other members of his family in Alsace, Jews who had stayed there and were now German citizens. It was not a leap to question whether Dreyfus could ever "really" be French as his brother officers were French.

The senior ranks of the army had, in fact, a strong Catholic bias, for many of these officers had been drawn from old Catholic families and educated by the Jesuits – at a time when the Jesuit Order in France was very strongly anti-Semitic. Anti-Semitism had also been given a marked impetus some years before when an important financial institution had gone bankrupt, to the substantial loss of many Catholic investors. It was firmly believed that the failure had been brought about by Jewish financiers. The historic picture of the wandering Jew, tied to no country and with no allegiance except to his co-religionists, became a very popular one, particularly among Catholics. This anti-Jewish sentiment had become so marked that when, in 1886, a leading anti-Semite published the book *La France Juive* (Jewish France) it sold 100,000 copies in two months.

Within the army, one of the centres of conservatism within the state, Dreyfus provided the perfect natural culprit. Nobody within the army at this early stage considered Dreyfus guilty because he was a Jew or because he was from Alsace, but once he had been accused of guilt, the accusation became acceptable because he was a Jew, an Alsatian, and an outsider.

Now followed discussions at the highest level of the army to decide whether there was enough evidence to charge Dreyfus. The problem was that if the case was pursued, it had to be successful. The worst thing that could happen would be to finish up with a questionable result. The suspicions were strong but not the evidence. Still, General Mercier gave orders for Dreyfus to be arrested. It was, by now, Friday, 12 October; the weekend was coming up, and he had had the matter in his hands now for five days. It seems probable that despite the paucity of solid proof, he considered that for both military and political reasons, a traitor could not be allowed to move about Paris freely, entering military establishments with further access to the army's secrets. An arrest too soon seemed much safer than an arrest too late. It now was essential that evidence be found.

The following day, Saturday, two handwriting experts gave their opinions. They did little to clarify the situation: one concluded that Dreyfus was not the writer; the other came to the opposite conclusion. Still, when Mercier returned he stood by his decision to have Dreyfus arrested. Within the army, from the top down, everybody involved was now certain that Dreyfus was guilty. Now they just had to find the evidence to prove it! If only there were more to go on than the bordereau.

The task of having Dreyfus arrested was given to Commandant du Paty de Clam. Over the weekend a note was sent to Dreyfus to present himself to the office of General de Boisdeffre, the chief of staff, on Monday morning. It was unusual to be called in with so little warning, but Dreyfus had been in the army long enough to know that it made its own rules; the summons caused him no concern. He spent a normal weekend with his wife and two young children, leaving home on Monday morning very cheerfully, without the slightest idea that his whole world was about to cave in.

When he was shown into Boisdeffre's office, the general was not there; instead, he found Commandant du Paty de Clam and three men in civilian clothes. Du Paty de Clam told him that the general would be along shortly, and in the meantime he asked Dreyfus to sit down and take some dictation for him, giving as explanation that he had hurt his hand. Du Paty de Clam then dictated to him a letter that contained a number of words that appeared in the bordereau. After a while, Du Paty de Clam noticed that Dreyfus was shivering and appeared to be ill at ease. On being questioned, Dreyfus said that his fingers were cold, but his reactions were taken to be those of a guilty man. By the time Dreyfus had finished writing, he realized that the atmosphere was abnormal. But all the same, he was astonished when du Paty de Clam stood up and in parade-ground voice shouted: "In the name of the law, I arrest you. You are accused of the crime of High Treason."

The horrified and confused man was then questioned; they demanded that he confess his guilt. They showed him a half-concealed revolver and implied that he should take the proper way out and finish it for himself. Dreyfus held to his innocence, quietly and firmly at first, then more vehemently and emotionally as time went on and he realized the terrible danger that he faced. The four men refused even to listen to any suggestion of innocence or any possibility that a mistake had been made. Finally, when the "traitor" persisted in his denials and refused to take the gentleman's way out, he was handed over to Commandant Henry, the big tough ex-ranker, well decorated for bravery, who had first discovered the bordereau. Dreyfus was taken to prison immediately.

Later, Henry, du Paty de Clam, and others who had been involved in the day's work were interviewed by General Mercier, who still seemed somewhat uneasy about whether he had done the right thing in arresting Dreyfus, at least at this time. But those who had taken part assured him that they had been watching the man and his reactions; they confirmed to Mercier that the Captain had behaved as a guilty man would do. But once more in the Dreyfus case, because the man was assumed guilty from the beginning, facts were ignored or misinterpreted that might have been the basis for objective doubt. For instance, one of the men present at Dreyfus's confrontation was named Cochefort. When he observed Dreyfus's dictation and questioning by du Paty de Clam, Cochefort was already convinced of the traitor's guilt, mainly because Sandherr, the head of the intelligence agency, had told him so and that evidence existed to prove it. He assumed that this evidence must be compelling and that it was the result of a thorough but secret inquiry. Further, he was aware of the existence of the handwriting expert's report that the writings were the same, but he was not aware of the other expert's report that they were not. So when Dreyfus entered the room to be confronted by du Paty de Clam and the three civilians, one of whom was Cochefort, the latter already "knew" him to be guilty. Everything that he saw was interpreted accordingly. Mercier had a high opinion of Cochefort's judgment and would take comfort in his expressed opinion that Dreyfus had acted like a guilty man. But this only compounded the errors already made, and each error committed the army more solidly to proving that Dreyfus was guilty.

So Dreyfus was in prison, secretly. There was still no public knowledge of the case. But it had moved no further forward within the army; everything still depended solely on the bordereau and on conflicting expert opinions about whether Dreyfus had written it. Nor could any

reason be found that would compel Dreyfus to be a traitor: he was in-
dependently wealthy, his military career was progressing well by any
standards, and he had always shown every sign of patriotic loyalty.
There were unproven rumours that he gambled; one, based on wild
imagination, maintained that he had betrayed his country for the sake
of a beautiful Italian spy; others claimed that he had had affairs with
women – which he admitted, but he argued that they had taken place
before he was married. If this alone was to be the basis for suspected
treachery, much of the French Army (and the French Cabinet, for that
matter) could have been considered equally suspect. By 28 October,
some two weeks after Dreyfus's arrest, du Paty de Clam had no choice
but to advise General de Boisdeffre in a report that the evidence was insufficient to make conviction a certainty and that it might be necessary
to drop the matter before it went too far. But General de Boisdeffre was
made of sterner stuff, or perhaps he just realized that to withdraw now
would be such an embarrassment that heads would roll and careers
would suffer. Whatever the reason, he told du Paty de Clam firmly that
things had gone far too far now to pull back – there was to be no retreat. Dreyfus was guilty and deserved death; he was not to be allowed
to get away with his treachery!

In the meantime a special secret file was being prepared from the
records of the intelligence agency. Over the years, all sorts of pieces of
correspondence and paper had been collected and delivered by low-
level spies like the cleaning woman. In the case of Schwartzkoppen as a
source, a mass of documents had been retrieved over a period of eight
years, including highly personal correspondence, drafts of intimate letters, and important documents that would be of significance to any spy.
Since many of these documents contained a snippet of information here
or there that did not as yet fit into any known pattern, they had been
filed away. At this point all these files were reviewed to see if there was
anything in them that related to the newly discovered bordereau. The
gleanings, anything that even remotely pointed in Dreyfus's direction or
that could be doctored or modified to do so, were collected in the new
secret file that was to play such a disastrous role in the Dreyfus Affair.

Within these gleanings, it appeared that three items shed additional
light on the puzzle of the traitor. All three of these documents came from
earlier correspondence between Schwartzkoppen and the Italian military
attaché, a man named Panizzardi. At the time, Austria-Hungary, Germany, and Italy had a common treaty of alliance, so there was a natural
affinity and a common interest in the exchange of information. Beyond

this, Schwartzkoppen and Panizzardi were close personal friends and thus wrote freely to each other. The first item was contained in a note from the German to the Italian. It mentioned someone named "D" (referred to as "that scoundrel D") who had given Schwartzkoppen plans of the French fortifications at Nice. The second was a record of notes from the Italian to the German that seemed to indicate that Panizzardi had been approached by a French officer willing to sell secrets – at best, an ambiguous item. The third was a letter, from the Italian to the German again, saying that if Schwartzkoppen had to concern himself over a particular matter with "his friend," he should be careful to make sure that a certain Colonel Davignon knew nothing of it. Davignon was the head of one of the General Staff bureaus, and he was also the officer in the French headquarters who was responsible for liaison with the foreign military attachés.

As the secret file was being put together, all three of these documents were interpreted as referring to Dreyfus. He must be the "D" of the Nice secrets. He must be the French officer who had approached Panizzardi. And he must be Schwartzkoppen's "friend." To the officers responsible for assembling the evidence against Dreyfus, these three items alone did not prove that he was the traitor, but in light of the bordereau, the items all seemed to fall into place. Dreyfus had worked under Davignon in the General Staff. For them, these three new facts obviously referred to the same man. If they had needed any further convincing about Dreyfus's guilt, these three details did it. But while these added weight, they still were not enough by themselves, or even with the bordereau, to carry the proof of guilt in a courtroom. More yet was needed.

If this proof could not be found, it had to be created. Objectively, this was a terrible step to take. But to some of the officers immediately concerned, it seemed the honourable thing to do. They were certain that Dreyfus was guilty of the most heinous crime an officer could commit. His cleverness, and the cleverness of the German enemy, had managed to hide the essential proof of his guilt, they argued to themselves. And since the traitor must not go free, it would be a patriotic and honourable act to confound him and his allies by creating the evidence that would damn them all. It is known who created it, a man named Guénée, a former police agent who was serving with the intelligence agency at the time. It is not known who else was involved, but certainly one or more others must have been, for Guénée could not have acted alone in initiating and carrying out the forgery now about to take place. The most likely accomplices were Commandant Henry and Colonel

Sandherr and possibly even General Mercier. The consequences of creating the forgery were twofold: it would help to imprison Dreyfus, but it would also necessitate a conspiracy among all involved in its creation; from this time forward mutual solidarity was essential for their own collective and individual safety.

This document was actually created by Guénée out of two earlier reports that he had written. The deputy military attaché at the Spanish Embassy was a man named Val-Carlos, a Spanish nobleman who was very pro-French. For some considerable time, he had been providing the intelligence agency with information on the other military attachés, including Schwartzkoppen and Panizzardi. Based on this information, Guénée had in late March 1894 prepared two reports for transmission up the line. He now took back these reports and doctored both them and the texts from Val-Carlos on which they had been based. The result was that everything now showed that in March 1894, the intelligence agency was already aware that the Germans had a French officer who was giving them important information. This, of course, had not been the case. Although the revised papers did not name Dreyfus, the changes did give the later, newly discovered fragments a new validity as proof.

There was also more evidence on the handwriting by now. One of the experts maintained that there were differences between the handwriting in the bordereau and Dreyfus's own writings because he had deliberately disguised his writing in the bordereau. This had the convenient advantage of "proving" the documents to be written by the same hand through their similarities while explaining away those differences that existed. Other experts gave other opinions: one new expert said that it was clearly the handwriting of Dreyfus; another said that it definitely was not. The adverse opinions were set aside.

Dreyfus could not be found guilty and punished by his superiors alone; no matter how convinced they were of his guilt, he had to appear before a legally constituted court of officers in a court martial. True, the members of the court were chosen by senior officers, and to some extent their own careers would depend upon how they carried out their task. Nevertheless, the military judicial system had to be satisfied, by evidence, that the man was guilty. This evidence, such as it was, was now put together by du Paty de Clam for General Mercier, who would make a final decision about whether to proceed.

Everything seemed to be under control when suddenly, Mercier's freedom to choose was cut out from under him. On the evening of 31 October and the morning of 1 November, several newspapers came out and openly said that a Jewish officer, Captain Dreyfus, was under arrest for treason. Until this time, Dreyfus's imprisonment, and the whole affair, had been secret, at least officially. Certainly, the rumours had been spreading in both government and military circles, but now that the affair was public, there was no turning back. The newspapers had the bit between the teeth and were off and running. The path of the future was already typified by one headline: "We have, nevertheless, a consolation; it was not a true Frenchman who committed the crime."

Mercier had now lost any freedom to delay or ponder his decision. The newspapers of France were numerous, often violently factional in political or religious matters, and commonly vitriolic in their opinions. Since many of them invented "facts" that suited their opinions if they were denied them from valid sources, it was unwise for any source to keep hidden what information could be revealed; otherwise, the source would find itself the object of attack. Mercier knew all this. He had to make an immediate decision either to proceed now with a prosecution of the case or to be in the almost impossible position of saying why he could not proceed. Further, to say that he could not proceed for lack of evidence was to say that there was a traitor on the General Staff of the French Army and that they did not know who it was. Both nationally and internationally, this was a humiliation that neither the army nor France could accept. From this time forward, the army, and the entire government, would be enslaved in the pursuit; nobody could back out. The die had been cast. On the 3 November 1894, with the complete backing of the government, the decision was made to try Dreyfus by court martial.

No longer was this a military matter; it was now a matter of national pride. It was stunning and appalling to the whole of France that treachery was abroad in the highest reaches of the army. This same national pride could only be satisfied by a terrible punishment, a national purging. This was no longer a matter, either, of a single French officer having disgraced his uniform. From the first hours that the news became public, he was identified as a Jew, and with him, all French Jewry came under violent attack. Henceforth, the Dreyfus case was driven as much by anti-Semitism, by Catholic bigotry, by religious issues, by politics, by national pride, and by the honour of the army as it was by the insignificant figure of Captain Dreyfus. From this time forward, these different immensely powerful forces each had a compelling interest in finding Dreyfus guilty. Even to suggest that there was the slightest doubt of guilt was itself a sign of treachery.

From the very beginning, most of the press assumed that Dreyfus was guilty. They knew little of the facts, so this gave them a wide-open opportunity to invent all sorts of fictions about how Dreyfus had gone about betraying France. Everything was done to convince the public of his guilt well before his trial. Each time something was said in his favour, it was turned against him. When his mother-in-law protested that he was innocent and asked why a rich man should commit such a terrible crime, the cry was raised that the Jewish conspiracy was coalescing to defend one of their own. When again the question was raised of why a rich man should commit such a crime for money, the response was that he must have got rich in this way. And if it was then demonstrated that he had always been rich, this was taken as proof that he must have committed his treachery for hatred of France, which was an even more heinous offence. When the German Embassy maintained silence on the accusations that were being made against it for spying on France through Dreyfus, their agent, it was taken as acceptance of complicity. When they did in fact claim total innocence, it was argued that the claim should be ignored because this was exactly what they would do if they were guilty.

Then as November dragged on, General Mercier himself came under increasing criticism. The whole affair seemed to be proceeding at too slow a pace for a press-driven public infuriated against Dreyfus and insistent upon trial and punishment. There were suggestions that he had arrested the man too soon, before he had sufficient proof, that some of the proof had been lost or stolen, and even that the delay was because he had been bought over by the Jewish moneymen. He responded with a public statement in late November that Dreyfus had been selling secrets to the Germans for three years.

This public statement was typical in its own way of the Dreyfus Affair. There was no truth to it, but once made by a man in Mercier's position, it became accepted truth, almost impossible to overcome. At the same time, it became a truth that had to be defended both by the army and by the state because if it was not the truth, doubt would be cast upon the whole foundation and honour of the state. From the day that Dreyfus was first under suspicion, he was found guilty in the eyes of the army. From the day that his arrest was known through the press, he was found guilty by the public. From the time that Mercier intervened publicly, the members of the court martial became obliged to choose between the minister of war and Captain Dreyfus. From this time on, a pattern was formed. Each time Dreyfus's opponents, particularly the army, came under attack, they responded with a new release of secret and unproven information. And each such unsupported statement had so much authority behind it that to question the statement was to question the unquestionable source.

The court martial of Captain Alfred Dreyfus began on 19 December 1894. When Dreyfus entered the court, he was said by those present to look much older than his thirty-five years. The prosecution asked that the court be cleared and that the hearing be in private because of the danger to public order. Despite the objections of Dreyfus's lawyer, this was done. Only two spectators remained: the prefect of police and a Commandant Picquart, who was the war minister's representative and who would play a major part in the Dreyfus Affair in the following years.

Dreyfus's judges were military officers, as was always the case in court martials. Evidence was presented to indicate that Dreyfus had acted in a suspicious manner and could have had access to all the items in the bordereau. The sinister habits of the prisoner were described: he was curious about matters outside his area of duty; there were frequent and unexplained absences from his work; he asked questions of detail about matters that did not concern him; he hung about when information was available that he had no need to know. These behaviours fitted a spy. (They also fitted the inquiring mind of an officer who wanted to know every aspect of his profession, but this was not the purpose of the evidence.) Then, of course, there were those items about his personality that caused others to find him aloof. Underlying the personal evidence of these witnesses were two facts, "Jew" and "Alsatian," unmentioned but read into every word. Only a few of his fellow officers stood by him and stated his virtues.

The case against him had four main elements. First was the bordereau with the supporting testimony of most of the handwriting experts that Dreyfus was the author. Second, Dreyfus had access, or could have obtained access, to all the information in the bordereau. Third was the evidence presented by the imposing military figure of Commandant Henry, who accused Dreyfus theatrically and impressively: "The traitor, there he is," he thundered to the court, pointing to and towering over the diminutive prisoner. Then he went on to hint at secrets that he could not disclose, a point well appreciated by a group of fellow officers used to the necessity for secrecy. The senior officer of the court, obviously accepting this need for secrecy, could not ask Henry to support his allegations with facts, but he could at least ask for an assurance, a confirmation, that these secret facts proved Dreyfus to be guilty: "Do you affirm on your honour that the treasonous officer was Captain Dreyfus?" he asked. Henry turned, pointed to a picture of Christ on the wall of the courtroom, and with absolute conviction, in a loud firm voice, declared, "I swear to it." In this court of military officers, this single unproven, unsupported affirmation probably outweighed in its impact all the other evidence presented during those days. Henry, the man who had access to all the secrets and who could certainly not divulge them, had sworn on his military honour as an officer that those secrets proved Dreyfus guilty beyond doubt.

This all might have been enough to find the prisoner guilty, at least if not too many penetrating questions were asked. But Mercier, on his own behalf and that of the army, could not afford even the possibility of doubt. It was far too late for doubts. So the fourth component, the secret file, was shown to the military judges – in secret and without the knowledge of the defence. It was a procedure that was totally illegal.[2]

Even today, the contents of the dossier shown to the judges are not all known for certain. The president of the court was handed a sealed envelope. It contained certainly most, if not all, of the documents already noted, and it was accompanied by a memorandum prepared by General Mercier himself explaining the documents and their relevance.

The reason for the secrecy would be clear to the judges. It contained correspondence between the military attachés of Germany and Italy about espionage in France. It would be clear that France had some sort of access to this correspondence, access that was valuable for the future and that should not be lost through public knowledge. The judges and the judges alone must be permitted to see the dossier. But the very fact that these, at best, ambiguous documents were so secret gave them a validity regarding Dreyfus's guilt that was well beyond the strength of their contents. To military officers like the judges, because of the gravity and pressures of a treason trial of a fellow officer, the dossier alone would have been proof.

Proof it may have been, but the secret provision of documents to the judges was completely illegal. In years to come, among all the other things that had to be covered up, the secret dossier was one of the greatest, for on the one hand, it was the principal reason for finding Dreyfus guilty, and on the other, it could never be admitted to exist or to have been used. The use of the dossier was a measure in itself of how weak the army itself knew its case against Dreyfus to be.

It was on the basis of all these "facts" that Dreyfus was declared guilty. Some two weeks later, Dreyfus's public degradation took place. By mid January, he was on his way to Devil's Island.

The one man who drove the "Dreyfus Affair" from the time of the conviction to the very end was Mathieu Dreyfus. This marvellous brother was determined to prove Alfred to be innocent. He threw himself into his task, sparing neither himself nor his fortune. It was a lonely task. In the beginning, virtually his only supporters and friends were the rest of the Dreyfus family. Even the Jews, so much associated by the press with Alfred Dreyfus, were in large part inimical to his cause. In their eyes, not only was he guilty, but his guilt had reflected unjustly upon the whole Jewish community in France. Only a very few Frenchmen were with Mathieu in seeing no motive for Alfred to have committed treason, but to these few, without motive, the crime was both unreasonable and unlikely.

Mathieu was armed, at first, only with his money and the same unrelenting determination as his imprisoned brother, Alfred. His task, he realized, was to identify the man who had really written the bordereau. Only then could he hope to have Alfred's case reviewed. His efforts at first were conducted in secrecy, using paid investigators to conduct inquiries into whether there were any other officers who might have been in a position to pass the information in the bordereau to the Germans and who might have had motive to do so. But the inquiries could not be totally hidden, and to Dreyfus's enemies, the inquiries were seen not as a search for the truth but as an attempt to find a straw man, a stooge, on whom the crime of Dreyfus could be unjustly pinned. This raised increasing apprehension that Mathieu Dreyfus and his few allies were conspiring and intriguing to place the traitor's guilt on some innocent man.

But when the first tiny break came in the case against Alfred, it was due not to Mathieu but to a military officer, a Commandant Georges Picquart. Although the first breach was very small and it would be another three years before the dam burst, it was Picquart who opened it. He was an unlikely catalyst, for he was himself both an army officer and a member of the General Staff. He was an Alsatian Catholic and the protegé of General de Boisdeffre. He had been present at Dreyfus's court martial as the representative of the war minister, one of the two people permitted to stay when the court martial went into closed session. Apart from this, he had nothing to do with the investigations into Dreyfus or the preparations of documents for the trial. Like practically every other army officer, he was convinced of Dreyfus's guilt. He was not a man to whom the "Dreyfusards" would naturally look as an ally.

Picquart's direct involvement came about purely by chance. Colonel Sandherr, the strongly anti-Semitic head of the military intelligence agency, retired with a terminal illness at the end of June 1895, some six months after Dreyfus's conviction. Commandant Picquart was appointed in Sandherr's place on 1 July and was promoted to lieutenant colonel. Upon his appointment, Boisdeffre told him that the Dreyfus family was active, that the affair could not be considered closed for this reason, and that he should keep an eye on the case and on the Dreyfus family. He soon discovered that he had further cause to keep the case in mind: from continuing interceptions of papers in the German offices, it became apparent that there were new leakages of information. Dreyfus was not the only spy, it appeared; there was a second one. Picquart, at this time, had no thought that Dreyfus might be innocent, only that there might be another case of spying on their hands. Naturally, however, he would look to see whether the two were connected.

What threw an entirely new light on the whole affair for him was that in March 1896, nine months or so after his appointment, he received from Commandant Henry some three months worth of the collected pickings of the same woman who had found the bordereau in Schwartzkoppen's wastepaper basket. One of the items, also from Schwartzkoppen's fruitful throw-aways, was a letter-telegram on blue paper in thirty or forty pieces; it became known as the "petit bleu." The written document had been ripped up and thrown away without being sent. On the address side, it showed the name and address of a Commandant Esterhazy. Within a few days, a second letter was received, also from Schwartzkoppen's basket, also ripped-up, also addressed to Esterhazy, although not in Schwartzkoppen's hand. To Picquart, the question seemed obvious: was this the second spy? In August 1896 he told General de Boisdeffre that he was following a case similar to the earlier one and that he was investigating Commandant Esterhazy. Boisdeffre approved and told him to carry on.

Esterhazy was not hard to find. Apart from the fact that Picquart had his address from the first ripped-up letter, he was well known in military circles in Paris. A serving officer, he had been through the General Staff course in the past, so he was well known to other officers in the ministry. He would have known, or could have known, the facts in the bordereau. Picquart took the proper steps to have Esterhazy placed under surveillance and followed, and by the end of August he was satisfied that the man was a spy for the Germans. But in addition, the surveillance had come up with some of Esterhazy's correspondence in his handwriting. Now it so happened that Picquart had in his desk a photograph of the bordereau. When he compared Esterhazy's handwriting to that in the bordereau, to his astonishment he realized that they were not merely alike; they were identical! He realized right away that the bordereau had not been written by Dreyfus but by Esterhazy. The implications of this were appalling.

He took the next obvious step and called for the contents of the secret file that had been prepared and used at Dreyfus's trial. General Mercier, the minister of war, had ordered that these contents be split up among several files so that nobody would know that the file had ever existed, but Colonel Sandherr had disobeyed this direct order. He had sealed the file including du Paty de Clam's commentary and placed it under lock and key. When Picquart retrieved and reviewed the file in light of his new knowledge, he quickly came to the conclusion that nothing in it pointed to Dreyfus's guilt. Once the bordereau was established to have been written by Esterhazy, the other "evidence" had no weight at all against him.

Now, on 1 September 1896, Picquart went back to his superior, General de Boisdeffre, to report his disturbing findings; he handed over the report personally. By this time not only was he satisfied that an injustice had been done, but he also had the evidence to support his case. He had no reason, at this time, to believe that documents had been forged or that his superiors had any knowledge of these matters. So when he went to Boisdeffre, he probably assumed that the general would be as shaken as he had been by the discovery and as concerned as he was that steps should be taken to relieve the innocent man with the least damage to the reputation of the army as possible for having made a grievous mistake.

Seen from Boisdeffre's viewpoint, the horse took on an entirely different colour. If Picquart had come to him with his first suspicions, the general might have been able to take steps to divert the inquiry into safer channels. He would have had many options. Perhaps he might have removed the matter from Picquart (who might well have been happy to be relieved of the unwanted responsibility). Perhaps he would have handed it over to a special investigation team under Henry or du Paty de Clam – which would have ensured a safe result. As it was, the instructions that Picquart received can have done little to ease his mind; he was told to pursue the Esterhazy inquiries but "to keep the two affairs separate." His instructions really meant that he was to pursue Esterhazy but to leave the Dreyfus case alone. He was caught in a dilemma, for he was now fairly certain in his own mind that Captain Dreyfus might well be innocent. The orders that he was receiving were inconsistent with his own conclusions and his conscience.

Picquart now pursued the Esterhazy trail actively, certainly far more actively than his superiors wished. It was not an easy task. Esterhazy's commanding officer stated that he was a perfectly satisfactory officer. He was recognized to be a skillful man, and he had high-level friends to whom he could appeal against "harassment," so Picquart's inquiries had to be discreet; nothing that amounted to proof of guilt emerged. More open inquiries were risky in light of the quarry's connections, and Picquart was constantly told to act cautiously. He was forbidden, for example, to employ a handwriting expert to come and give an expert opinion about whether the "petit bleu" was written by Esterhazy – so far the whole suspicion against him rested on Picquart's own conviction that the handwritings were the same.

But, at this same time, Mathieu Dreyfus's machinations were having results. His public affirmations that his brother was innocent had by now created a hostile reaction in a section of the Paris press. It called for an end once and for all to any suggestion that there was the least question of Dreyfus's guilt. This gradually built up to a demand that the matter should be put to rest by telling the public the grounds on which the judges had found him guilty. As this demand developed in the newspapers day by day, it became clear to the public that documents had been shown to the judges that had influenced their decision but that had remained secret so far. The tenor in the press was not that there was doubt about his guilt but that the public had the right to know that he was guilty beyond any doubt; releasing the documents would serve this right, and the matter would be put to rest.

While the existence of secret evidence had long been suspected by Mathieu and his friends, this was the first time that these suspicions had been confirmed publicly. This evidence would prove vital to the Dreyfus case; its use at his trial, in secret, was illegal. If it could be proved to have existed, a new trial could be demanded. However, the army could neither deny the existence of the file nor admit it, so it did nothing. The silence made a few people wonder what was going on, albeit only a very few, but they were enough to form a base of support for the future. Meanwhile, Madame Dreyfus appealed to the Chamber of Deputies on grounds of a mistrial. The newspaper published her appeal. The Dreyfus Affair, with all its questions, was now a highly public issue.

In the army, someone at this time began to suspect Picquart himself of being the secret source of the information that the press was revealing. Since his appointment, he had become increasingly unpopular within his military circle. Henry and the other officers of the intelligence unit had quickly grown to dislike him as he continued to take an unwanted interest in the history of the Dreyfus case. Knowing their own guilt, they recognized the serious threat to themselves. But Picquart would not let go of his bone. He persisted in continuing his investigations of Dreyfus and Esterhazy against the clear wishes of Boisdeffre. From the viewpoints of both his subordinates and his superiors, Picquart was being too independent by far. It was not a stretch for his brother officers to see this secretive and individualistic colonel as the source of leaked information, for whom the press was a means of getting around the official restrictions imposed on him.

There was absolutely no reason to suspect him, in fact. The secret documents had been known to a number of people from the very beginning, including Alfred's judges. The word had spread within official circles at the political levels. Once silence was breached, there were many who were prepared to pass on the details. And to most, the existence of the secret papers was proof of Dreyfus's guilt. Nobody except the judges had seen them, but everybody "knew" that they contained incontrovertible proof of guilt. Things finally came to a head in the first days of November 1896 when a pamphlet written by a convinced Dreyfus supporter was sent to all the leading politicians and personalities of influence in Paris, including journalists. It revealed openly and clearly that it was not the bordereau that had convicted Dreyfus but secret documents revealed only to the judges. A few days later one of the Paris newspapers published a copy of the bordereau itself.

Picquart's superiors, suspicious and fearful, were now convinced that the source was Picquart himself. There was even suspicion that he might even have arrived at the conclusion that Guénée's Val-Carlos documents had been forged. The copy of the bordereau that they thought Picquart had released to the press probably came from one of the handwriting experts. But the fact that he had conducted his investigations secretively and sometimes against the wishes of his superiors gave the impression that he was untrustworthy to his caste. He was viewed as having been both disloyal and suspect. When his superiors, and his own hostile staff, cast about to look for a culprit, he (like Dreyfus) seemed to fit.

Everybody concerned, from the generals down, had to get rid of Picquart. This would not be too difficult, as he could simply be sent on a military mission of some sort that took him out of circulation and away from Paris. Initially, he was sent out on an inspection of units in the east of France, and later he was sent off to North Africa, where the army was fighting a bitter campaign; there were reasonable prospects that he would not survive. He was told that this was all temporary and that he would come back to his old position. But Picquart was no fool; he knew that he would never be back as head of intelligence, and he fully expected not to survive at all once he was sent abroad. Commandant Henry took over his position on a "temporary" basis.

Picquart's activities had done much to open up the Dreyfus case and to cause consternation in the higher ranks. He would suffer for this: first, there was North Africa, which he survived, then later a court martial on the grounds that he had made public secret information about the case, and then dismissal from the army. (When Dreyfus was finally found innocent, Picquart's true and honourable work was recognized, and he was reinstated – in time to become minister for war. But at present these events were years ahead.)

Meantime, throughout 1897, Dreyfus was still almost universally considered guilty by the public, but the constant revelations in the press kept the case alive when the military might well have hoped it would disappear from public consciousness. Questions about the secret file were by now being raised in the National Assembly. This must have caused palpitations in the hearts of those in the know. True, the questions were easily enough dealt with by the minister: Dreyfus had been found guilty by a legal court, he said. The facts that had led to a secret trial still obtained: national security prevented any further details being provided. The debate was conducted in a climate of general anti-Semitism, and Madame Dreyfus's request for a retrial was refused.

Still, with increasing disclosures in the press, one or more of the conspirators concluded that new and additional proof must be found that Dreyfus was guilty. Who it was that first proposed a new forged document is unknown to this day. Perhaps Henry, the ever-loyal soldier, came up with the idea himself? What is certain is that Commandant Henry worked at home and created a new forgery. He took home with him a number of documents that had been retrieved at different times through his cleaning woman. One of these was a letter from the Italian

Panizzardi to the German Schwartzkoppen. It was written in blue pencil in the summer of June 1896 and read: "Here is the manual. I paid for you (180) as agreed. Wednesday, eight in the evening at Laurent's place is fine. I have invited three from my embassy, including one Jew. Don't miss it." Henry also had available an envelope from Schwartzkoppen's basket that was addressed in Panizzardi's hand to the German and that had the Italian's seal on the back. Now he took a sheet of blank graph paper of a similar kind, the one commonly used by Panizzardi, and forged onto it a text of his own: "I have read that a Deputy is to pursue questioning about Dreyfus. If Rome is asked for new explanations, I will say that I never had any relations with the Jew. If they ask you, say the same, for no one must ever know what happened with him." This text was, as best he could, written in a copy of Panizzardi's handwriting. Where he could do so, he employed traced copies of words used in previous Panizzardi letters. The two pieces of paper were carefully glued into one. To an unsuspecting eye, the document appeared to be exactly what it was intended to be – more proof beyond question that Dreyfus had been a spy. But Henry was not an accomplished forger; an exacting inspection would in time reveal that the graph papers had slightly different coloured lines and that the squares were of slightly different size. These differences would cost Henry his life.

By October 1897 a tiny part of public opinion was beginning openly to question Dreyfus's guilt. This forced the military to take action in another direction. By now the investigations that Picquart had initiated into Esterhazy were confirming the suspicions that he was a spy. These suspicions were still kept close secrets within military circles. The army was afraid that accusations against Esterhazy might appear in the press – which would only increase claims from Dreyfus's few supporters that he was innocent and that Esterhazy was the true guilty man. Their fears proved well founded. By mid November, his name was put forward as that of the true spy in a letter published in *Le Figaro* by Mathieu Dreyfus. Esterhazy was told secretly by army authorities that he should fly and that he would be looked after. These acts were traitorous to France. The officers who took part, led by Henry but supported by his superiors, were leading the army into an ever-deepening quagmire. Perhaps not surprisingly, Esterhazy took a different position both then and afterward. In effect, he said that there was no need for him to fly: since they had to protect him in order to protect themselves, he would continue life as usual. The more that Esterhazy's forced allies did to support him and the more forged documents that they produced to affirm

Dreyfus's guilt, the more they placed themselves in Esterhazy's hands. By now he was making it very clear to them that he could ruin them by telling all he knew. So the military officers who had committed crimes, and those above them who had at least connived or turned a blind eye, more and more became potential victims of a man whose sole concern was to save his own skin.

Meantime, in the latter part of 1897, the original tiny band of those who had always believed Dreyfus to be innocent was very gradually being augmented by politicians, artists, intellectuals, and above all, journalists and authors. It was one of the notable features of the Dreyfus Affair that the press – both the massive bulk against him and, at this time, the tiny portion in his favour – played a part much greater than ever before in such an issue. As Jean Bredin says in *The Affair*: "For the first time the press exercised a major influence on the political life of the nation, dramatising and fueling the event, supporting or denouncing the authorities, exercising pressure and various forms of blackmail." At this time, the most famous, and in the long run the most influential, of Dreyfus's champions was Émile Zola, world-famous popular novelist and an influential journalist of great note. Already he was striking verbal blows in his newspaper articles for a finding of innocence in Dreyfus's case. There were other supporters, too, who gradually came forward, among them the politicians Georges Clemenceau and Jean Jaurès. These men, like all leading politicians, were active writers in the daily journals and had leadership of their own papers. So their views were widespread and influential. And as such men came forward, a new element became more obvious. The Dreyfusards were, in general, challengers of traditional authority and anti-clericals, which in France at the time meant that they were against the Catholic Church. This is hardly surprising. The French church was in this matter allied to the French Army. As questions of Dreyfus's innocence were raised, it became almost an article of faith to continue to insist on guilt. The church became ever more closely allied with the elements in society that were anti-Jewish. For them, to be against Dreyfus was to be for the nation and for France. To be pro-Dreyfus was tantamount to being a traitor to the nation, an enemy of all that was sound, reliable, and traditional. The country was beginning to split along political lines.

By now, public questions about Esterhazy could no longer be ignored. "Who is protecting Esterhazy?" demanded Clemenceau – the man who would become France's great leader in the First World War. These events virtually forced the army and political authorities into a position of ordering an investigation – not of the facts against Dreyfus but of the accusation that Esterhazy was the author of the bordereau. In the meantime, supported by his senior officers, who told him he would be protected, Esterhazy demanded a court martial to clear his name. The central points of the court martial were closed to the public. Esterhazy was declared innocent. Still, Henry and his fellow conspirators had cause to worry about what any further investigation might uncover. But for Dreyfus's supporters, this was a grave blow. Esterhazy's public "innocence" was but a confirmation of Dreyfus's public "guilt."

It was at this lowest point, just two days after the declaration of Esterhazy's innocence on 12 January 1898, that the bomb that would ultimately blow apart the Dreyfus Affair was exploded. The great French novelist Emile Zola had a worldwide reputation and readership and enormous public and international influence. He was appalled by the refusal of the government and the army to reopen the case against Dreyfus. From the time he had first heard that a secret dossier had been given to the judges at his court martial without Dreyfus or his lawyer ever seeing it, Zola had held that the whole case against the accused man was based on illegal processes. The court martial finding on Esterhazy's innocence now compelled him to enter the battle and speak out in the strongest terms, no matter what the cost. In Clemenceau's paper, *L'Aurore*, he published his famous denunciation, "J'Accuse," an open letter to the president of France, in which paragraph by paragraph, he accused the government and the army of illegalities, falsehoods, and errors and demanded that the Dreyfus case be reviewed. Zola knew that he had put himself up against the most entrenched forces in the land and that he would be made to suffer for his bravery. But he also knew that his worldwide reputation was so great that his accusations could not be ignored – everybody would know of them.

Zola's denunciation stated: "A court martial, acting on orders, has just dared to acquit such a man as Esterhazy. Truth itself and justice itself have been slapped in the face ... History will record that it was during your Presidency that such a crime against society was committed." In the long opening to the letter, he went on to pull no punches. "One wicked man has led it all, done it all: Lieutenant-Colonel du Paty de Clam ... He *is* the entire Dreyfus Affair." And so it went on until he came to his famous list, each item headed by "I Accuse": "I accuse Lieutenant-Colonel du Paty de Clam of having been the diabolical agent of a miscarriage of justice (though unwittingly, I am willing to believe) and then of having defended his evil deed for the past three years

through the most preposterous and most blameworthy machinations."
"I accuse General Mercier ... I accuse General Billot ... I accuse Generals de Boisdeffre and Gonse," and so on, until he says, "Finally, I accuse the first court martial of having violated the law by sentencing a defendant on the basis of a document which remained secret, and I accuse the second court martial [Esterhazy's] of having covered up that illegal action, on orders, by having, in its own turn, committed the judicial crime of acquitting a guilty man."

It is a document that is as startling and as compelling today as it was then, even if he had mistakenly exaggerated the position of du Paty de Clam as the prime mover.

This open letter to the president of the Republic had two principal effects. Zola's international reputation raised the whole question of Dreyfus's guilt or innocence to a new public high, both in France and internationally. It also forced those named to take highly public legal action against him (as it was designed to do), ensuring that the subject could not fade from the public mind.

Zola's letter raised a whirlwind that would not die down, but its immediate result was that within a month, he was on trial for making a false accusation against the court martial. His trial was a great public affair that he could not win – nor did he expect to. But it did publicly raise all the questions that he and the Dreyfusards wanted aired. The judge carefully steered away as much as possible from the Dreyfus case to concentrate on Zola and the specific accusation against him. However, one point came out that was, in later days, to have great importance. The letter that Henry had forged from whole cloth was referred to for the first time publicly. And the longer that the case existed in the public mind, the greater the risk grew that sooner or later the false evidence and the forged documents would be revealed.

The Affair would not die. The sentence against Zola rebounded against Dreyfus's enemies when Zola appealed the verdict on seven legal points and won. The High Court of Appeal ordered a new trial to take place in May of 1898. Although he would lose his case once more, the old questions were raised once more as well. Convicted yet again, Zola fled to England to escape his sentence in mid July of that year. But the Dreyfus Affair was now fully alive and growing in the public mind day by day, dividing the country, becoming now an element in the rise of the Socialists, who began to see the importance of a battle that pitted the individual against the authoritarian state and church.

A new government had been elected in May 1898, and in this government a man named Cavaignac was appointed minister of war. He was a clever and determined man, absolutely convinced of Dreyfus's guilt. He decided that it was high time to put the Dreyfus Affair to an end once and for all. He determined to have all of the facts and records of the Dreyfus case analyzed for him with a view to proving to everybody what he already "knew" to be true: that the pro-Dreyfus case was built on lies and false accusations. As the minister, he called for the secret file and asked the head of the army, de Boisdeffre, whether he had checked all the documents for authenticity. The general, already at least in part aware of the cover-up, recognized that Cavaignac's questions could lead to the whole case unravelling. But he had no choice but to say, to the minister's amazement, that he had not done so.

Cavaignac's response was to appoint an officer to review every detail of the file and ensure that it was complete and valid beyond question. Every step that he took at this time was sound and appropriate. In his own mind, he was sure that the file would be found to be in perfect order and would indeed prove Dreyfus's guilt. This certainty was further supported by an army officer who, at the time of Dreyfus's sentencing, had claimed that Dreyfus had confessed his guilt. The officer now came forward again with a sheet from his notebook that recorded the confession's having taken place. The confession itself, of course, was not produced, nor could it be – it had never taken place. But the affirmation added to Cavaignac's certainty about all that he was doing – so much so that before the secret file had been reviewed, he made a speech in Parliament on 7 July stating his own firm conviction that Dreyfus was indeed guilty and reaffirming Dreyfus's "confession." He also tabled three documents, one of which was fraudulent and forged (although he did not know it), and concluded by saying that he was going to bring forward "proof of the truth." This speech, innocent enough on the surface in light of all that had been said over the years by so many people, was in fact a significant step. As a minister of the government, he had personally vouched for the accuracy of the documents and the existence of the Dreyfus "confession." Until this time, although the case had been discussed many times by many people in the House, it was really the army that had been the main protagonist. The ministers in their capacity as the ministers of the government had remained supportive but, in effect, quiescent. Now Cavaignac had raised the stakes to a level higher. He had inadvertently combined the government's and army's positions on the affair, and the prime minister now led and passed a vote to post

the speech in every part of France. This would not create a problem if
the army's case was sound and honest, but it would place the government in a very difficult position if the army's case was fraudulent.
Cavaignac was an honest man. If *his* facts were questioned and found
to be false, then his position, and that of the army, and that of the government would be at enormous risk.

The "facts" that he presented were immediately questioned. The first
to act after the speech was the great Socialist Jean Jaurès. He attacked
Cavaignac's facts in the press and once more argued that Dreyfus had
been convicted illegally because the secret documents had not been provided to him to defend himself. He went on to say that if the supposed
"confession" was seen by the minister to be so important, was it not
strange that it had never been properly recorded and attested to by the
army? And he raised the issue that at least one of the documents that
had convicted Dreyfus was a clear forgery. This was followed shortly
afterward, on 9 July, by a letter from Picquart to the prime minister
stating that he could prove some of the documents in the file to be false.

These events did not sway Cavaignac in his certainty of Dreyfus's
guilt. On 13 August, however, the dam finally burst. That night, the officer charged with reviewing the documents in the secret file discovered
that Henry's letter was a forgery. By a trick of the lighting by which he
was working, it became evident that the single letter was written on two
different pieces of paper joined together. It was well enough done that
when he showed it to others under different lighting conditions, the differences could not be seen until he recreated the lighting as it had been
at the time of his discovery. The officer, a convinced anti-Dreyfusard,
nevertheless felt that he must inform the minister that a principal document against Dreyfus, one whose validity Cavaignac had proclaimed to
the whole nation, was in fact a forgery. When Cavaignac was told, he
seems to have accepted the fact of the forgery but still felt that the rest
of the case against Dreyfus was convincing. Perhaps in light of his public statement, he could not live with any other conclusion. But how far
was the General Staff implicated? He had to know.

Looking back from this distance, and with the facts that we now
know, it is hard to understand how Cavaignac could still have believed
Dreyfus to be guilty. How could the greater part of the country indeed
have believed him to be guilty? Emotion, of course, was part of it and a
sense that if he was not guilty, many honourable men must themselves
have committed crimes to make him so. Pride of country, religion, belief
in the army: all these factors made it difficult for those who had been

convinced three and four years ago to now admit that they might be wrong. So in many minds it was not a question of Esterhazy *or* Dreyfus being spies. Even *if* Esterhazy was himself a spy and traitor, Dreyfus could also be one. Many of the "facts" that his supporters had brought forward in Dreyfus's favour could be explained away by Jewish money having bought supporters or even forgeries. Esterhazy himself went on claiming that he was innocent and that the Jews had created all the evidence against him. So, until this time, at least, even while the affair was crumbling about the ears of the army, Cavaignac still believed that although errors had been made, the man was guilty and should not get away with it. But the situation for Cavaignac got worse still.

Henry was now called before him on 30 August. Under intense questioning, he began to fall apart and finally admitted the forgery. This big, rough soldier hero, after heavy questioning by the minister, finally admitted his guilt of forgery and offered an explanation: "My superiors were very worried ... I wanted to calm them, give them some serenity ... I told myself: Let's add a sentence; if only we had proof in the situation in which we find ourselves. Moreover, no one knew anything about it ... I acted solely in the interests of my country." He was arrested. Cavaignac released a communiqué to the news agency Havas revealing Henry's confession. Boisdeffre resigned, saying that he had been deceived. The next day Henry committed suicide by slitting his throat, taking many of his secrets with him. Other compromised officers, including Esterhazy, were openly revealed as part of a conspiracy to all who had open minds. Esterhazy himself had already been dismissed from the army by Cavaignac, who had no time for him; after Henry's suicide he fled to England, where he would lead the rest of his life in lies and sleaze. All this should have been the end of the affair. But it was not.

Meantime, far from being vilified for his forgery and his suicide, Henry had become to many a hero. Eulogies lauded him as a martyr who had sacrificed himself, misleading "your superiors, your friends, your colleagues, your compatriots for the welfare and honour of all." And further, "Your ill-starred 'forgery' will be counted among your best feats of war, and that which is most lamentable, its failure, has been paid and overpaid by your blood." The Jews were responsible for his death.

Cavaignac was replaced in an election by a new minister of war. Despite all the revelations, he, in turn, refused to give in to increasing demands for a review of the Dreyfus case. There was a new factor that influenced the decision: reopening the Dreyfus case, it was believed, could mean war (a testament to how far the case of this little French

army captain had grown in the intervening years). This last seems somewhat surprising, but in the mass of falsehoods and rumours that surrounded the case over the years, the accusation had been made that the
German Kaiser himself had instigated Dreyfus's actions, that Dreyfus
had worked directly for him, and that he had become personally involved in covering up Dreyfus's guilt. It was one thing to see such rumours in the press, but to see such accusations against the German
emperor raised in an official inquiry was, in the eyes of those who believed the rumours, to invite war with the Germans.

So, by this time, although the Dreyfus case centred around one small
and rather insignificant-looking man, it had split France in two, affecting
French politics and even international relations. Things had reached the
stage where many honest people in France felt that even if there was the
possibility that Dreyfus was innocent, the stakes connected to reopening
the case were so high for the country that it was better to let things lie –
that the state was more important than the individual. "It was better," as
the High Priest said of Christ, "that one man should die for the people."

The dilemma faced by the prime minister was enormous. Where did the
best interests of the country lie? Not until a month after Henry's death
did he become convinced that a review was necessary. The Cabinet was
split and the country in turmoil – something had to be done that would
move the situation forward without indicating or taking a firm decision
on Dreyfus's guilt or innocence. So on 26 September 1898, a month after
Henry's death, the president referred the matter to the High Court of Appeal. He made no declaration of guilt or innocence but simply required
them to look at the facts surrounding Dreyfus's court martial and to deliver a legal decision on whether it had been conducted in accordance
with all due processes. In this manner, he took the affair out of the realm
of politics and placed it in that of the law. The public result at least was
further violence and riots in the streets.

The law takes its time in such matters, as it did on this occasion. And
while this was going on, the split in the country solidified. But it was no
longer based primarily on Dreyfus's innocence or guilt. The divide was
much wider still. On the one side were those who supported change and
intellectual questioning of French life, the challengers to the established
authority. And on the other were the church, the army, and the traditional state. The Dreyfus case had changed France with effects still felt
today; the forces of 1789 – a free and just society based upon individual
freedoms – were juxtaposed against those of authority, control, and
raison d'état.

But finally, the law laboured and brought forth a decision – of a sort. On 3 June 1899 the court rescinded and annulled the verdict rendered on 28 December 1894 against Alfred Dreyfus and required that his case be judged in a new court martial to be held at Rennes. After all these years, Dreyfus was to come back from Devil's Island and to be granted a second attempt at justice. On 5 June 1899 Dreyfus was informed that his rank would be restored, that he was no longer judged guilty but instead had the status of a suspect, and that he would be returned to France to be allowed to defend himself at a new court martial in Rennes. Within a few days he was taken on a French cruiser back to France, where he arrived in the middle of the night and was immediately taken by train to Rennes. There, still under arrest, still sick, white-haired, terribly aged, finding it hard to speak because over the years in his isolation he had lost the ability, he was permitted for the first time in nearly five years to see his loyal wife, who had worked for him unceasingly.

This should have been the end. He should have returned in some measure of triumph; the review of the facts in open court should have exonerated the innocent man. But it was not to be. The army showed not the least signs of contrition for anything that had been done, and in many military quarters it was clearly the intention to defend the army, this most sacred bulwark of France. This court martial was to be as unjust as the first one. As one politician/journalist wrote, "On the one hand there is Dreyfus' honour; on the other, there is the honour of the ministers and generals who have sworn to Dreyfus' guilt." At the trial, everything raised against Dreyfus originally was raised again as though nothing had happened in the meantime (shades of Grandier). Still they came forward and repeated as facts all the unsupported accusations and in the name of national security said that they could not table the proof that they had. In their view, Esterhazy was only a straw-man introduced into the case by the Dreyfus family to divert attention from the real culprit. At 4:45 P.M. on 9 September 1899 the court martial delivered its verdict. Dreyfus was guilty and sentenced to ten years of detention. The whole world was shocked.

But deep in the psyche of France, things had changed. It was obvious that Dreyfus's broken health would not survive the disgrace of a second public cashiering and that he would die if imprisoned once again. Many in power recognized that in the court martial the army had judged itself and had found itself innocent in the national interest. But this was not justice! The government could not overturn the court martial, but it could grant Dreyfus a pardon. It was true that in accepting a pardon he was implicitly acknowledging that he must have been guilty in the first place. However, he was persuaded by his friends and family that it was better to live and seek further justice than to die for nothing, as he would certainly do if imprisoned once again. On 19 September 1899, ten days after the court martial verdict, the government issued a statement of pardon.

It was another six years before further investigations supporting Dreyfus's innocence finally persuaded the courts and the government to overturn the Rennes court martial and find Dreyfus innocent. On 12 July 1906 the High Court unanimously overturned the Rennes finding. On 13 July the Chamber and Senate voted to reinstate Dreyfus and Picquart to the army. Dreyfus was made a lieutenant colonel, and Picquart went on to become a general and the minister for war. On 20 July Dreyfus was presented with the Legion of Honour in a military ceremony on the same parade ground where twelve years earlier he had been cashiered – for all that he had suffered, he got this paltry medal. A year later, he resigned from the army in a state of ill health. On 2 August 1914 he rejoined and served throughout the war. The postwar years were spent quietly with his wife, and he died on 12 July 1935, aged seventy-five.

The beginning of it all was really the shocking defeat of France by Germany in 1870 – Germany the constant enemy. The lost provinces had to be regained. The reanimated army was the nation's pride and hope. Then there was the discovery of a traitor serving the Devil by revealing his country's secrets to the great enemy, a traitor who was in the French Army, in a position of great trust, and thus a threat to the nation. He had to be discovered, to be arrested, to be punished before further damage was done and before the existence of the spy became public; an undiscovered traitor would be disastrous for the nation, the government, and the army. The pressure to find the guilty man was overwhelming. This was what led to Dreyfus being quickly but mistakenly identified. And now new factors entered. His guilt became more easily believable because he was a Jew. Dreyfus was not popular with his fellow officers, making him even more acceptable as a suspect. So the common initial conditions that would lead to a witch hunt were present: fear and hatred, this time of the Germans. Added to this was another feature frequently associated with witch hunts: he belonged to a despised or rejected group, Jewry in this case.

Once started, this witch hunt exhibited a standard symptom: the accused was assumed guilty. Once Dreyfus's handwriting was "identified," there was no search of any kind for anybody else. There was no evidence against him beyond the handwriting (from the beginning a disputed issue), but his guilt was taken for granted. The only task remaining for his accusers was to find the evidence that would prove the guilt.

From now on, the characteristics of a witch hunt followed almost automatically. All evidence that cast doubt upon his guilt was ignored or argued away. Possible differences between his handwriting and that in the bordereau were explained away by the "fact" that he had disguised his handwriting, a perfect solution for the army – the similarities were explained and so were the differences! The opinions of the handwriting experts were inconclusive, but the army ignored the conflicting opinions and relied only on the opinion that suited their case. When he was asked to take dictation, his apparent unease was taken as a sign of guilt and used against him. Nothing that spoke in his favour had any value. There was no motive suggested for why he should have betrayed his country, but the fact was ignored. Conversely, anything that could be used against him was given undue weight. Every judge at his court martial simply accepted Henry's word that he knew Dreyfus to be guilty and that the security interests of the nation prevented him from stating what he knew. Worst of all, the secret file was illegally accepted as proof against him without his even knowing that it existed.

And then there were the forgeries, the creation of false evidence, which is so common to witch hunts. A conviction could be assured only if evidence was forged against the accused; it became essential to his being found guilty. The Devil was so clever that he would escape unless good men took action to outwit him, and since the man was known to be guilty, he must not be allowed to go free to continue his evil. It became justifiable – indeed, honourable – to create false evidence and to include it in a secret file that was itself used illegally. Then after his conviction, he was accused by an officer of having confessed to treason. There was no record kept of the confession, only the officer's word, which was false, too.

Finally, there was the perceived danger of accomplices and supporters. In this case whoever supported the accused man risked becoming himself accused as an agent of the Devil. To be on Dreyfus's side or to speak out for him was to be a part of the Jewish conspiracy and disloyal to France. This was true of friends, family, and the gradually growing mass of people who came to question his guilt. This was true of Émile Zola and even more noticeably of Commandant Picquart. All of these evils were compounded when the true questions of innocence did arise and became a public issue.

The Dreyfus Affair was a terrible one marked by the demand for an instant culprit, a decision of guilt before there was any credible evidence, a refusal to accept any evidence that did not support guilt, the creation of false testimony and documents, and a complete closing of the ranks against any suggestion of innocence. It bore all the hallmarks of a witch hunt.

9

If It Walks Like a Duck

The Dreyfus case was a witch hunt. Of course, a witch wasn't involved but a traitor. This traitor was as real a threat to society in 1895 as the witches of Bamberg and Salem had been some two centuries earlier. Dreyfus was to France as much a witch as Grandier had been to France. The proof is that they treated Dreyfus exactly as they had earlier treated witches. His case met all the characteristics of a witch hunt that we saw earlier.

Chadwick Hansen, in *Witchcraft at Salem*, gives a good definition of a witch hunt: "When a community looks only for evidence of guilt and ignores or suppresses all contradictory evidence, the result is a witch hunt." But for more certainty, we need to expand upon this by adding the characteristics of a witch hunt that we have already seen. We know that a witch hunt is in progress when the witch hunters:

1 judge an accused person guilty *before* seeking evidence;
2 apply whatever pressures are necessary on suspects, including beatings and torture, to extract confessions and obtain accusations against others;
3 accept *any* incriminating evidence, however dubious or vague;
4 emphasize what they want to hear and ignore testimony or evidence inconvenient to their theory;
5 create or employ false evidence if necessary to convict;

6 threaten anyone speaking in favour of a defendant as a suspected accessory;

7 treat the accused as having no normal rights because he or she is so dangerous;

8 are prepared to accept secret accusations, to hide the accusations from the accused, and to protect the identity of the accuser;

9 expand the hunt in order to find other witches, acolytes, and supporters, always assuming that the accused witch is only the tip of the iceberg;

10 justify and excuse all errors by appeals to national security, the protection of society, or the good of the state.

So, expanding upon Hansen, we can say: *a witch hunt takes place when a community looks only for evidence of guilt, when it ignores or suppresses all contradictory evidence, and when its conduct meets most of the characteristics of a witch hunt.*

Using this definition, all the cases that we have seen were "witch hunts." The witch, in Dreyfus's case, was a traitor, and in cases yet to come we will find (alleged) gang-rapists and terrorists, but the illegal treatment that each suffered fits the definition. As the saying goes, "if it walks like a duck, swims like a duck, and quacks like a duck, then it probably is a duck."

There are people who hold that we cannot have a one-person witch hunt. They say that to have a witch hunt, there has to be a mass of witches. The Grandier and Dreyfus cases, they say, were not witch hunts but "miscarriages of justice." Those who take this position don't define a witch hunt, and they don't define a miscarriage of justice. But we have defined a witch hunt; now let us define a miscarriage of justice: *when laziness, stupidity, overeagerness, cupidity, inexperience, a desire for fame or promotion, personal prejudice, or similar compounds of human error result in failures in proper procedures or due process that lead to an innocent person being found guilty, a miscarriage of justice has occurred.*

The difference is that in a witch hunt the accused is judged guilty because he is "known" to be guilty, so any action, illegal or otherwise, is deemed justified in an effort to find or create the evidence necessary to get a guilty verdict. A witch hunt is a state of mind.

By comparison, a miscarriage of justice is a matter of stupidity and human error. We read every day of verdicts, sometimes years old, overturned and recognized as mistakes. True, the cases, once reviewed and all the facts are known, may meet some of the characteristics of a witch hunt, but this is true of only a few of them, and usually they result from hidden or ignored evidence and failures in procedures. The state of mind is quite different from that occasioning a witch hunt.[1]

The Grandier case was clearly not simply a miscarriage of justice; it was not a mistake but a witch hunt. So was the Dreyfus Affair. In fact, it is insulting to call the Dreyfus case a miscarriage of justice, a sort of "Oops guys, we goofed. Sorry about that!" Miscarriages of Justice arise from errors, stupid errors, culpable errors, perhaps, but errors nonetheless. Witch hunts arise from deliberate decisions to find a specific person or group guilty.

"For Brutus is an honourable man; So are they all, all honourable men," said Shakespeare in *Julius Caesar*. And witch hunters, too, often act out of the highest of motives. But can liars and torturers be honourable men?

Witch hunting is a state of mind that makes honourable men perform illegal acts because they "know" that the accused is guilty and may get away without punishment to commit further terrible damage. We saw this clearly in the Dreyfus case. In his trial, as in many witchcraft cases, it was not evil men who created false evidence but men of good intention who knew that only with the creation of lies and hiding of favourable facts could the guilty man be found guilty and punished. It was their duty, they thought, to save society no matter what it cost them!

To men like Sandherr, Henry, du Paty de Clam, and the generals Boisdeffre and Mercier, their actions were patriotic, honourable, justified. They had, in their eyes, discovered a traitor. But treason was difficult to prove – by its nature it was most secret and conducted by clever men. By its nature, too, much of the true evidence of treason was in the hands of the enemy, those for whom the traitor was working, and therefore could never be discovered. This was the problem with which they were faced. They "knew" who the traitor was but had only marginal proof. Military secrets of the highest order were at risk, but they could not reveal what had been discovered and passed on precisely because they were secrets. They had to remain secrets lest they reveal something new to the enemy. To these men, certain of Dreyfus's guilt, it seemed a necessary step to create and change documents in order to prove guilty the man whom they knew to be guilty.

It was (and is) this same witch-hunting state of mind that so often made torture appear acceptable, even necessary, torture approved by honourable men, as we saw in Bamberg. Torture was seen as necessary to reveal the truth, necessary to find accomplices, necessary to obtain confessions so that the culprit could be imprisoned, hanged, or burned. It is this willingness on the part of honourable people to do despicable things in the name of good that makes witch hunts so frightening and threatening. True then. True now.

There is nearly always secrecy in witch hunts. The Dreyfus case was shrouded in secrecy from the beginning. It had to be. So many facts that were used to condemn him were questionable and could not stand the light of day. There were the forgeries, the secret file that was revealed to the judges, and Henry's resounding statement to the court martial that national security prevented him from revealing the facts but that he would swear to his knowledge of the man's guilt. The whole process of the five-year fight to prevent any review was a cover-up, a constant rearguard action to maintain the secrets – some of which remain unknown to this date as a result of Henry's suicide.

As Benjamin Franklin said, "Three may keep a secret, if two of them are dead." Secrecy becomes an outstanding characteristic when governments or important government agencies are involved because national security or some equivalent protection can be invoked so easily at this level. We have all heard the police spokesman on some heinous crime say of a suspect that "we cannot reveal all the facts, but we have our man." Beware if ever you hear someone say "if only I could tell you all I know."

There will be times when national security overrides the public's right to know or when the police or justice authorities cannot reveal all. But as we saw in the case of Dreyfus, and shall see later in the case of Maher Arar in our own times, under the cloak of secrecy and national security, society may sometimes be improperly protected and great injustices may be hidden – sometimes witch hunts can be carried out.

10

The Scottsboro Boys

The case of the Scottsboro Boys began on 25 March 1931 in the American state of Alabama. It never really ended, or at least it never ended in the sense that their clear innocence was declared in a court of law. Nevertheless, long ago it became recognized that the nine young African Americans involved were innocent of the charge of rape for which they were repeatedly tried and condemned to death and for which they spent many awful years in prison.[1]

By 1931 America was in the depths of the Depression. Work was often impossible to find, and many Americans (mostly men) drifted from place to place, seeking work, seeking a new place to beg and panhandle, seeking new fields for petty crime that would give them enough to live on, or just seeking new adventures. The railroads were one of the commonest means of transportation for the "hoboes" of the time; empty rail cars on the freight trains could take them right across America if that was where they wanted to go.

On 25 March 1931 the nine young African Americans who would become the "Scottsboro Boys" were riding the rails from Chattanooga to Memphis on a freight train that passed through the state of Alabama. Four of them, teenagers, had heard of possible work in Memphis, and the five others were from various parts of Georgia; most of them did not know each other. There were young white men on and in the railroad cars as well. And two young white women, Victoria Price and Ruby Bates.

Not long after the train crossed into Alabama at its leisurely pace of twenty-five miles an hour or so, one of the white youths who was jumping from one car to another stepped on the hand of one of the blacks, Haywood Patterson. A stone throwing fight ensued, and the blacks evicted the whites from the train – all except one, Orville Gilley. He was about to be forced to jump when the train reached a speed at which he would be in danger. Patterson pulled him back in.

The ejected whites went to the stationmaster at the closest station to report that they had been assaulted by a gang of blacks, and the news was in turn telegraphed to the next station, a place called Paint Rock, Alabama. By the time the train got there, a posse had been formed – a large one with dozens of men who rushed the train as soon as it was stopped and rounded up the nine black youths. They were tied together with rope, put on a flat-bed truck, and taken to the jail in Scottsboro. What had created the posse was anger over the fact that a bunch of blacks had had the temerity to fight young white men and eject them from the train. That neither group should have been on the train in the first place was immaterial. In Alabama at the time, blacks were automatically inferior to whites; if they attacked whites, whatever the circumstances, they could expect anger and retribution. What would happen in the coming years was rooted in these racial feelings and fears. From the beginning, the case of the Scottsboro Boys was both coloured and infected by the history of Alabama. These young men and boys were already guilty by virtue of having fought white boys, even before there was any suggestion of rape.

While the posse was still gathering up the boys, they came across two young white women who had got down from the train, Victoria Price and Ruby Bates. We do not know whether the women volunteered the information on their own or gave it as the result of a question, but the two of them said that they had been raped by a gang of twelve black boys and men armed with knives and pistols. Price said that she had been raped by six of them, and the assumption was quickly made that the other six must have raped Ruby Bates. (Since only nine of the blacks were on the train when it arrived at Paint Rock, it seemed that the other three had managed to get off the train before it arrived there. They were never found – if they ever existed.) The young women's story was that they had spent the previous night in Chattanooga at the home of a Mrs Callie Brochie. The next morning they went looking for work in the local mills, without success. They decided to return to Huntsville, their hometown. To get there they boarded a freight train, first getting into an oil car and later climbing over to what was called a gondola, an open topped car partly filled with gravel. They said that they met seven white boys there and started talking to them. Somewhat less than half-way to Huntsville, according to their story, twelve young blacks climbed into the gondola from another car in front, started a fight with the white boys, and ejected all but one of them from the train. (There were in fact various figures provided by different witnesses about the total number of blacks and whites in each "gang," but given the nature of the fight, the numbers could well have been confused. Relevant to our story is that by the time the train reached Paint Rock, there were nine African Americans present.) Victoria Price said that one of the blacks, Charlie Weems, had a gun and had been waving it about. She also said that all the whites but one (Orville Gilley) were forced off the train. Then the blacks turned on the two women, attacked, and raped them. She said that while Weems was the leader and had the weapon, it was another of the men who first attacked her (Clarence Norris). She said that he raped her while the others held her down and that the others then each took turns – Charlie Weems, she claimed, was still in the act of raping her when they arrived at Paint Rock.

In May 1931 Hollace Ransdall, a teacher, journalist, economist, and activist went to Alabama at the request of the American Civil Liberties Union (ACLU) to report on the trials of the Scottsboro Boys. Her record is a fascinating contemporary document. In it she raised the question of when the two young women had accused the men of rape. One investigator, after the trial, said that they did not make any charge immediately against the blacks but only did so after they themselves were taken into custody and when they sensed the spirit of the armed posse. This is quite possible, for both women had some history of prostitution. They were no doubt aware of the danger of being charged with vagrancy, or worse, after having been found on the train.[2]

As for the women themselves, Victoria Price was the leader (she claimed various ages but was probably twenty-seven; Ruby Bates was seventeen). Victoria was much the more outgoing of the two, a bubbly character who liked to be the centre of attention. Ruby was quickly pushed back into the position of confirming what Victoria said rather than speaking for herself. Victoria was certainly shrewd, clever, and a match for any lawyer, as she would prove in the various trials that followed.

Nobody was prepared to question the validity of their story. Not in rural Alabama. White women were not just at a different level from all

African Americans within this society; whites were on a different plane entirely. And in this white society, it was taken as a given that all black men wanted to rape white women. It did not matter that Victoria and Ruby were both low-class, poor whites who lived among blacks and were in effect their social equals. To the white society of Alabama, their accusations were not only believable but had to be believed. There was no need to question the facts that the women presented because the men were guilty from the time that they were accused – anything that might be said in their favour was ignored. The accusations were given the weight of testimony. Indeed, the accusation was in fact the only evidence required by the people of Paint Rock, of Scottsboro, and of Alabama in general. To many of them, a trial was not even necessary. That night a crowd of several hundred men milled around outside the jail in Scottsboro and worked themselves up for an old-fashioned lynching. Only the action of the governor of Alabama prevented this when he sent in the National Guard to protect the jail and the nine terrified young boys.

The pleasant people of small-town Scottsboro became transformed when they learned that nine blacks had raped two white women. As Ransdall put it in her account: "The thing that stands out above everything else in their minds is that the black race must be kept down; as they put it, 'The Nigger must be kept in his place.'" So, early in the morning, twelve days after the alleged rapes, 118 members of the National Guard took the men from the local jail, where they had been held, to the courthouse. Eight to ten thousand people came from all around to be present at the trial scene, lining the square outside the court where armed soldiers held them back. Only those with a special permit were allowed inside the court. The public mood was intensely hostile. The blacks were defended by two lawyers who were by any standards incompetent to perform their task. They failed to cross-question the two women adequately despite contradictions in their testimony and offered only the defendants themselves as witnesses. This was a serious error, for the young men stumbled through their testimony, incoherent, rambling. Worse, while six of them denied raping or even having seen the two women, the three others admitted to the rapes, having, they said, performed them under threats from the others. Clarence Norris attested that: "They all raped her, everyone of them." The Boys were not all tried at once but in small groups, so there was a succession of trials, with the nine appearing as witnesses at the different ones. But it was Victoria Price who really controlled affairs in the courtroom. Ransdall tells us that she gave her testimony "with such gusto, snap and wisecracks, that the courtroom was often in a roar of laughter. Her flip retorts to one of the attorneys for the defence especially caused amusement. The sentiment of the courtroom was with her, and she knew it and played up to it."

Price was the principal witness. Ruby Bates and Orville Gilley (the one white male who had stayed on the train) also made minor appearances. The other witnesses of significance were two doctors. They testified that the girls were examined shortly after they were taken off the train and showed no lacerations, tears or wounds, or other signs of brutality or severe manhandling, nor did they show any significant signs of severe stress. Victoria had one minor scratch and a little bruising. Since multiple rapes had occurred as the girls were being held down by a number of men on a bed of sharp-edged stones, the lack of bruising or surface wounds was surprising, but these peculiarities were ignored. The doctors also revealed that both of the women had had recent sexual intercourse, evidenced by the presence of semen. Another witness, a farmer, testified that he had seen the black men and the girls on the train as it passed his farm and that he "had seen a plenty."

Of course, what overrode all other testimony was the admissions of rape on the part of the blacks. With these, no matter that they contradicted each other in large part, there could be no other verdict but guilty. When the verdict was given on the first trial (the trial of Clarence Norris), the second was still in progress. The people in the courthouse could hear the loud cheers from the crowd outside; there was little doubt about the outcome of the trials yet to come. In the third trial, five of the boys were tried together and found guilty. The only significant new evidence was provided in the case of Willie Robertson: he was suffering from such a severe case of venereal disease that it would have been most painful for him, if not impossible, to have had sexual intercourse.

By the end of three days, eight young blacks had been sentenced to die in the electric chair; all were under twenty-one, and four were under eighteen. Only the youngest of the nine, thirteen-year-old Roy Wright, was spared. A mistrial was declared in his case because the jury held out for death when the prosecution, in view of his age, asked only for a life sentence. He was sentenced to life imprisonment.

At their first trial, the Boys were not closely questioned on their own testimony, and Victoria Price was far too clever to be caught by the two inept lawyers at Scottsboro. Yet the initial trial raised many questions, particularly in the North.

Ransdall wrote about the Boys: "I visited them in their cells in the death row on May 12, locked up two together in a cell, frightened children (they could neither read nor write) caught in a terrible trap without understanding what it was all about."

True, the trial had conformed to the letter of the law: it was held in open court with a jury duly selected, and the youths had legal counsel. But when one of the defence lawyers had asked for a change of venue and been refused, the verdict was never really in doubt. The all-white jury in this time and at this place would find any blacks guilty who were accused of raping white women. Moreover, the defence lawyers were pitiful. One of the two did not want to be named as the defence lawyer, seeking only to be identified as an adviser – understandable in a climate where defending blacks in such a case implied trying to get the guilty set free despite their guilt. Being too closely connected with the defence would isolate him from the rest of the society in which he had to live and find clients.

The judge set the date of execution of the eight for ninety days later, the earliest permitted under the law, to allow for appeals. And there were appeals, initially at least without effect. In January 1932 the Alabama Supreme Court upheld the sentences. But when the cases were appealed to the United States Supreme Court, new trials were ordered on the grounds that competent legal counsel had been denied by Alabama. But it would be many months before the next trials began.

All of these events took place in America at the height of the Depression. As the trials and the Boys became more widely known, they also became a part of the politics of the time. At first the National Association for the Advancement of Colored People (NAACP) was expected to become heavily involved. But this was not a good case for them in which to act as public champions; if even one of the blacks turned out to be truly guilty, it would do the association grave harm in the South. So it was the Communist Party that grasped the opportunity. Unfortunately for the Boys, the Communists were almost universally detested in the South. Still, whatever else might be said, they had good defence lawyers from now on. The lead man was Samuel Liebowitz, a New York lawyer with an amazing record of seventy-seven acquittals and one hung jury in seventy-eight murder trials. Further, Liebowitz had no connections with the Communist Party and was indeed a well-known Democrat. He was assisted by Joseph Brodsky, the Communist's chief attorney. Two years passed between the first set of trials for the Boys and the beginning of the second. This second trial was quite extraordinary for its ending, which was totally unexpected.

The prosecutor was Alabama's newly elected attorney general, Thomas Knight Jr, and Liebowitz would be the principal defence lawyer – this trial now had a very high profile nationally. The choice of the judge was equally important. Judge James Horton was a man of high legal reputation, described in his hometown newspaper in Alabama as having an "unusually equable nature, great legal ability and fairness." His appointment was well received by everybody. The trial would be held in Decatur, Alabama. In this community, Liebowitz, the New York Jewish lawyer paid by the Communist Party, would most certainly be seen as a "foreigner," no matter how high his legal reputation stood elsewhere. The defence had asked for the trial to be held in Birmingham, a city of substantially greater size than Decatur. The smaller town was some fifty miles from the birthplace of the Klu Klux Klan, right next to the county from which the two accusers came. As Linder puts it: "Residents expressed to visiting reporters a willingness to give the Scottsboro Boys a fair trial, but at the same time warned they didn't want to hear any 'arguments about race equality or the right of Negroes to serve on juries.'"

Who were these Boys? Patterson, who started the fight from which everything followed, was eighteen when the event took place; he had left home when he was fourteen and had ridden the rails looking for work as he went. The prosecutors saw him as the most defiant, and the most guilty, of the boys, which is why they put him on first. He entered jail illiterate, but within eight months he was reading and writing. He was clever, without doubt, but subject to mood swings – not surprising given all that was happening to him.

Clarence Norris had gotten only as far as second grade; by the age of seven he was working in the cotton fields. In 1933 he was nineteen. He had held a job in the Goodyear plant, working up to sixteen hours a day until his girlfriend left him and he took to the rails. He said that "on the night before his first trial, he was removed from his cell, beaten and told to turn state's evidence if he wanted to save his life." He testified that the other blacks had raped Price and Bates and that he alone was innocent.

Andy Wright was eighteen when he was arrested. He had gone to school until sixth grade and then to work to help support his family after his father died. He lost his job after seven years when his employer's insurance company learned how young he was and raised the rates. He and his young brother, Roy, together with Patterson and Williams, all boarded the freight train together to go to Memphis to look for work. He denied ever having seen Price or Bates until he got off the train. His brother, Roy, was thirteen when arrested and eventually got a life sentence in view of his age. At the first trial he said that he had seen other defendants rape the white girls. But he later said that he did this only after being threatened and severely beaten by authorities.

Charles Weems, at nineteen, was the oldest of the Boys. He had endured a hard life. He was four when his mother died, and only one of his seven brothers and sisters reached adulthood. He had finished fifth grade and had worked in a pharmacy. Ozzie Powell was sixteen. He claimed not to have known any of the other Boys before his arrest and that he witnessed the fight but was not involved. He had an IQ of 64 and could write only his name. He had worked in lumber camps for nearly three years before his arrest.

Olen Montgomery was seventeen; he had gone to school until fifth grade. He would claim that he was riding alone in a tank car throughout whatever happened. Eugene Williams was thirteen and had worked as a dishwasher. He boarded the train with his two friends, the Wright brothers, and with Patterson. He claimed that while he had fought with the white boys, he had not seen Price or Bates until he was arrested.

Willie Robertson was seventeen. He was suffering from a severe case of syphilis that would have made intercourse painful and unlikely. He had to use a cane to walk and was certainly not in a condition to leap from car to car as was alleged. He had left a job as a busboy in a Chattanooga hotel to look for something better. He claimed to have been in a boxcar by himself.

What we see, then, at the Decatur trial in 1933 are eight young illiterate men and boys,[3] all black and in a hostile community – none of them was likely to strike anybody with the appearance of innocence. Some of them claimed later to have been threatened before the first trial, beaten up, and instructed to accuse others of the rapes. This is almost certainly true. The result was that when they were being tried in their first trial, not all their stories were consistent, and some of them said in testimony that they had actually seen others committing rape – shades of Bamberg and Wurzburg!

At Decatur the earlier "confessions" of guilt would always be something that Liebowitz had to overcome. All depended on whether Liebowitz could raise real doubts about Victoria Price's innocence and veracity. Would the judge and jury believe Victoria Price once more? Or could Liebowitz in effect place her on trial?

The first to be tried was Haywood Patterson, selected by the prosecution from the beginning because he had the appearance of being an angry young tough who might be quite capable of raping a white woman. The courtroom was crowded with over 400 people; those who could not get in milled about either in the corridors or around the building. The black section of the courtroom held 100 African Americans. The place was well guarded.

Liebowitz started by demanding that the indictments be quashed because there were no blacks on the grand-jury rolls – in other words, only whites could be selected to be on the jury for these young men. There was no legal written prescription against blacks being on the grand-jury rolls; it was simply the practice in Alabama to see that the names of blacks did not appear on the list. Not that Liebowitz expected Judge Horton to rule in his favour, for no judge would ignore Alabama Supreme Court decisions upholding the lawfulness of the state's jury-selection system. He was laying the groundwork for an appeal later if his clients were found guilty.

Before the jury was selected, Horton spoke to the potential jurors, closing with these words: "If any of you are tempted, remember that they would consider it a disgrace and a shame upon the fair name of this and the other counties of this State to have anything happen here to reflect upon the administration of justice in our courts. I expect from you proper restraint and a fair decision according to the law and the evidence. We must be true to ourselves, and if we be true to ourselves we can't be false to any man." Judge Horton was going to follow these words no matter what the jury did.

When the trial proper started on 2 April 1933, Haywood Patterson was the first to be tried, and Victoria Price was the first prosecution witness. In response to the prosecution lawyer, she repeated the essence of her testimony from the first trial.

Haywood Patterson, she said, had come into the gravel car, where she and Ruby Bates were seated, from the top of the next boxcar. He and the others, she claimed, "come running ... toward the engine and jumped over our heads." The prosecutor, Attorney General Knight, then asked her, "What happened immediately after these colored men jumped in that car?" She answered, "They commenced fighting and knocking off the white boys." The prosecutor then asked, "What, if anything, did this defendant, Haywood Patterson have in his hand as he got in the car?" She replied, "He had a gun." Then in answer to other questions, she said that in the fight with the white boys, "he helped knock them off and throwed his gun up and him and the other one shot a time or two over the gondola" before throwing seven of them off the train, leaving only Orville Gilley, who "said he was scared he would get killed if he jumped off, and said he was going to stay in there, and if us girls died he would die too." The questions and answers went on:

Q: After the boys were put off the train, the white boys all except Gilley, then what if anything did this defendant do?
A: He helped take my clothes off.
Q: Helped take your clothes off?
A: Yes sir.
Q: What clothes did you have on?
A: Overalls, shirt, three dresses, pair of step-ins, girl's coat and girl's hat.
Q: What clothes did they remove from your body, this defendant you say helped?
A: Pulled off my overalls and tore my step-ins undone – tore my step-ins apart.
Q: What happened then Miss Price?
A: Well one of them held my legs and one held a knife on my throat while one of them raped me.
Q: Did Haywood Patterson on that occasion while one of those boys had a knife at your throat, and the other one holding you by the legs, did he have sexual intercourse with you?
A: Yes sir, he was the third one, or the fourth one, I won't be positive.
Q: This defendant had intercourse with you?
A: Yes sir.

When she had finished, Liebowitz began his cross-examination. Victoria Price was uncooperative, hostile, and flippant. She was argumentative about her age and lied about it, saying that she was twenty-one when, in fact, she was twenty-seven. She agreed that she had been married twice. Then he turned the questions to the rape itself, clearly with the intention of raising doubts about her veracity on this issue:

Q: They didn't spare you in any way, didn't try to make it comfortable for you in any way?
A: No sir.
Q: Just like brutes?
A: Yes sir.
Q: You lay on your back there for close to an hour on that jagged rock screaming?
A: Yes sir.

Q: Was your back bleeding when you got to the doctor?
A: I couldn't say.
Q: When you got to the jail did you find any blood on your back?
A: A little bit.
Q: Are you sure about that?
A: I ain't sure, that has been two years ago.

These questions were designed to raise doubt about whether a multiple rape could have taken place in the conditions that she described with so little physical damage for the doctor to find when he saw her so shortly afterward. Liebowitz moved from there closer to an equally important point of doubt, namely the general history of her morals and, most important, whether the semen that was found in her could have come from somebody other than the black boys. He asked Victoria Price whether she had known a man named Lester Carter before she boarded the train. She denied ever having seen him before she arrived at the Scottsboro jail, where (for reasons unstated) he had been detained. He changed tack for a little while, asking questions about another man, Jack Tiller. He intended to show that she had in fact known both Jack Tiller and Lester Carter before she even boarded the train and, what is more, that she had had intercourse before she got on the train.

First, he accused her of having earlier been convicted of lewdness with Jack Tiller, and when she denied this, he produced the certificate of conviction. He was attacking her credibility and her morals, but he had only just begun, for he now began to tie Tiller and Lester Carter together and, despite her earlier denials, to show that Price had in fact known both of them before she and Ruby Bates left Huntsville on the fatal morning. Liebowitz asserted that Jack Tiller and Lester Carter had come to her home with Ruby Bates (and he would later support this with other evidence) and that two or three days later, the four of them went to an area of railroad tracks that had a bad moral reputation. Then he continued his questions:

Q: Isn't it a fact that three days after you met Lester Carter you and he [and] Tiller and Ruby Bates went walking along the L&N Railroad tracks?
A: No sir, we never have been on the railroad together.
Q: Isn't it a fact that you had intercourse with Tiller on the ground while Ruby Bates had intercourse with Lester Carter right beside you?
A: No sir, I didn't.

Q: A day or possibly thirty six hours before you were examined by the doctor?
A: I never was in Lester Carter's company before I was in Scottsboro in jail.
Q: Did you have intercourse with Tiller a short time before you left Huntsville?
A: No sir.
Q: On the railroad yards?
A: I have told you three times, and I am not telling you any more – no sir I didn't.

Liebowitz's questions were designed to show that Victoria Price had had intercourse with Jack Tiller twenty-four to thirty-six hours before she got on the train. He then took her through her journey from Huntsville to Chattanooga, where she met up with Orville Gilley (the white boy who was the only one left on the train when the others were thrown off). He asked her about the night before she and Ruby had first climbed on the tank car to continue their journey. His purpose now was to show that she had intercourse again that night, this time with Lester Carter:

Q: Didn't you and Gilley and Lester Carter and Ruby Bates then go over a trestle near the railroad yards in Chattanooga and down a valley to where there was a clump of trees?
A: No sir.
Q: To a place called in Chattanooga, Hoboes Jungle?
A: No sir, I stayed with a woman by the name of Callie Brochie.
Q: Isn't it a fact you all went over in the jungle there and built a fire?
A: I didn't go to any jungles.
...
Q: Isn't it true that Gilley had intercourse with you in the jungles?
A: He absolutely did not – I told you, that is the seventh time I wasn't in any jungle.

By now Liebowitz had laboriously done all that he could to bring into question the morals and veracity of Victoria Price. But he had also begun to lay the grounds for explaining where the semen came from that had been found in her when examined by the doctors. From one of them, Dr Bridges, he later managed to establish that the doctor had found semen in both Price and Bates (much more in Bates than in Price). But he also testified in response to Liebowitz that the semen was

"non-motile." Sperm normally live from twelve to forty-eight hours after they have been deposited in the female. Non-motility of the sperm
would be quite consistent, therefore, with a time of deposit before the
supposed rapes had taken place. The defence lawyer had established
that intercourse could have happened before the women had boarded
the train in Chattanooga or even before they had left Huntsville.

But had he persuaded the jury? Or, perhaps more directly relevant,
could they be persuaded? Were they even open to persuasion? He was
an outstanding lawyer with an outstanding record, but he was a northerner, he was a Jew, and he was working for the Communist Party. The
locals seem to have made little distinction between his being employed
by the Communists and being one himself. On every account he was
anathema to them. He had been parachuted into a community where all
of his strengths and accomplishments worked against him and his clients.
Victoria Price's ability to stonewall him and his inability to break her
down might well be seen as a well-deserved comeuppance and a defeat
of the outsider. In any normal case the accused would have been assumed innocent until proved guilty; here, the reverse situation reigned:
the accuser was assumed to be innocent and the accused assumed to be
guilty. In these circumstances it might not be enough to raise doubts
about Victoria Price's veracity; to be successful he would have to try to
prove her falsehoods beyond a doubt. This was the problem with which
Liebowitz was now faced.

Of course, the crux of the issue was the rapes, or more properly, the
alleged rapes. Liebowitz was setting up to argue that they had never
taken place, that the women had made false accusations, that their testimony against the Boys could not be believed, and that particularly Price
was a woman of ill repute. The task of the prosecution was to find witnesses who would prove that the blacks had been seen with the women,
preferably during the course of the rapes. So the prosecution called a
farmer, Ory Dobbins, who claimed to have seen the train passing his
farm and the young black men attacking Bates and Price. He said that
he was on his farm, about forty yards from the train track, and that he
saw negroes and two white girls on a gondola car. Talking then of one
of the women on the train, he said:

It went by and when it went by I saw this here fellow grab her and throw
her down in the car.
Q: You saw a negro grab her?
A: Yes sir a negro.

Q: How did he grab her?
A: Around the waist.
Q: With his arms?
A: Yes sir.

Many objections from Liebowitz against this man's testimony were supported by the judge, but he just went on ignoring the adverse rulings. The details of the testimony show that this man was hostile to the defence; he was clearly a man determined to say whatever he wished to say exactly as he wanted to say it. But despite the repeated interventions by the judge, the problem that he posed for the defence was that he seemed to establish a physical connection between the women and the black men that they had denied existed. Liebowitz had to refute his testimony, or the case would be lost. When he started his cross-examination, he worked on where Dobbins was standing in relation to a barn and to the train and determined that the amount of time that Dobbins had to see any event was very limited. Then he began to question Dobbins about how far he really was from the train and about what he was now saying that he saw, compared to what he had testified to having seen at the first trial. His questioning showed that Dobbins's testimony here was totally at variance with his earlier statements. He had stated at the first trial that he was one hundred yards from the track; now he was saying forty. There were contradictions in his statements about how many girls he had seen and about what was happening to them. Then the questioning proceeded to the subject of what the women were wearing:

Q: You know it was a woman don't you?
A: She had on women's clothes.
COURT: She had on women's clothes?
A: She had on women's clothes.
Q: What kind of clothes, overalls?
A: No sir, dress.

The earlier questions to Dobbins had raised considerable doubt about what he had seen, but his last few lines proved that what he said was totally unreliable. There was no question at the trial that both Ruby Bates and Victoria Price were dressed in overalls, and everybody who had followed the case knew it.

The task of the defence when it had the opportunity to present its own witnesses was to prove that the word of Victoria Price was so

unreliable that there was no case against the Boys. Dallas Ramsey, a defence witness, was put on the stand to refute Victoria Price's assertion
that she had never visited the "hobo jungle" in Chattanooga. Ramsey,
who lived in the immediate vicinity of the railroad, testified that he had
seen the two young women in the hobo jungle early on the morning and
that later he had in fact seen them board the train. Then Liebowitz
called George Chamlee. Whereas Ramsey was a black man, Chamlee
was white and could speak with authority in this court not only because
of his colour but because of his own history and background. The colour should have made no difference, but Liebowitz seems to have felt it
necessary to establish that Chamlee was a witness on whom the jurors
could rely; he had been an attorney for forty years and district attorney
in Chattanooga, he had lived in the South all his life, and his father had
fought for the Confederacy against General Sherman.

Victoria Price had said that in Chattanooga she and Ruby Bates
had spent the night at the house of a Callie Brochie, at a certain
address. Chamlee, with his detailed knowledge of the part of Chattanooga in question, testified that neither the boarding house nor Callie
Brochie existed.

Six of the accused Boys were then put on the stand by Liebowitz. This
time, all of the accused young men claimed not to have seen the women
on the train and not to have raped them. But during cross-questioning,
they were faced by the prosecution with the evidence that they had
given at the trial in Scottsboro, when various of them had admitted to
being present while the women were raped. Now they were reversing
their testimony, all claiming that they had not seen the women raped
and, in some cases, that they had been in different railroad cars from
each other and had not even seen the women at all. Either they were
lying or they had been framed, as Patterson claimed under questioning
from Liebowitz: "Yes sir, I was framed at Scottsboro."

What could the Alabamian jury make of all this? They likely regarded
Patterson's claim to being framed as an insult to justice in Alabama.
They probably saw nothing improper in the attorney general of Alabama hectoring a black who was accused of rape. They likely saw the
strong objections that Liebowitz made to the hectoring of witnesses by
the attorney general as evidence of northerner, New Yorker, and Communist sympathies with black people. They no doubt saw Patterson's
reversal of testimony that he had given at Scottsboro as nothing more
than lying. Faced with two opposing testimonies from the same witness,
they would take the version that was consistent with the accusations of

Victoria Price. And here at Decatur, only Victoria Price appeared and restated her accusations, for Ruby Bates had disappeared, and nobody seemed to know where she was.

Later the defence lawyer brought a young man to the stand. This was Lester Carter, the man whom he had earlier said had had intercourse with Victoria Price. His testimony was needed by Liebowitz to cast further doubt on Price's morals and on the reliability of anything that she said. He stated that he and another young man, Jack Tiller, were with Victoria Price and Ruby Bates in Huntsville two nights before the "rapes." Liebowitz asked: "What occurred in the jungles that night?" Carter answered: "I had intercourse with Ruby Bates and Jack Tiller had intercourse with Victoria Price." He went on to say that they had first had intercourse "in the jungles, in the woods ... on the grass ... about eight or nine o'clock" (a little more than thirty-six hours before the "rapes"). Later it started raining, and "We came back down to the N.C. Railroad and got in an empty box car and remained there the rest of the night ... We had a couple more intercourses with the girls." The next day, he said, Price, Bates, and Lester Carter went to Chattanooga, and there they met Orville Gilley. The four of them spent the night in the "jungles" there, and on that night, Lester Carter testified, Orville Gilley had intercourse with Victoria Price.

By this time Liebowitz had established without doubt that on one night in Huntsville, Victoria Price had sex with Jack Tiller and that on the following night in Chattanooga, she had done the same with Orville Gilley. Further, she had been in jail briefly on a charge of lewdness and had lied about it in this court. She had lied also when she said that she had only met Carter for the first time after the alleged rape and again when she said that she had spent the night in Chattanooga at the Brochie house, which did not even exist. Any objective observer must have wondered how much faith could be put in this woman's words.

The prosecutor, Attorney General Knight, recovered some ground during cross-examination. His task was to shake faith in Carter's testimony by suggesting that he was in the hands of the Communists and northerners and that he had received money and support from them. He established that Liebowitz's assistant, Brodsky, had paid for a room for Carter in New York, that he had arranged for him to be driven back for the trial, with his expenses and meals paid, and that he had paid for the new clothes that Carter was wearing at the trial.

The next witness called by Liebowitz was a staggering surprise to everybody in the court. Just when everybody thought that he had completed his defence and was about to rest his case, the doors opened, and to the astonishment of all, in walked the missing Ruby Bates. In her testimony she said that she had gone to New York and had met a famous minister of religion there. Troubled by her conscience, she had confided in him. At his urging, she had now returned to tell the truth. Her testimony supported the case that Liebowitz was putting forward. She had known Victoria Price for some time; she and Price had spent one night having intercourse with Carter and Tiller in Huntsville and the next night, the night before the "rapes," in Chattanooga with Carter and Orville Gilley. Then Liebowitz proceeded to the day of the alleged rapes:

Q: [D]id the negroes come in that car where you were?
A: Not that I know of.
Q: Did any negro attack you that day?
A: Not that I know of.
Q: Did any negro attack Victoria Price that day?
A: Not that I know of.
Q: Did you see any negro attack Victoria Price that day?
A: No sir.

Next she was asked questions about her earlier testimony against the Boys at the first trial:

Q: You testified at Scottsboro that six negroes raped you and six negroes raped her, and one had a knife on your throat; what happened to her was exactly the same thing that happened to you. Who coached you to say that?
A: She told it and I told it just like she told it.
Q: Who told you to tell that story?
A: I told it like she told it.
Q: Who told you to do that, who coached you to do that?
A: She did.
Q: Did she tell you what would happen to you if you didn't follow her story?
A: She said we might have to lay out a sentence in jail.

Now Knight, the attorney general of Alabama, questioned Ruby Bates, asking about her clothes, her fashionable coat, her hat, her shoes. He was suggesting that the defence had paid for her clothes – and for her testimony. She did not have the assurance of Victoria Price on the stand, and some of the spectators sniggered and laughed at her to the point that Judge Horton had to intervene. Throughout the proceedings, the judge was watching her closely, judging for himself the quality and truthfulness of her evidence. The jurors were making their own judgments. Both in her case and in that of Lester Carter, Knight did everything that he could to make it appear that they had in fact been "bought" by the defence, "bought" by the Communists, and that their evidence had no value.

Ruby was the last witness. Then came the closing arguments. Liebowitz appealed to the jury for a just verdict: "I shall appeal to your reason as logical, intelligent human beings, determined to give even this poor scrap of colored humanity a fair, square deal." But perhaps he doubted already whether this appeal would be answered by the jury. It is clear from the record that he was conscious of the fact that he was appealing to them as an outsider when later in his summation he attacked the approach that the prosecution had taken: "What is it but an appeal to prejudice, to sectionalism, to bigotry," he said. "What he [the Attorney General] is saying is, 'come on boys! We can lick this Jew from New York! Stick it into him! We're among our home folk.'"

The attorney general, in response, said: "I do not want a verdict based on racial prejudice or a religious creed. I want a verdict based on the merits of this case." And then he completed his statement: "On that evidence, gentlemen, there can be but one verdict, and that verdict is death – death in the electric chair for raping Victoria Price." It was an interesting final statement. It appears that Ruby Bates's testimony had been accepted by the prosecution to the extent that she was no longer considered to be a victim of the multiple rape. She was just ignored, as though she did not exist. And ignoring her meant that only Victoria Price was left. All her accusations were still taken as true.

Judge Horton had overseen the trial as honestly and fairly as he could, given the superheated prejudices within his courtroom. And his charge to the jury now reflected this same deep desire for justice. He tried to convey this to the jurors: "Take the evidence, sift it out and find the truths and untruths and render your verdict. It will not be easy to keep your minds solely on the evidence. Much prejudice has crept into it. It has come not only from far away, but from here at home as well." Even he, with all his reputation within the community, felt it necessary to stress that he, too, was a southerner: "I might say that a great many of us, and I together with you, a great many of our forebears came here with the earliest settlers, and I happen to be descended from one who was the first that came down to this country. On both sides, as far back as I know, my people have always been a Southern people, and I have no desire to live anywhere else. I am getting old, and it is my home, my native land, and I want to see righteousness done and justice done, and we are going to uphold that name."

The written verdict came on Sunday morning and was presented to the judge. It read: "We find the defendant guilty as charged and fix the punishment at death in the electric chair." Horton was stunned.

The next day the court convened again. It was anticipated that Judge Horton would sentence Patterson and then begin the next trial. Instead, he said, in effect, that the whole atmosphere was not conducive to continuing immediately with the trials of the other accused: "No court, regardful of its duty to see that trials must be fair and impartial, could under such baneful influences permit the trial of this case to proceed at the present time. It, therefore, becomes the unquestioned duty of this court at the present time to enter of its own motion a continuance of this case." So there would be delay. Those who wanted to read between the lines guessed that Judge Horton was not happy with the jury's finding in the Patterson case. But most of those hearing and reading his words were confident that it was just a matter of delay – justice would be completed at a later date when the other trials would be held.

Some weeks later, Judge Horton convened the court again; it was 22 June 1933. When he spoke, he raised the question that had been occupying his thoughts for weeks now – "whether the verdict of the jury is contrary to the evidence." As the judge, he had to decide whether there was sufficient credible evidence presented at the trial upon which to base a verdict. And then he began to specify his own concerns, which must have been tearing at him all this time:

How can the physical condition of Price be reconciled with the gang rape she claimed to have suffered? Why did the jagged chert [the stones on which she was lying while being raped] not bruise her back? Why did the pistol lick on her head not leave a visible wound? Why was no semen found in her pubic hair? Why was the spermatozoa in her vagina non-motile? Why was her respiration and pulse normal less than two hours after the rapes? Why was she not hysterical or crying?

When we consider, as the facts hereafter detailed will show, that this woman had slept side by side with a man the night before in Chattanooga, and had intercourse at Huntsville with Tiller on the night before she went to Chattanooga; when we further take into consideration that the semen being emitted, if her testimony were true, was covering the area surrounding her private parts, the conclusion becomes clearer and clearer that this woman was not forced into intercourse with all of these Negroes upon that train, but that her condition was clearly due to the intercourse that she had on the nights previous to this time.

How do we make sense of the glaring contradictions in the testimony of Ory Dobbins, the farmer who claimed to have witnessed the assault from his barn near Stevenson? Why did he testify that the woman he saw attacked was wearing a dress when Price was wearing overalls? Why did he say the attack occurred in a coal car when Price claims to have been raped in a gondola filled with chert?

This is the State's evidence. It corroborates Victoria Price slightly, if at all, and her evidence is so contradictory to the evidence of the doctors who examined her that it has been impossible for the Court to reconcile their evidence with hers.

Horton went on to raise other doubts about the testimony and then to question the morals of the women and to say "the common experience of mankind teach[es] us that women of the character shown in this case are prone for selfish reasons to make false accusations both of rape and of insult upon the slightest provocation for ulterior purposes." He concluded all this with something totally unexpected but within his rights as the judge: "It is therefore ordered and adjudged by the Court that the motion be granted; that the verdict of the jury in this case and the judgment of the Court sentencing this defendant to death be set aside and that a new trial is hereby ordered." This was a stunning decision. Judge Horton's conclusion came close to saying that the Boys could not get justice in Alabama. He was a southerner by birth and history, yet in his decision he was going against the prevailing southern instinct of the time. He had little doubt that he would pay for it, and he did. He lost the next election, although previously he had been unopposed.

For the second time now the trials of the Scottsboro Boys had been overturned, first on the grounds of inadequate defence lawyers and now based on the decision that the guilty verdict was inconsistent with the evidence. Their lives were saved, at least for the time being, but they would remain in prison until they were tried again. And tried again they would be; Attorney General Knight immediately and angrily declared that the state had every intention of pursuing this to the end, adding that Patterson would go back on trial as quickly as it could be managed.

It was an extraordinary decision; the witch hunt, once started, must not be halted. It was now incumbent on the state, it seemed, to try the Boys once more – not because they were guilty but because they could not be found innocent. Southern society could be protected only by pursuing the cases to the acceptable end. White women had to be protected. White society had to be protected. Everything that the Confederacy had fought for had to be protected. Everything that their grandfathers had passed on to them had to be protected. There was only one acceptable end: a verdict of guilty and the death sentence. It had started off with an apparent clear-cut case, in local eyes at least, of blacks raping two white women. But this was really no longer the issue: now the issue was that even the suggestion of blacks raping whites had to be stamped out. The blacks had to be put in their place, the northerners had to be kept at bay, the Communists had to be defeated lest they gain a foothold with the blacks, and the northern Jews had to be kept out. The barbarians, it seemed, were at the gates in the form of these few young black boys and their supporters who wanted to change the southern world. Guilt and innocence were no longer the issue: what mattered was the verdict, and it had already been decided in Alabama. All that was needed now was another trial.

Within the next few months, Knight arranged for Judge Horton to be excluded from judging the case. A new judge was appointed, Judge Callahan, a man acceptable to Knight. Callahan acted like a prosecutor rather than a judge, overruling just about every defence objection. Liebowitz again defended the Boys, but the judge would not allow him to raise any inquiry into Victoria Price's morals, character, or reputation, and he cut the lawyer off when he tried to suggest that the woman had had sex before the supposed rape. Orville Gilley, a witness this time, corroborated that Price had been raped. Professor Linder suggests that Gilley's testimony resulted from the fact that Knight had been sending weekly cheques to Gilley's mother and that he was now calling in his chips. When it came time for Callahan to give instructions to the jury, he told them that "they should presume that no white woman in Alabama would consent to sex with a black."

Given these facts, it is not surprising that first Patterson and then, in a second trial, Norris were found guilty and sentenced to death. Judge Callahan did not proceed with the other trials for the time being on the grounds that the first two cases were going to be appealed and that he would wait on the results before proceeding. The grounds for appeal were on a subject that had been raised in the previous trials but that had not been pursued, namely that both in fact and in practice, no blacks were allowed to sit on juries in Alabama and that there had not been, therefore, nor could there have been in practice, any blacks on this jury. Nothing in law prevented the inclusion of black jurors, but the lists of potential jurors were prepared and handled in such a way that the names of no blacks appeared, resulting in all-white juries. This argument finished up at the Supreme Court of the United States, which decided in favour of the appeal. The finding in their judgment was that "upon the proof contained in the record now before us, a conclusion that their [the blacks] continuous and total exclusion from juries was because there were none possessing the requisite qualifications, cannot be sustained ... and in view of the denial of the federal right suitably asserted, the judgment must be reversed and the cause remanded for further proceedings not inconsistent with this opinion."

So there would be yet a fourth trial. And meantime the Scottsboro Boys would remain in prison. This legal bouncing back and forth between Alabama and the United States Supreme Court seemed as though it could go on forever.

But things had changed. The original charges had been laid back in 1931. When the cases were tried again in Alabama for the fourth time, five years had passed. The state was not by any means prepared to let the young men go free, or at least not all of them, but neither did it desire to continue to demand that the last ounce of flesh be given up. The truth was that for years now, Alabama had been the subject of criticism and vilification, particularly in the North, which was having political and economic consequences that outweighed the benefits. Those most immediately concerned within the state wanted to see an end to it. Alabama, and Alabama justice, had to be satisfied, but the sooner it could be done and the faster the dirt could be swept under the carpet, the better it would be. The first major sign of change came when Haywood Patterson, tried once more and found guilty once again, was sentenced to seventy-five years in prison instead of being given the death-sentence, which had always been his punishment before. Andy Williams was sentenced to ninety-nine years in prison. Clarence Norris did get the death sentence, although it was never carried out, and Charlie Weems got seventy-five years. Ozzie Powell pleaded guilty to a lesser offence and received a lighter sentence. These were terrible punishments, but apart from Clarence Norris's sentence, they were, to the public mind, a far cry from what had gone before.

Offsetting these sentences were the pardons granted to four of the young men – an indication of how much the authorities were now prepared to compromise. Olen Montgomery, who was seventeen at the time of the "rape," had consistently claimed throughout the years that he had been riding alone in a tank car when all the events took place and that he had known nothing about them at all. By 1937 all the prosecution lawyers appear to have quietly accepted that he was in fact innocent, so he was pardoned and released the same year. Eugene Williams was thirteen when he was arrested. He admitted to having been involved in the fight but said that he had never seen Bates or Price. The charges against him were dropped, and he, too, was released. Willie Robertson (the boy with the advanced case of syphilis), who had been accused directly by Victoria Price of holding her legs apart while she was raped by the others, consistently testified that he was alone in a boxcar. Ultimately, the prosecutors gave up pursuing his case, and he was likewise released. Finally, Roy Wright, also thirteen at the time of the original events and the youngest of the boys, had all charges against him dropped in 1937.

In hindsight, it is apparent that these decisions were totally inconsistent with all that had gone before. In earlier trials, each of these young men had been found guilty of rape and had been sentenced. Now they were released and permitted to go free – as though the trials and sentences had never taken place, even as though the rapes had never taken place. It cannot be forgotten that from the very beginning, all nine were supposed to be in the case together and equally guilty. If four were allowed to go free, could they really be less guilty of rape than the others, and if they were as guilty, then why were they let free? Certainly, Victoria Price had accused Willie Robertson of direct assistance in the rape. So did his release not imply that the veracity of her testimony was in doubt? And so the questions go.

The five Boys who were still jailed in Alabama eventually found their ways out, either by escape or by parole. Charlie Weems was kept in prison until 1943, when he was paroled. Andy Wright was paroled in 1944 for the first time and was subsequently in and out of jail for parole violations until 1950, when he was finally released, the last of the Boys to leave prison. Ozzie Powell (whose IQ was measured at 64) was finally released in 1946.

The outstanding member was Haywood Patterson. Patterson was always seen as the most guilty and the most defiant of the men accused. He was the natural prime target of the prosecutors. In all, he spent sixteen years in prison awaiting trials and serving his sentence. In the years leading to his final conviction, he had been sentenced to death three times. He once spent a night that had originally been scheduled for his own death in a cell watching and listening as another man was electrocuted. He escaped prison briefly in 1943 and then again in 1947. He was free for three years before being recaptured by the FBI. Alabama requested his return, but the governor of Michigan refused extradition. Later, Patterson was arrested in connection with the death of a man in a barroom brawl. The result was a manslaughter conviction for which he was imprisoned again. Less than a year later, in 1952, he was dead of cancer.

Clarence Norris's death sentence, given in his fourth trial, was commuted to life imprisonment by the governor of the state. He was paroled in 1944, broke his parole and was returned to prison, and was paroled for a second time in 1946. In time, he settled, married twice, had a family, had a permanent job and a decent living. As the years went by, there developed an increasing demand that his innocence be officially and legally recognized. This came about ultimately in October 1976 when Governor George Wallace handed to Clarence Norris a full pardon on behalf of the State of Alabama in recognition of the fact that he had never raped anybody. It was, in effect, a recognition that all of the Boys had been innocent. He lived until 1989, the last of the Boys to die.

So they lived and were not executed. But they spent many years in jail. Most of them entered as boys; they left as men, psychologically scarred and damaged. As boys, when they were first held for trial, they were terrified, the crowd outside howling for their blood and threatening lynching. They were ill-treated in the days and nights to come, some of them beaten to gain confessions or accusations against the others. When they finally came to trial, it was to be sentenced to death, then after appeal, they faced trial again, and then a third time – always with death ahead of them. Finally, after the last trial, the sentences were for imprisonment, forever, with sentences of up to ninety-nine years and seventy-five years, in harsh, brutal prisons. Even Dreyfus was not treated as terribly as this.

So the story of the Scottsboro Boys never ended in a conclusion of finality; it just petered out. The Second World War and other events took over.

It is now recognized that the Boys were innocent, even though there has been no formal statement to this effect. This is something commonly found in "witch hunts" both now and in the past. By the time the "witches'" conviction took place, the authorities had become so committed that to admit their error would have been to cast doubt on the probity of the authority and even on the state itself. The state ultimately released the victims, but it fought long rearguard actions to avoid saying officially that an injustice had been done. But great harm was done to the individuals. Some never recovered. None of the Boys ever really managed to live a normal life after all the injustices that had been done to them both by the "system" and by their years in prison.

What would have happened if these nine young boys and men had been poor whites rather than blacks? Would Victoria Price's and Ruby Bates's accusations of rape still have been accorded a halo of truth that could not be tarnished when their own backgrounds and moral history were established? Probably not. Would there have been an immediate danger of lynching because the Boys had to be guilty? Almost certainly not. Would the police and the juries have ignored the claims of some that they had been in different parts of the train and had no knowledge of events? Probably, they would have at least considered the stories as possible. Would Ruby Bates's retractions have been ignored by the jurors if the Boys had been white? And would all the contradictions in Victoria Price's testimony and statements have destroyed her credibility? Nobody can know for sure, but it is certainly highly probable that if all the participants had been white, things would have been different. Here we see in black and white the obvious differences that colour made in this tragedy.

From the very beginning, as soon as the women accused them, the Boys were guilty. In those courtrooms, testimony against the accused Boys was accepted virtually without question; testimony in their favour was ignored or argued away to nothing. And when it came to trial, it made no difference that the whole original case was built on false evidence. Even an open retraction by Ruby Bates was ignored. She admitted perjury, swore that neither she nor Victoria Price had been raped, and declared the innocence of the accused boys and men. And all of this was after Price's veracity had already been put into severe doubt. But Ruby Bates's testimony was ignored by the jury as though it had never been given – as though she had never appeared, never existed.

The admissions of the Boys at the first trial, when they accused each other of having raped the women, were to hang over them from trial to trial no matter how much they were later retracted. The jurors must always have been saying to themselves that the Boys told the truth the first time and that the rest was all lies to save themselves. But the Boys were very nearly lynched that first night – a terrifying experience.

Afterward, there were the threats and the physical beatings in the jail. Threats and torture brought about these "confessions," one of the common symptoms of a witch hunt, just as they did in Bamberg, Wurzburg, Salem. For the witch hunters, the crime was so great that it seemed permissible to do anything to get a confession.

Judge Horton was never reelected but lived on to devote himself full time to his farming; he lived an honoured and respected life. He died in 1973, aged ninety-five. Ruby Bates continued in the North to speak for the innocence of the Boys whom she had once accused. She married in 1940. Later she went back to Alabama, where she died in 1976, aged sixty-three. Victoria Price, the evil genius of the whole case, died in 1982. She never admitted that she had been the cause of such terrible injustice.

11

The Witch Hunters

The case of the Scottsboro Boys was a typical witch hunt, but it was unusual in one respect: although there were nine of them, they were actually treated as though they were one individual. So you can have a multiple-case witch hunt where the "witches" are treated as one person. Thus it is not the number of people targeted that defines a witch hunt but whether the characteristics of a witch hunt are met.

Of course, somebody might say that the case of the Scottsboro Boys was not really a witch hunt because there wasn't a hunt involved – they were found on the train. But this protest suggests an unnecessarily literal interpretation of a "hunt." The case of the Boys met the characteristics of a witch hunt very clearly. They were "guilty" as they got off the train and were met by the posse, and they were treated as guilty all the way through, necessitating false evidence, forced confessions, the works. This was indeed a witch hunt.

The real originator of a witch hunt is never the "witch"; it is the witch hunter. It is the witch hunter who first declares the witch to be a witch. And the hunter does this when he or she decides that somebody is guilty and is to be pursued to the end and then publicly announces this view. It all starts in the mind of the witch hunter when he or she first decides guilt without evidence. This is why witch hunting is really not an activity but a state of mind – the witch hunter's mind.

We have seen some of the things that drive witch hunters: fear, anger, hatred, to start with, brought about by some terrible event that impels them to act and to decide on guilt.

Sometimes their decision of guilt is coloured by the fact that the person whom they are accusing belongs to a despised group, a Jew in Dreyfus's case and blacks in Scottsboro. There, the root of the case was fear in the white local population that given the least opportunity, the blacks would rise, rape, and pillage. Feared they certainly were! But despised, too. To the vast majority of the local whites, the blacks, and certainly these poor blacks, were a subclass – a dangerous subclass. Only by the severest of treatment could white society be protected. To this end it became justifiable to the society of Alabama to force confessions, to subvert the normal justice of trials, to lie, and knowingly to accept the accusers' lies as the truth. As the trials dragged on, it must have been increasingly obvious that Victoria Price was lying, yet her lies were accepted, even if not believed. If somebody is despised (especially if they are feared and despised), their ill-treatment is made more acceptable. Further, if somebody or some group is described as evil, their ill-treatment is made quite acceptable – as the Bamberg and Salem witches discovered and as Grandier did, too. The true witch hunter associates a sense of evil with his or her victim – a sense of the victim being despicable, inhuman – that justifies all kinds of psychological pressures and physical tortures. This might be called "the axis of evil" syndrome.

Good witch hunters are not necessarily bad men. Indeed, they usually are not. Their motives are often of the highest: a desire to protect society from evil men, the protection of the Godly state, the knowledge that they are "on the side of the angels." This sense that they are protecting all that is best in their society against its greatest enemy is what drives and sustains them. This certainty is what impels them to undertake improper and illegal actions to rid their world of what is threatening it.

Of course, there are other motives – baser and more human ones: ambition, personal profit, promotion, public praise. And in big cases, like Bamberg, witch hunting becomes an industry that gives tangible benefits to its members. Moreover, there is what one might call the fighter-pilot mentality: some of the most famous witch hunters became renowned for how many witches they could burn. Laubardemont, for instance, in the Grandier case came to Loudun with an established reputation for the "body count" of witches whom he had burned during an infestation of witches in Navarre.

The Guildford Four and the Maguire Seven, our next case study, show witch hunters again fulfilling the descriptions that we have just seen.

12

The Guildford Four and
the Maguire Seven

The Irish Republican Army (IRA) fought a decades' long war against British rule in Northern Ireland. Their acts of terrorism (or freedom fighting, depending on which end of the telescope you are looking through) have included urban guerrilla war in the towns and countryside of Northern Ireland, the 1979 assassination of Earl Mountbatten, a relative of the Queen of England, and a nearly successful rocket attack on the British Cabinet in 1984. Within mainland Britain itself, the ordinary population was subjected to random bombings over many years. As early as 1968–69 British troops were sent into Northern Ireland in large numbers; the province became a war zone for at least the next twenty-five years as a brutal war of mutual terror ensued there. Only in the early 1990s did both parties begin to edge toward some kind of peace.

It was within this context of planned violence and terrorism on both sides that in 1974, the IRA undertook a major bombing campaign. The first of these attacks took place in the town of Guildford, in England, on 5 October. Two bombs were placed in pubs popular with both men and women army recruits from local barracks. The bomb in The Horse and Groom exploded at 8:30 P.M., killing five people and injuring many others. The bomb in the other pub, The Seven Stars, went off an hour later, but the owner had already cleared his pub in light of the earlier bomb, so there were no casualties. A month later, on 7 November, another bomb went off in The King's Arms in Woolwich, London. Two people were killed in the attack.

The most frightening incidents took place on 21 November 1974. Two bombs were placed in Birmingham, a large provincial city in the English midlands. Both exploded at about 8:20 P.M. The first was in The Tavern in the Town and killed eleven people. The other went off in The Mulberry Bush and killed ten. There were, in addition, 161 serious injuries.

Over many years, particularly after the Irish Famine of 1846–50, there had been extensive emigration from Ireland to the great cities of England and Scotland. This had continued in the post-Second World War years. Sections of all the major cities had substantial Irish populations, particularly Birmingham, which at the time of the bombings was home to an Irish community of 100,000. This series of attacks set off a wave of fear and anger in the English population. All the hysteria and prejudice that had been building over the years against the incomers suddenly came to a head. At the local level, in Birmingham, it resulted in reprisal incidents against this immigrant population. At the national level, in Parliament, a bill was introduced – the Prevention of Terrorism (Temporary Provisions) Act – that swept away the legal protections of the individual that had been constructed in British law over centuries. Within a week of the Birmingham bombings, the bill was introduced. It was passed through the Commons within twenty-four hours, with the Lords taking only three minutes to complete the task. The Birmingham attack took place on 21 November, and the Prevention of Terrorism Act came into effect on 29 November. Its effects were draconian. Membership in or support of the IRA became an offence. The word "terrorism" was redefined to include threats of violence not just to people, but also to property and to anything that "causes a risk to the health and safety of anyone." It gave the authorities powers to restrict the movements of designated persons, but much further, it gave the police power to arrest anybody, without warrant, whom they reasonably suspected was concerned with terrorism, even where they had not assembled sufficient evidence to make a specific case. Moreover, the Act gave the authorities the power to hold suspects without charges for up to seven days and in effect prevented them from communicating with anybody. This, by itself, removed rights and protections that went back in England to the Magna Carta of 1215.

Certainly, the intense fear and anger were justified. Clearly, the British government had to take drastic action in response to the attacks in order to satisfy the public and to protect its people. As it turned out, however, not only did the Prevention of Terrorism Act give the police and the justice system enormous powers; it also took away the protections of the innocent along with those of the guilty.

The Act produced immediate results. Within hours the first arrest was made under its provisions. A Belfast-born man named Paul Hill, who was then living in north London, was arrested in Southampton at the home of his girlfriend. The following day, a friend from Belfast who had spent the months from August to October that year in England was also arrested at his home in Belfast and taken to Guildford in England. His name was Gerard Conlon. Subsequently, two others were arrested, Patrick Armstrong and Carole Richardson. All four would go on trial for the Guildford bombings, would be convicted and imprisoned, and would become known as the Guildford Four.[1]

How were Paul Hill and Gerry Conlon identified in the first place? At the time of the trial the police did not need to make public anything about why they were interested in Hill; they had only to say that they had acted on information received. But it would appear that Hill was believed to have played a peripheral part in the abduction of a man in Belfast who was later found shot dead. So his name was known to the police. When an informer was paid in connection with the Guildford bombing, Paul Hill's name came up. This is one theory, but not the only one. There are other variations on the story of how he came into the picture, extending to the suggestion that Hill was suspect to the Provos (an extremist wing of the IRA) and that his name was given across as a suspect for the Guildford and Woolwich bombings in order to take the heat out of a search for the real perpetrators. This complete uncertainty about the facts is indicative of the pressure that the police and the other authorities were under to find the culprits and to find them immediately. It was a case of "full speed ahead and damn the torpedoes."

Why Gerry Conlon became initially suspect and involved is equally obscure but again seems to have originated with an informant. There is some suggestion that he had attended a meeting with a couple of men from the IRA and that this became known to the informant, who was ready to sell his knowledge. But, once more, there is no certainty about this. Clearly, however, once the authorities had the names, they were already certain that they had the bombers. With the provisions of the Prevention of Terrorism Act in hand, they had the means to deal with them. All that remained was to find enough evidence to obtain a guilty verdict.

After the Guildford bombings, the police put a great deal of work into interviewing all the survivors who had been in the pubs. From more than 300 statements, they established in considerable detail who had been where in each pub, who was next to them, and everything that they saw. It was a fine piece of police work, from which they established that at The Horse and Groom a man and a woman had been present who had not been accounted for and that at The Seven Stars the same was true of a man and two women. There seems to have been little doubt that these were the people who had carried out the bombings. But when it came to descriptions of these people, they did not tally. In the case of The Horse and Groom, for instance, three people gave solid descriptions, but they were not the same. Police-artist sketches were attempted but did not fit any of the people arrested. Eight witnesses from The Horse and Groom failed to identify Carole Richardson in a police line-up, and for some reason the other three suspects were never put into line-ups at all. Despite all this work, there was no material-witness evidence against the members of the Guildford Four at their trial. Further, there was no forensic evidence. The police had only confessions of the four arrested suspects, and it was on this evidence that they were all convicted. All four were alleged to have made voluntary confessions to the police. That they "confessed" is certain. That they later repudiated these confessions is equally certain, and they did so on the grounds that the confessions had been made under duress. Hill maintained that he had been subjected to brutal treatment both by the Surrey police (Guildford is in the county of Surrey) and by police of the Royal Ulster Constabulary, who had been brought across from Ireland to interview him. He talked of a gun being held to his head. He also claimed that both he and his girlfriend (who was pregnant with their child) were threatened and that he was beaten. Under this intense pressure, he claimed, he signed statements confessing to involvement in both the Woolwich and the Guildford bombings.

Armstrong, in turn, said that he had been extremely frightened and was punched by the assistant chief constable of Surrey. Richardson also said that she was beaten and afraid of what was going to happen to her if she did not confess, although she made it clear to the police that she had not even been in Guildford on the night of the event. As for Conlon, his defence lawyer argued that he had been slapped in the kidneys and the testicles and that threats had been made against the Conlon family back home in Belfast. Today, there is no doubt that the members of the Guildford Four were brutally beaten.

The confessions had their own weaknesses. There were some elements that simply did not hold up to scrutiny. Hill for instance talked of a bomb factory in a place named Brixton; but the factory was found not to exist. People were named as being present at particular times who were later proved not to have been there. Carole Richardson confessed to being present at the Woolwich bombing; later it was found that she had not been there at all. The lawyer who led the prosecution got around these inconsistencies neatly. He argued that the police were being deliberately misinformed by the accused in these parts of their confessions (and hence by the Provos, their masters) in order to confuse the issue with a clever mixture of truth and falsehood so that the authorities would not know the truth at all. (When Jeanne des Anges and the other nuns confessed to Laubardemont that they had falsely accused Grandier, the commissioner held that this was the Devil acting through the nuns in order to confuse the issue and support Grandier's false "innocence.")

As Woffinden points out in *Miscarriages of Justice*, "there were over a hundred discrepancies in the 'confessions.'" He notes that the prosecution told the jury that "their separate stories, given in the confessions, fitted together like a jigsaw." The Crown thus argued both that the confessions had an erratic relationship with the truth and that they were truthful and reliable. In the end, Hill, Conlon, Armstrong, and Carole Richardson were convicted on the basis of the "confessions" being both "voluntary" and "true."

Carole Richardson, in fact, had a very firm alibi proving that she was not present in Guildford at the time of the bombing but, in fact, far away. The principal supporter, a man named Johnson, claimed that he had been in London with Carole Richardson on that evening along with other named people. The police, satisfied that Richardson was guilty, did not believe him. He was held by them on more than one occasion, interrogated repeatedly, threatened, and at one point charged with offences under the Prevention of Terrorism Act. They certainly did not want to have him come forward with (supposedly false) evidence that the charges against Carole Richardson were invalid. Eventually, after having been in custody for some seventy-five hours, he was released with a warning that if he turned up in court to give evidence, they'd make sure that he got years of imprisonment for attempting to pervert the course of justice. (He did in fact come forward to give evidence for the defence and stuck to his original statement.) Others, too, supported the alibi at the trial. But by now the Crown's whole case depended on Carole Richardson being one of the Four. If the case against her were to fail, the case against the others would be equally suspect. The prosecution managed to squeeze past the problem by arguing that the timing of the events would have allowed Richardson to have just managed to get from where she was in London to Guildford. In fact, it might have been possible if this had taken place in the middle of the night with empty roads and in a police car with sirens blaring, but on a Saturday night it would have been out of the question. Still, the jury accepted the police case.

The fact is that the case itself was not really being tried at all. Given the horrifying bombing, the IRA connections, and the universal demand for an immediate solution to the crime and punishment of the criminals, guilt was assumed by everybody from the time that the accused were taken into custody. It was not a question of listening to evidence and judging its value; the mindset of the whole population was to accept any evidence against the accused as valid. At worst, in the climate of the times, if there was doubt about some item of evidence, it could be ignored because everybody knew that they were guilty and that the guilty should not be allowed to go free because they were clever enough, manipulative enough, to be able to cloud the issues.

Many years later, the passage of time smoothed over the fear and anger and dampened down the immediate hatred and instinctive demand for revenge. Only then did a significant number of people begin to have serious doubts about whether innocent people had been convicted in a trial that had all the elements of a witch hunt. Questions mounted, and although it took yet more years, eventually serious, formal, and objective investigation began. An official inquiry was instituted under Sir John May on 19 October 1989. In his final report, it became evident that the police and the prosecution had found the Four guilty and then looked for evidence – first the verdict, then the trial. The public pressures to find the terrorists had made proper investigative procedures virtually impossible, these having certainly been set aside. The accused, three men and a woman, were judged guilty from the start; if they were to be saved, it was up to them to prove themselves innocent, and under the circumstances and in light of the forces against them, this was impossible. It was impossible because extraordinary (and illegal) threats and brutality were used against the accused and because witnesses in their favour were ignored or threatened with imprisonment as accomplices, as was the case with those corroborating Carole Richardson's alibi. Any testimony in favour of the accused was disregarded and hidden, improperly kept from the defence team, as the later inquiry discovered. The police, the whole legal system, and indeed, the population of Britain in general, having made up their minds from the beginning that the Four were guilty, heard only what they wanted to hear from that time on and ignored any contrary facts or evidence.

The heinous nature of the crime had, of course, much to do with how the investigation and the trial proceeded, but as in many witch-hunt trials those who were accused started off being both despised and feared – despised because they were Irish and immigrant, feared because they were IRA, or so it was universally believed.

After the Four were found guilty and imprisoned, there was certainly a sense of just retribution having been achieved – at least as far as it could be. There is little doubt that if, at the time, the death penalty had still been in effect in Britain, it would have been applied to the Four with widespread satisfaction. Nevertheless, the terrible sentences handed out did give a sense of closure. This sense was one factor that led the "establishment" to bitterly oppose reopening the case years later. It was not just a case where the whole system had been derailed by the events and emotions of the time, although this was certainly true; nor was it solely that to reopen the case was to raise enormous questions about how British justice would be viewed in light of the mistakes, although this certainly applied. The problem was that by reopening the case, those who had been believed guilty would be proved innocent, with nobody to take their place. The sense of closure would no longer exist.

Something else in the Guildford Four case exactly paralleled the witch hunts: the search for accomplices – indeed, the demand for accomplices even where they did not exist. During the 1600s and 1700s this was achieved by torture and by the demand for names of those who had attended Sabbaths. In this case the need was met by brutality amounting to torture and by the demands for the names of those who had provided the bombs. Just as witches must have adherents and accomplices, so IRA "witches" must have them, too. Just as the witches of earlier times (as in Bamberg and Wurzburg) "created" accomplices and gave names to the inquisitors to escape further torture, so, too, in the case of the Guildford Four were accomplices created and names provided to escape the beatings and the threats.

This is also how the so-called Maguire Seven were created and identified, leading to yet another terrible injustice – terrible because if it could happen to Anne Maguire and her family, it could happen to us all.[2]

Anne Maguire was born in Belfast in 1935 and brought up there. She was one of eight children, and the family lived in modest, hard-working circumstances. They were Catholic and, of course, Irish. As she grew up, she would have liked to continue her schooling but had to leave to take up work; as the second eldest, her income was needed in the growing family. She sewed army tunics and uniforms, later got a job weaving, then moved to work in a hospital. Her boyfriend, Paddy Maguire, was three years older than she was, her first and only boy-friend. He joined the British Army at the age of eighteen and served in England and Cyprus. About a year and a half after he got out of the army, having completed his term, he and Anne were married. He was always proud of his service in the British Army; neither he nor Anne had any time for the IRA, then or later.

By this time he was living in London, where they had moved after the wedding. It was 1957, and she was twenty-one. There, Anne and Paddy had their children. In 1974 Vincent was the oldest at sixteen, John was fourteen, next was Patrick at thirteen, and the baby, Anne-Marie, was eight years old. They were ordinary working people, good neighbours, honest and well-respected folk. By 1974 they had been living in their current modest house for the past four years, and they worked hard at what work they could get to provide a respectable living for their fam-ily. Anne made income from cleaning; she had five part-time cleaning jobs. Paddy was unemployed for the first time in his life, having been without a job since September. It was early December, a bad time to be out of work with Christmas coming on. They had lived in England for many years now, and as much as Anne loved Belfast, she had no great wish to return there to live, given the "troubles."

On 3 December 1974, an ordinary day, there was some tension in the home between Anne and Paddy; she wasn't used to his being about the house, and it annoyed her that he was there, smoking and drinking in the daytime – even though he was never a drunkard. She felt that he should be out trying harder to find work – a fairly typical wifely reaction.

Anne was planning Christmas presents while working at her cleaning a couple of blocks away from their house. When she got home, the tele-phone rang; it was a close friend of theirs, Pat O'Neill. His wife had gone into hospital to have another baby, and he asked whether she could look after his three little girls, which she agreed to do. Two of them could go to school with Anne-Marie, and she would take the youngest out with her. Later, after working on her other cleaning jobs, she returned home and started her own housecleaning; she was very house-proud. In the sitting room, she found a suitcase that she did not recognize. She asked the children whose it was. The last thing that she needed was an unanticipated guest when she already had to cope with tension in the house between herself and her husband and three addi-tional little girls to care for after a hard day's work.

She still did not know who the visitor was until later when she was washing her kitchen floor and her husband came in with his brother-in-law, Giuseppe Conlon. Giuseppe looked tired and sick, which wasn't surprising, for she knew that he had been suffering from tuberculosis for some years. He had arrived unexpectedly from Belfast that afternoon. His son Gerard had been arrested, and he had come to bail him out. The son was Gerard Conlon, who had been arrested as one of the Guildford Four.

Gerard was a seventeen year old with a brief history as a small-time criminal and a petty thief, so it did not surprise Anne to hear that he had been arrested. What did shake her was Giuseppe's news that it wasn't this simple: Gerard had just been arrested a couple of days before on suspicion of being involved with the Guildford bombings at the beginning of October, some two months earlier, in which five innocent people had been killed and many others injured.

They could hardly believe it to be possible. Gerard? Her nephew? The son of Paddy Maguire's sister? Certainly, he had caused his parents grief with his petty thieving and his drug habit, but such things were a far cry from bombs and murder! Giuseppe was certain that his son had played no part in the bombings.

The Maguires called Paddy's brother and his wife, Hugh and Kitty Maguire, who lived locally, because Giuseppe had sent them a telegram saying that he was coming, and since his arrival he had not been in touch with them. There was no reply at their house to the telephone call. When they called other friends looking for them, one of them said that there had been no reply because the police had taken them away on Saturday morning (this was now Tuesday). They had been in custody all this time without the family knowing. In fact, as it later turned out, Hugh and Kitty Maguire had been taken into custody because Gerard Conlon had once stayed with them. Anne Maguire states that these relatives were in custody for a week, during which the police ransacked their house. When they were finally released without any charges being laid, they returned home to discover this invasion of their home. Anne Maguire writes that "always hard working people, their lives were destroyed by what happened. Kittty's nerves were shattered and she has never recovered."

These events are all so quickly covered in words, but the reality was frightening. These were innocent people, taken without warning from their home, questioned and bullied by the police for a whole week on something that they knew absolutely nothing about, without anybody knowing that they had been taken, and then released to find that their home had been invaded and ransacked by the police, without redress. And all this being said, they would be the lucky ones within the Maguire family.

At about six o'clock that evening or a little later, Sean Smyth, Anne's brother, arrived. He was staying with them and was working twelve-hour days to make money so that he could go home to Belfast for Christmas. He was shocked by the news of Hugh and Kitty, but he, in turn, shocked Anne when he said to her, "You know, love, they'll be coming here next." It had not even occurred to her that her own family might become involved. They had not had much to do with Gerard Conlon, and they certainly knew nothing about bombs or bombings, nor did they have any IRA connections or sympathies.

Sean ate his dinner, but Pat O'Neill didn't want any, nor did his three little girls; they were not fond of stew. So Anne went out to buy some chips to make up egg and chips for them. Pat stayed long enough to eat a little. Meanwhile, the three Maguire boys, Patrick, John, and Vincent, went out, Patrick and John to the youth club and Vincent to his night class. Later, all the men went over the road to the local pub, Paddy Maguire, Giuseppe Conlon, Pat O'Neill, and Sean Smyth. This left Anne and her little daughter, Anne-Marie, in the house, along with the three O'Neill girls – a good opportunity to do the laundry. While she was do-ing this, her son John came home from the youth club. As she was fill-ing the washing machine, the doorbell rang insistently, to be followed immediately by banging on the door. A nightmare that was going to last for nearly seventeen years (and that, perhaps for the Maguire family, has never ended) was about to begin.

Anne-Marie, just eight years old, ran to answer the door, but it came flying in as she went toward it; if she had been a little closer, she would have been knocked over and injured. The police crowded in, most of them in plainclothes, except for the ones behind with sniffer dogs. The lead policeman asked the mother if she was Annie Maguire (not the name that she usually went by, but Gerard Conlon as well as family and friends in Belfast called her Annie). Anne-Marie was screaming in ter-ror, and the three little O'Neill girls were crying in fear. Anne managed to get the girls quietened down while the police were ordering the dogs upstairs with their handlers. She asked the men who they were, what they were doing there. The plainclothesmen asked her to switch off the washing machine and go through to the sitting room. By this time, she tells us, the place looked like a police station. She remembered Sean's remark and asked them if they were there because of Gerard Conlon, and they said yes. They asked what she knew about him, and she told them that she really knew very little. They seemed surprised when she told them that Conlon's father had arrived that afternoon and would see a solicitor the next morning about his son and that in the meantime he was staying with them. The chief of the policemen, a man named Mundy, asked who else was staying in the house. She told him of her husband and four children and that her brother Sean was staying with them as well as Giuseppe and the three O'Neill girls while their mother was in hospital. He asked where the men were now, and she pointed to the pub down the road. The police made it clear that they had been watching the house. In this case, thought Anne, she could not understand why they had not seen Paddy and the others going down to the pub. They arrived so shortly after the others had left that they must have passed them. "At the trial," she says, "the police made out that the men had gone over the wall from our back garden into Ilbert Street to dispose of explosives. Despite their claims that we had possessed explosives in our house, they never found any, either there or in the whole surrounding area which they searched later that night."

Meantime, the police were searching the house with the aid of the dogs, looking for explosives. They found nothing. And while this was going on, they questioned Anne about Gerard Conlon. She told them that she hardly knew him, that he lived in Belfast and she in London, and that she had seen very little of him. It must have been evident to her by now that these were not the questions, nor was this the tone, that would be associated with the police looking for assistance; she and her family were in some way suspect through their association with Conlon. Any doubt about this was removed when the policeman Mundy asked her whether anybody could look after her children while she was taken down to the police station for further questioning. He was insistent that not only she, but also her three teenaged sons, must go there, sixteen-year-old Vincent, fourteen-year-old John, and Patrick, who was only thirteen. She became hysterical at this involvement of her own young children, whom she knew to be innocent of anything at all.

Eventually, she arranged with a neighbour to look after little Anne-Marie and the three O'Neill children, but it was hard to put the little ones to bed and leave them, particularly her own little eight-year-old girl, who was fighting back tears as her mother left. And while this was going on, the policewoman started to look in the drawers and cupboards. It so happened that Anne Maguire would buy damaged cans of food cheap and store them for use later. One box contained cans of baked beans without labels and the policewoman remarked that she had plenty of food. Mrs Maguire replied, "Yes, for the boys," meaning her sons. Quite a different interpretation of this innocent reply would later be offered by the police, who maintained that she was referring to the "boys" in her supposed IRA terrorist cell. When she was taken downstairs to go to the police station, her three boys were there surrounded by police. In so short a time, an ordinary family had changed from an everyday existence of minor joys and problems to a nightmare that was still in its early stages and that would be marked by consequences that none of them, in their innocence, could even have imagined. Anne Maguire herself was taken in a police car, and the three boys followed in a police van, a "meat wagon" as it was commonly known. She thought that they might be away for an hour or so before being allowed to return home. She had confidence that the police were the public's protectors, and she knew that she and her family would have nothing to fear once all this was sorted out.

When she got to the police station, the boys were taken off to some other section, and the police started to take swabs of her hands. The substance that they used hurt her, and they remarked upon it. She told them that she had dermatitis. They took her fingerprints and scraped under her nails. They questioned her more about Gerard Conlon, but she repeated that she knew very little about him. When they took her back to her boys, she thought that they were going to go back home. She felt that their work on her had been excessively thorough, but she says, "I still trusted the police and had confidence in them. I just told myself it was their job." Mundy walked in at this point with his hands full. He had some wigs and wanted to know whose they were. Anne Maguire told him that they were hers. He asked her, too, about some disposable gloves that he had found in a drawer, and she told him that she had dermatitis and that she used them when she was cleaning and dusting. She had thrown some old gloves out, she added, and she told him where he would find them in the garbage can. It wasn't until later that she discovered why Mundy was interested in the wigs. The police were looking for a blonde-haired woman in connection with the Guildford bombings, and one of the wigs was what Anne called a "dirty blonde" colour. Wigs at the time were quite in fashion for a while, so to possess and use them was not at all unusual. Friends had given them to her, but she had never worn them, except as jokes. Certainly, that night at the police station the wigs and the plastic gloves seemed innocent enough to her, but she did not know that these items would later be used as evidence against her and her family.

She was not, in fact, to go home that night. The boys were sent home, protesting that they wanted to stay with her. But the police kept her. She still thought that it would be a matter of an hour or two before she would follow them. When they took her to a cell, she realized that things would not be so simple. She did not sleep that night but lay there wondering why they were holding on to her like this. Was it just because she was Gerard Conlon's aunt? This didn't seem to make any sense. The next morning they came and asked her whether she could make longer-term arrangements for somebody to look after her children. She questioned why; after all, she would be back home with them herself in a few hours. She was told that she wasn't going back home; she was going to be taken to Guildford for further questioning. They put it to her plainly: if she didn't make arrangements for Patrick and Anne-Marie, they would be put "into care." Her peace of mind was crumbling. If her own situation was frightening, it was much more terrible for her to realize that her children were at risk, threatened by the very authority that she had always believed was there to protect the innocent.

By the time that she arrived in Guildford in the police car, she was in a state of shock. As they drove, the police would ask her whether she recognized one building or another or the route. She told them that she had never been to Guildford, that she had never even heard of a place with this name before reading of the bombings in the paper; the only Guildford that she knew of was in Northern Ireland. When they got to the town, the car went toward the police station. The policeman in the back of the car with her advised her to pull her coat over her head when she got out so that her face would not be seen. She said that having done nothing wrong, she saw no need to cover her head. In front of her she saw a police van. Her husband and Sean Smyth, her brother-in-law, were in it; she could make them out waving at her through the rear window. As she got closer to the police station, she could hear shouts from a crowd: "Hang the Irish bastards! Hang them!"

Inside the station, she met with still more policemen, particularly two named Powell and Robinson. It was Robinson who shouted "Get her in here," just as she was about to be given a drink of water. And now the interrogation began in earnest. Did she know why she was there? Yes, she answered. Because she was Gerard Conlon's aunt. She repeated that she knew that his father, Giuseppe Conlon, had arrived at her home the previous day to help his son and that he had said that Gerard was not involved in the IRA. Then he asked what she would say if he told her that Gerard Conlon had "implicated" her and had made a statement saying that she had showed him how to make bombs. At this stage they didn't tell her that Conlon's statement had been supported by Paul Hill; this came only later. For the moment, she replied that if Gerard Conlon had truly stated such a thing, then he was lying. Her husband, she said, had served in the British Army and was regarded by some as being "pro-British." They mocked her, saying that her husband had told them that she didn't have five cleaning jobs and that she earned her money prostituting herself. They said that Gerard Conlon had told them that she had gone to Guildford with others and planted bombs. "No sir," she responded, "he is telling lies." She says that she always respectfully called them "sir."

They brought in an older man, very badly beaten. She didn't know him. Then they brought in Paul Hill. "When I say 'brought in,'" she tells us, "I mean dragged in. They practically had to carry him and then hold him up, as he couldn't stand. I don't think he could even have spoken, his face was in such a mess. His eyes were swollen up like balloons, and I don't even know if he could see me. He didn't say anything, just stared, eyes glazed, straight ahead. I had seen him once before but, because of the state he was in, I only recognised him by the jacket he was wearing, the same one he had had on before. I said that it was Paul Hill. At that they turned him around and they dragged him out again." The police told her that Hill had also accused her of teaching him in her kitchen how to make bombs. She told them that he had never been in her kitchen and that this would quickly become evident if they asked him to describe it.

She had, in fact, met Paul Hill once before, some weeks earlier. Paddy's brother, Hugh, had persuaded them to get out and go to an Irish dance that was on that night. Gerard Conlon was there. He was with a group of friends from the hostel where they were staying in a part of London named Kinburn, often referred to as "Little Ireland" because of the number of Irish who had settled there. Anne Maguire was not fond of her nephew and had little to say or do with him at the dance. One of the friends who was with him did speak to her for a little while, and it turned out that she and his mother had known each other quite well back in Belfast in her early years. This was Paul Hill, and until the police station in Guildford, this had been her only contact with him. When Hill was taken away, they brought in Gerard Conlon. Anne Maguire tells us, "To this day, Gerard's recollection of that event and mine are different. He was not in as bad a state as Paul Hill. At least he was able to walk in. I asked him 'Did you write that statement, son?' He said to the police, 'You've got what you want.' I told him, 'Gerard, you know this is lies. Why don't you tell the truth?' Then he looked at me and said, 'You tell the truth,' and they led him away. I forgive Gerard and Paul, but I cannot forget what they brought upon our family and other families."

Her interrogation went on for a week. She lost track of time. She was disoriented through shock and lack of sleep and fluids. They beat her around the head from behind, and when her eyes hurt, they pulled her head back by her hair and shone bright lights in her eyes, calling her a murderous bastard and humiliating her in every way that they could. The simple housewife and mother was no longer an innocent victim; she had been turned into a murderer, a terrorist, an enemy to be granted no quarter. She was so hated and despised by the policemen who surrounded her that despite the lack of evidence against her, they would not even consider the idea that she might be innocent. Public pressure made it essential to find the people who had committed the Guildford bombings, and once they had beaten from Hill and Conlon a confession and an accusation against Anne Maguire, they asked no further questions of themselves. From the very first moment that the "confessions" were beaten from the men, Anne Maguire was "guilty." All that remained was to find enough "evidence" to support the verdict at which they had already arrived. The very fact that she was "Irish" was enough to prove her guilt in the eyes of her accusers, such was the climate of the times. And it is a measure of the volume and success of the IRA bombings of those days that to be accused on the weakest of grounds and to be one of the feared and despised "Irish" was also to be guilty. The truth is that given the climate of fear and demand for retribution that existed, and given the powers provided to the police in the Prevention of Terrorism Act, Anne Maguire had no chance of justice.

"They had taken my shoes and tights away," she tells us, "and would make me stand spread-eagled against a wall, arms and legs outstretched. I was weak and had a very heavy period. I kept falling down. They would just kick and kick me, using foul and abusive language, telling me to get up. Their kicks struck around the lower back and kidney area. I would somehow manage to get up, but not for long. Soon I would collapse again and they would grab me by the hair, pulling and kicking me around the room. When I arrived in Brixton after being charged later the same week and was seen by a doctor, they noticed huge clumps of my hair were missing. My kidneys have never been right since, on account of the kicking and the lack of fluids during that week." Anne Maguire was charged with murder. "Here was I, a working wife and mother who loved children, being charged with killing some mother's child. I kept fainting and coming round again, going from faint to consciousness. I wanted to wake up and realise it was all a nasty dream. But it wasn't."

The two police officers, Powell and Robinson, told her that if they could not make the murder charge stick, they would get her on the gloves. The murder charge was made on the grounds that she had been directly involved in the bombing of the Guildford pub, and the case against her was not a strong one because they would have to prove that she was present. But if this failed, the two policemen were confident that they could prove that she had been involved in bomb making because they had her plastic gloves, which, according to them, had traces of explosive materials on them.

For the first time now since she had been taken from her home, she was allowed to see Patrick, her thirteen-year-old son. When he came in with her solicitor, "he just looked at me and froze. Then he launched himself at Officer Powell. Poor little kid – he no doubt decided that nobody was going to treat his mum like that." The next day, for the first time, Anne met Carole Richardson, one of the so-called Guildford Four. Anne was put into a police van and found this other young woman already there. When they did not speak to each other, one of the policewomen asked her if she wasn't going to say hello to her friend. Carole said that they didn't know each other, had never seen each other, and when Anne asked her who she was, Carole told her and said that she had been charged with the same crime and that she hadn't even been in Guildford (which years later was proved to be true). "My God," Anne burst out, "but you're only a child"; Carole was seventeen. From this time on, Anne unconsciously adopted the young girl as though she were her own daughter.

Anne and Carole were transferred to Brixton, where they would await their trials. As they entered, they moved past the row of cells. Carole was put into one, and Anne was about to be put into the next one when she saw some other officers approaching her. "I froze to the spot and begged them not to touch me, not to hit me any more." They assured her that they would not beat her. She was in prison custody now, not police custody. And however terrible her overall situation, her treatment certainly became much more humane and decent.

Christmas passed, the first without her family. The two youngest children were with an aunt, so she at least knew that they were safe and

cared for. And slowly the weeks went by. Once a week they would
be taken to Guildford for a court hearing in order to be remanded for
a further week. Her husband, Paddy, together with Pat O'Neill, her
brother Sean, and Giuseppe Conlon were also under arrest and awaiting their trial but on different charges. Anne would appear with Gerard
Conlon, Paul Hill, Paddy Armstrong, and Carole Richardson because
all five of them were charged with murder for having bombed two pubs
in Guildford. Then sometime around the beginning of March 1975 at
the Guildford court, Mrs Maguire was informed that the murder charges
against her had been dropped. For a short time that day, it seemed that
she might be going home at last, but this hope was short-lived, and in
some ways the nightmare was to become even more terrible. They were
about to charge her with bomb making, based on the traces of explosives on her plastic gloves. Worse was to follow. "We have your two
sons down the road and are also charging them." The police had Vincent
and Patrick under arrest and were charging them with having traces of
explosives on their hands, too; the assumption was that they, too, were
involved in the bomb-making factory supposedly run by their mother.
"That day they removed the charge they had laid on me, as they
couldn't make it stick, but they added two other intolerable burdens.
They charged two of my sons with something which, like all of us, they
had not done." What perhaps made it even worse was that one of the
two charged was her youngest son, Patrick, who was only thirteen (and
who, as it turned out, would be the youngest person imprisoned under
the Prevention of Terrorism Act). Mrs Maguire believes that Patrick
was charged, rather than her older son John, because of a confusion
over names. One was named Patrick Joseph, and the other John Patrick.
The police confused the two, she thinks, and having made the mistake, they could not admit it – so the younger, Patrick, would be the
one imprisoned.

The boys were released on bail, and eventually, so was Anne, but bail
was refused for Paddy, Sean, Pat O'Neill, and Giuseppe Conlon – even
though Giuseppe was seriously ill by now. Carole Richardson, the
young girl of the Guildford Four, had hoped that when Anne Maguire
had the murder charge removed, she, too, would be treated the same
way. But it was not to be. They added more charges to her list. So the
months went by awaiting trial.

This was Bamberg all over again, the search for accomplices among
family, friends, and acquaintances. It all started with Gerard Conlon
and Paul Hill, probably through informants who were questioned and

provided their names for relief or benefit. Then it spread to Patrick Armstrong and Carole Richardson, apparently because of their living with Hill and Conlon. Then Conlon and Hill gave up the name of Anne Maguire, and the contagion spread from her to everybody connected with her who was in her home, however brief the contact. It spread first to her husband; then to her brother, Sean Smyth, who was living with them; then to Giuseppe Conlon, newly arrived that day; and then to Pat O'Neill, whose only involvement was that Anne Maguire was helping out with his children while his wife was in hospital – he just happened to be in the house. Finally, the two sons were added. From nothing, the coven had spread to eleven people in exactly the same way that it had spread so often and in as frightening a manner some 350 years before. Nor did the assumption of guilt decrease in this modern time when Anne and the children were out on bail. "Young Patrick had only to step outside our door and he was picked up by police in a van and beaten black and blue. For that year we were awaiting trial, not a day passed when they didn't abuse my child, on his way from school, on a message to the dairy or as he walked to or from his little part-time job in the shop across the road." In the eyes of the police, whether tried or not, he was guilty, and they treated him as such. There was no sense of innocent until proved guilty in their case.

Mrs Maguire's treatment shows us another aspect of the same mentality, and here it was not the police who were responsible but the public press: "We had already been tried and found guilty by some sections of the media, and many people simply assumed we were guilty. What was most hurtful was being avoided in the street by people I had known previously and even people I had helped in the past. If someone did stop to speak, the moment they saw anyone else that they knew approaching they would start to edge away. People didn't want to be seen with me. After all, they had read in black and white that our home was a 'bomb-factory' and that I was 'Evil Aunt Annie'. It must be true, mustn't it? I myself used to believe everything I read in the papers."

During September and October 1975 the Guildford Four came to trial. All of them were sentenced to long imprisonment. The evidence of witnesses who testified that Carole Richardson could not have taken part in the Guildford bombings because she was with them in London at the time was argued away on the basis that she could have been present if the timing of her transportation was perfect. It was essential to the police case that all four be guilty, and guilty they were found. The judge, Mr Justice Donaldson (who would be the judge in the Maguire Seven case at his own request), recommended that Carole Richardson should serve a minimum of twenty years, that Conlon should serve not less than thirty years, that Armstrong should not get less than thirty-five years, and that Paul Hill should never be released. His sentence was the longest in British history. None of this boded well for Anne Maguire and her family.

The trial of the Maguire Seven started on 12 January 1976 at the Old Bailey. The judge and the prosecutor were the same ones who had carried out the trial of the Guildford Four. Anne Maguire was still convinced that they would all be found innocent; she knew her own innocence and still believed that British justice would prevail. When she saw the paucity of the evidence brought against her and her family, she was sure that the case would be dismissed. But day after day they sat there in court, all seven of them, including her two boys. The trial lasted seven weeks. She and the boys were still out on bail, so she was able to go home with them each day; the others had to stay in jail.

She comments in her book that one of the police witnesses deliberately lied at the trial. Some time before any of the events began, she had been given, as a souvenir, a rubber bullet in Belfast used by British troops. She had kept this in the back of a drawer, half-forgotten, and she, in fact, had told the police about it. The policeman in his testimony claimed that the bullet was sitting on her table, presumably a proud ornament and proof of her IRA support. Although she immediately protested that he was lying, the judge silenced her.

But what convicted them was the plastic gloves. The forensic evidence provided to the court "proved" that each member of the Maguire Seven had minute traces of nitroglycerin on their hands. In the case of Mrs Maguire, the traces were on her plastic gloves. This scientific evidence was in fact almost the only evidence against her and her family. So it became of vital importance to them – then and later.

The story goes back to 3 December 1974, some fifteen months earlier. On the day that the police invaded her house, all of the Maguire Seven had their hands swabbed and scrapings taken from under their fingernails. These were sent for forensic tests to a laboratory at Woolwich that, belonging to the Royal Arsenal, specialized in explosive materials. The Thin Layer Chromatology (TLC) tests proved positive for six of the seven. In Anne Maguire's case, it was her plastic gloves that had traces of nitroglycerin. She had a large quantity of these because of her dermatitis. The gloves were taken to another laboratory where similar tests were done, with a supposedly positive result.

The bulk of the tests were done at Woolwich, where they were performed by a young technician of seventeen or eighteen who had been employed for only nine weeks. The judge referred to him as an apprentice, and everything was going to hang on his inexperience. Part of this inexperience had led to his using up all the samples, contrary to standing orders. No confirmatory tests could be done either then or later, when the real questions arose. But even at the time there were questions about the validity of the tests, questions that should not have been treated lightly since they came from the former director of the laboratory, who had devised the test in the first place. This Dr John Yallop, who appeared for the defence at the trial, made the sum of his evidence absolutely clear: "no competent scientist could do other than conclude that the hypothesis is incorrect; namely, that the pink spot ... is not due to nitro-glycerine. To do otherwise would be unscientific, illogical and pig-headed." Nor has any competent and independent scientist ever disagreed since that time.

Other evidence at the trial established that nitroglycerin was not the only explosive capable of giving a positive result. Another substance was detected by the tests, one used in commercial explosives and never by the IRA. This information alone should have invalidated the case against the Maguires. The judge failed to bring this to the attention of the jury, and he may not have understood the significance himself. There were other inconsistencies from the tests as well. Yallop pointed out, among other instances, that some of the accused seemed from the tests to have nitroglycerin under their fingernails but not on their palms – an inexplicable circumstance. The underlying fact is that the test was really designed for nitrates, not for explosives.

At the trial, evidence was provided for the defence that a number of perfectly innocent and innocuous items could give positive readings in the TLC tests, including a number of standard cleaning items and even tobacco smoke. But even more startling is another item of evidence provided by Yallop, who argued that if the Maguire home was in fact used for bomb making, a hand-held explosive detector would have confirmed any other tests: "This is a reasonable condition under which to use a sniffer and to expect to get a positive result. The fact that it gave a negative one is, to my way of thinking, another factor ... pointing away from the interpretation of nitro-glycerine." No trace of explosives was found in the house or in the surrounding area, even though Gerard Conlon said that he had learned to make explosives in his aunt's kitchen.

The prosecution's case was weakening all the time, but the judge and prosecution managed to shore it up. Young Vincent, for example, talked of a stick of chalk that his father had brought home for Anne-Marie. He said that it was under Sean Smyth's bed, which is in fact where it was found. But as the trial went on, the stick of chalk, for the prosecution, became a stick of dynamite. In fact, in his summing up, the judge specifically referred to it as "a stick of gelignite." He was echoing one of the prosecution witnesses who had suggested that what Vincent described seemed to fit the description of a stick of gelignite. When the judge summed up, he referred to this detail while failing to point out that the witness had gone on to say that it could not have been gelignite, for the sniffer dogs hadn't picked it up. In this way, the judge managed to get around the fact that the sniffer had failed to pick up explosives; after all, if the stick had been identified as gelignite by its appearance, surely this was enough.

The judge has been much criticized for his lack of impartiality, as has the prosecutor for his behaviour. Certainly, the jurors were convinced by what had been presented to them, however questionable it might have been. The earlier newspaper headlines about "My Aunt Annie taught me to make bombs" and "Evil Aunt Annie's bomb factory" could not have been forgotten by all the members of the jury. Above all, the climate of fear and hatred played its part. There was extreme public apprehension about the IRA, and justifiably so. As Mrs Maguire herself says, "We have to remember the climate in England at the time. I can't blame people for thinking the worst about us. The IRA had launched its vicious 'mainland bombing campaign' and there was an atmosphere of fear and revulsion, coupled with a desire that these people be caught and punished as soon as possible." On the very morning that the verdict was delivered, another train bombing took place. What jury could have released a group of supposed terrorists after such an event?

On 3 March 1976 the jury returned with guilty verdicts for them all. Anne was the first to be sentenced, receiving fourteen years – less, in fact, with remission, but she did not know this, and at the time it would likely have made little difference if she had. She was going to spend years in prison for a crime that she had not committed, and so were her husband and her two boys. And throughout this sentence she would be separated from her other son and her little girl, Anne-Marie. She fainted on the spot. Paddy, her husband, was given fourteen years as well. The other three adults were each condemned to twelve years. Vincent, her seventeen year old, was given five, and thirteen-year-old Patrick was condemned to four. The next day she was taken to the prison in Durham in the north of

England. On the way, the van that she was in stopped for gas at a service station. "When I looked out of the window, the whole place was cordoned off, and there were police vans and cars and motorcycles everywhere. I was such a dangerous criminal now, that I had a whole convoy of police vehicles and personnel accompanying me."

Anne Maguire began her sentence in Durham on 4 March 1976. She was released on 22 February 1985, having endured nine years in jail, nine years separated from her family, nine years of lost life. In her book she gives the details of these years, from her arrival, weak and doped up by the authorities, to her gradual adjustment to a prison life that was bearable only because there was no other choice and because she was a woman of great moral strength sustained by a deep faith. Her own story is well worth reading for many reasons but above all as a study of character. During these years life beyond the prison walls went on – without her. Some eighteen months after she entered Durham, her son John was married. In March 1979, three years after her own incarceration, her son Patrick was released, his own four-year sentence completed with remission for good behaviour. In October of the same year, her son Vincent got out of prison, his five-year sentence served. Three months later, Giuseppe Conlon died in prison – his only crime having been to come to England to help his son. In February 1984 her husband, Paddy, was released. Now only Anne herself remained incarcerated. She had been out on bail for months with her children before her trial while the other adults were imprisoned awaiting trial, so she had this extra time to serve. She was released one year after her husband.

Most people would have been bitter, vengeful, and full of hatred. But not Anne Maguire. Basil Hume, who was a Catholic cardinal, the archbishop of Westminster, and a highly respected churchman, described her in 1993 as she talked of her experiences to 200 young people: "As she told her story they listened to her quite spellbound. It was not so much her story, immensely disquieting as this is, but the quality of the lady who was speaking which impressed them. It was her dignity, her evident goodness and the total lack of bitterness which spoke more eloquently than her words ... Anne Maguire never lost faith in God and in humanity. Perhaps it took this ordeal to bring the best out of her, and she is, as far as I am concerned, a very exceptional woman whom it has been a privilege to get to know."[3]

Anne suffered not only directly; for all these years she was separated from her children, who themselves were going through experiences that would affect them throughout their lives. This must have been the greater martyrdom for her.

But for our purposes here, of concern are the continuing events of her incarceration and the gradual process that would one day lead to official recognition that these people were all innocent – which takes us back to the early days of their imprisonment and to the days of their appeal. This took place in the summer of 1977, when they had all been in prison for some fifteen months after sentencing. Three judges heard the case. The issue turned, in the first place, on whether there were traces of nitroglycerin on the hands of the defendants and, further, whether the defendants had had on their hands not merely traces of nitroglycerin but significant quantities, of which the traces were only microscopic parts. Once more the arguments on the validity of the tests were placed before the jury. Once more it was decided that justice had not miscarried, and the appeal was not allowed to go forward. The judges found "clear evidence of considerable scientific weight" to support the decision. Today, it is still difficult to understand how this conclusion could have been reached in light of the hotly disputed forensic propositions. It seems clear that what affected everybody connected with the judgment was the continuing fear and hatred of the IRA.

Another significant event preceded not only the appeal, but also the trial, of the Maguire Seven: the arrest of the Balcombe Street Gang.[4] On 12 December 1975 four men were arrested in London, ending what became known as the Balcombe Street siege. Some days previously they had been the quarry in a car chase through the West End of London and had finished up in Balcombe Street, where they held an elderly couple hostage for six days, finally giving themselves up to the police. The event attracted worldwide publicity. This all took place a couple of months after the Guildford Four had been found guilty of bombing the Guildford and the Woolwich pubs and some three months before the trial of the Maguire Seven. When arrested, the four all stated that they were IRA volunteers. However, they surprised the police when, having been asked what their first target had been in Britain, they said, the bombing at the Woolwich pub. The Woolwich and Guildford pub bombings were known to have been performed by the same gang. So the Balcombe Street Four were a mixed blessing to the police. It was soon established that they had captured the IRA's active service unit responsible for the intensive bombing campaign of the previous months, which was certainly a plus. But at the same time, if what they claimed about the Woolwich bombing was true, this meant that the Guildford

Four were innocent of the crimes of which they had been convicted. Worse still, if the Guildford Four were innocent, so, then, must be the Maguire Seven, for the whole police case against the family rested on the evidence forced from Gerard Conlon and Paul Hill. The Surrey police, who had investigated these two cases, must have got it wrong if the Balcombe Four were to be believed. As time went on, the gang became more specific, claiming that they had been responsible for both the Guildford and the Woolwich bombings, that others had been involved whom they would not name and who were still at large, that before reading the names of the Guildford Four who had been arrested and found guilty, they had never heard of them, and that those who had been accused were entirely innocent. The lawyer for the Guildford Four, together with a retired police inspector, interviewed the members of the Balcombe Street Gang. He was satisfied that they were trained guerillas and that they knew a great deal about the bombings that had taken place. They described the Guildford bombings, where their cars had been parked, who had been next to them in the pubs, and conversations that had taken place there. The Guildford bomb was found to be a carbon copy of another used in a separate bombing. For the lawyer of the Guildford Four, there was no doubt that his clients had been unjustly convicted. He interviewed the four Balcombe Street men separately (along with another who had agreed to be named by them) in the knowledge that the security measures controlling the men were such that there could not have been collusion. Their whole story hung together.

The Balcombe Street Gang came to trial in January 1977, a year after the Maguire trial. They were charged with twenty-five counts of murder, all of which took place between December 1974 and December 1975. They had in fact been actively bombing since August 1974, but by avoiding charging them with acts between August and December, the prosecution avoided raising the Woolwich and Guildford bombings, which had occurred during the earlier period. At the trial, they took the opportunity to set the record straight. One Joseph O'Connell said, "I refuse to plead because the indictment does not include two charges concerning the Guildford and the Woolwich pub-bombings – I took part in both – for which innocent people have been convicted." Two of the others made similar statements.

The prosecution ignored the Guildford and Woolwich bombings on the grounds that the men were not charged with them and that they were therefore not relevant. "Guildford and Woolwich are not a matter

for you ... [even though] it may be that O'Connell and Butler are anxious to claim their part in other bombings," he told the jury. This was
clever: in the first place Woolwich and Guildford were not matters for
this trial because the men were not charged with these crimes; moreover, the judge introduced a hint of why Woolwich and Guildford were
not relevant, having suggested that the Balcombe Four were trying to
confuse justice by claiming to be responsible for bombings in which
they had played no part. When the prosecution case was complete and
no witnesses were called for the defence, Joseph O'Connell was allowed
to speak to the court. He said, in part: "We are all four Irish Republicans. We have recognised this court to the extent that we have instructed our lawyers to draw the attention of the court to the fact that
four totally innocent people – Carole Richardson, Gerard Conlon, Paul
Hill and Patrick Armstrong – are serving massive sentences for three
bombings, two in Guildford and one in Woolwich which three of us
and another man now imprisoned have admitted that we did. The
Director of Public Prosecutions was made aware of these admissions in
December 1975 and has chosen to do nothing." He went on to accuse
one of the main prosecution witnesses, a man named Douglas Higgs,
principal scientific officer at the Royal Arsenal Research and Development Establishment, Woolwich: "Higgs admitted in this trial that the
Woolwich bomb formed part of a correlated series with other bombings
with which we were charged. Yet when he gave evidence at the earlier
Guildford and Woolwich trial he deliberately concealed that the Woolwich
bomb was definitely part of a series carried out between October and
December 1974, and that the people on trial were in custody at the time
of some of these bombings."

The jury found the men guilty of many of the charges but acquitted
them of those that they felt the prosecution had not adequately supported. For the police, it was less than a complete victory. Too many
unanswered questions remained, and too many falsehoods and inconsistencies had been made obvious.

The trial of the Balcombe Street Gang and their claim to have been
responsible for Guildford and Woolwich gave the Guildford Four
grounds to appeal. A successful appeal on their part would obviously
lay open the path to an appeal by the Maguire Seven since their case depended on the Guildford Four's being guilty. The Guildford appeal
opened in October 1977 and was argued on the grounds that the men
captured in Balcombe Street had admitted to the crime.

The appeal was dismissed – largely on the grounds that when one of the members of the Balcombe Street Gang was giving evidence, he had disagreed with the other three about details. In retrospect, the details seem to be of no great importance. Nevertheless, they were enough to convince the judges at the time. But the crux of the matter appeared in the judgment, which ran to over fifty pages. It noted that O'Connell, one of the Balcombe Street Gang, who had already been convicted of six murders, "had nothing to lose by accepting responsibility for a further seven." The theory was then put forward that the claim by the Balcombe Gang to have committed the Guildford and Woolwich bombings was a conspiracy concocted to bring about the release of the persons who had really committed the crime – the Guildford Four. "We are sure that there has been a cunning and skillful attempt to deceive the Court by putting forward false evidence. O'Connell [and the other members of the gang] had ample opportunity while awaiting trial to work out how the attempt should be made. Doing so was well within the intellectual capacity of O'Connell." The court did accept that the Balcombe Street members had played a part in Guildford and Woolwich, but they were deemed to have done so not in place of, but in addition to, the Guildford Four. The cases put forward by the police and prosecution had survived a dangerous attack, a very clever and carefully constructed conspiracy to release the guilty, something that would cost the Balcombe Street members nothing because they had already been found guilty of so many other murder charges.

The Maguire Seven, while a side issue in this series of events, were directly affected by the outcome. The failure to review the case of the Guildford Four, and perhaps to clear them, meant that the case of the Maguire Seven would also remain unchanged. So they languished in prison. Anne Maguire had suffered much from the police. But she is the first to point out that some did show her kindness and how much this meant to her. And the same was true in prison. At first, of course, it was desperately hard to accept unwarranted incarceration and the thought of years of separation from her family. Other prisoners helped her through these unhappy times, and gradually, as she accepted the unavoidable routine of prison life, she settled down to the long haul; this process took a year or more. Seven months after her arrival, she was even allowed a visit from her husband and the two boys; they were temporarily transferred to the men's prison in Durham for this purpose, although as she points out, there were some in the Home Office who did all that they could to make visits as difficult as possible. They were, of course, at the time classed as very high-risk prisoners and had to be treated as such. In her own story she does not talk about her own influence on others, but by the deepest instincts of her nature, she was a mother, and it is clear that she mothered the younger prisoners who needed it and was called "Mother" by many of them. This strength of hers no doubt had an effect over the months and years on prison staff as well as prisoners. And this would be increasingly the case as public questions gradually began to arise about whether a group of innocents had been imprisoned in a grave miscarriage of justice. But still, throughout these years, most people believed that the Seven were terrorists who had been justly convicted. Some of the worst times would come about when there were further acts of IRA terrorism in the outside world:

It was as if we were on the outside and personally responsible for the attack in the eyes of some officers and fellow inmates. We dreaded the reaction whenever we heard the news of another bomb going off somewhere. Anne and Eileen [two prisoners] and the others can still tell the story of how one prisoner barricaded herself in her cell when Lord Mountbatten (an uncle of the Queen's husband, Prince Philip, and the last viceroy of India) was murdered sailing his yacht off the coast of Ireland, as she didn't want to mix with "those IRA women." If people really believed we were convicted terrorists, it is not difficult to understand. I can't blame them.

Throughout this time, as tough as things were for her, Anne would not express "remorse" for her crime. She would not admit to committing a crime that she had not done. Yet without this step, she could not be eligible for parole and early release from prison. Plenty of people advised her to give in so that she could get back to her family, but she would not accept the easy way out. Nor did any other member of her family.

Gradually, outside, the first public questioning began about the justice of the cases of the Guildford Four and the Maguire Seven. There had of course always been a few who believed them to be innocent. One of them was Giuseppe Conlon's doctor back in Belfast, Joe Henderson. He had shared his belief with Gerry Fitt, who was the member of Parliament for West Belfast and who had long fought a nearly lone battle to generate active public interest in the case. The events that sparked public concern were the illness and death of Giuseppe, Gerard Conlon's father, who had happened to be in the Maguire house that fateful afternoon. He had been ill at the time of arrest and trial and had only grown sicker in prison.

What increasingly worried people – including members of Parliament – was that Giuseppe Conlon's constant declarations of innocence never stopped as his death approached. He died still proclaiming innocence. In response to his last requests, Gerry Fitt promised to clear his name posthumously, a promise that he was to carry out. And if Giuseppe was innocent, what of the rest of the Maguire Seven? As well, another man had become concerned and involved who also could not be ignored, Cardinal Hume, archbishop of Westminster, head of the Roman Catholic Church in England, a man of tremendous status. (The growing effect was similar to what had happened in Salem when people who had led good lives died proclaiming their innocence on the scaffold.)

Following Giuseppe Conlon's death, members of the Balcombe Street Gang repeated their proclamation that the Guildford Four were innocent. The case and the questions began to appear in the respected media and then in a debate in Parliament, where on 4 August 1980 three MPs urged the home secretary "to review all the circumstances of this case." For the first time in this debate, one of the MPs publicly and formally raised the possibility that the Guildford Four might in fact have been wrongly convicted. This had little immediate effect, but Gerry Fitt had been elevated to the House of Lords after many years of service in the Commons, and he continued his campaign with successive home secretaries. Again, there were no immediate results, but little by little public interest and concern increased. In particular, two television programs, one in 1983 and the other in 1984, discussed forensic scientific evidence. It was becoming increasingly clear that the tests performed on the Maguire Seven were highly questionable in their results. Meantime, first Patrick and then Vincent were released from prison in 1979, their sentences completed. "They were still classed as convicted terrorists and had to try to get on with their lives as best they could, without the comfort of even having their parents or a family home." Anne's husband, Paddy, was released in February 1984. Since she had been "decategorized" in December 1983 (i.e., no longer classed as a top-security terrorist), she was moved from Durham to a much more "pleasant" prison (if such a term can be used to describe the confines of an innocent prisoner). On 22 February 1985 she was released. She had served the whole sentence required of her by the law.

Outside the prison and waiting for her was a television crew from the Irish state broadcasting company; by now she and her case were sufficiently well known for her to be interviewed at "a big meeting, a sort of press conference, in a London hotel" that afternoon. The next day, she and her husband were flown to Dublin to do further interviews. They went on to Belfast to see her sick and dying father, who had determined that he would live to see his daughter free (he died two weeks later). When they returned to London, they did more interviews for highly respected interviewers; their case was becoming more widely known each day. There was a general feeling developing that some of the "Irish" cases needed to be reviewed; there were just too many questions in some instances about whether justice had been done.

Gradually, a campaign to clear the names of the Maguire Seven gained momentum, becoming associated in the public mind with the same questions that were already being asked about the Guildford Four. Meetings were held around the country to raise awareness and concern about these two cases and about the case of the Birmingham Six, another miscarriage of justice. More politicians also became active and raised the issues publicly and in Parliament. But perhaps the turning point came when Cardinal Basil Hume spoke out publicly; certainly, Anne Maguire considers this to be the weight that tipped the balance in the minds of both the public and the politicians. In October 1986 a book had been published by Robert Kee on the Maguire case titled *Trial and Error*. Following this, Cardinal Hume wrote a letter to *The Times*, and in July 1987 he led a delegation to see the then home secretary. He could not be ignored. Also in January 1986, 400 members of Parliament signed a "Motion 280 Miscarriage of Justice" calling for a review of the Maguire case.

Between 1987 and 1989, as the pressures increased, police from another jurisdiction entered the picture. The original inquiries into both cases had been conducted by the Surrey police. Now detectives from the Avon and Somerset police were called in to take an independent look at what they had gone on in the Surrey inquiry some fifteen years before. What they discovered from records, untouched for fifteen years, was that three instances threw doubt on the confessions of Paul Hill and Gerard Conlon, and since they had given the names of Armstrong and Richardson as co-conspirators, the convictions of these two were equally in doubt. The Avon and Somerset police found that Surrey detectives had fabricated evidence and had misled the 1975 trial in order to obtain convictions. There was by now virtual certainty that something was wrong with the convictions. Enough time had passed that the facts relating to these four people could be reviewed without being distorted by the fear, the anger, and the natural demands for immediate and harsh punishment present at the time of the bombings. The current home secretary

could no longer hold out, largely because of the findings of the appointed authorities. The criticism of the Surrey police for improper and
illegal actions was open and extremely severe. On 20 October 1989 the
Court of Appeal cleared the Guildford Four.

Given the new independent police report and views expressed in *The
Times* on 20 October 1989, when the Guildford Four were released
there was little doubt that the members of the police who had perverted
justice would have to be treated harshly and that it was not just a case
of misconduct by a few low-level policemen but a subversion performed
by experts; the suggestion was that more senior officials were deeply involved. (But justice could only go so far. The climate of the times and
the hatred and fear of the IRA would not permit too many questions or
too much redress. The offending police officers were in fact not subjected to the rigours of the legal system. The implication of the decision
was that public opinion would not accept that they be pursued.)

Two hours after the release of the Guildford Four, an inquiry was set
up under Sir John May to look into both their case and that of the
Maguire Seven. His task in connection with the Guildford Four was to
discover not whether they were guilty but how they had been found
guilty in the first place and what had gone wrong. His inquiry in connection with the Maguire Seven was to review whether justice had miscarried. It might have been expected that with the Guildford Four freed,
the Maguire Seven would also be totally exonerated. The Guildford
Four were now openly recognized to have been convicted solely on the
basis of the confessions of Hill and Conlon in court fifteen years earlier.
These confessions were now admitted to have been forced from them
and supported by false police statements at the trial. If the confessions
were false, then surely the confessions involving Anne Maguire and her
family were almost certainly false. Newspaper articles at the time of the
release of the Four pointed out that the two cases were connected and
that there were most likely another seven innocents. But an immediate
and urgent reassessment was not done. Rather, Sir John May was given
his task of reviewing the facts and history of both the Guildford Four
and the Maguire Seven.

He cannot be accused of adding to the delay unnecessarily. On 12 July
he produced an interim report. The trial judge at the original trial, Lord
Donaldson, was openly and severely criticized for his handling of the case
of the Maguire Seven. As at the original trial, everything centred around
the forensic evidence. But whereas originally the lab tests had been accepted as valid by the judge and jury, now all of the weaknesses identified

by the defence were recognized as having great weight, to the point that the scientists who had earlier given evidence were heavily criticized as being unscientific in both their approach and their findings. In retrospect, it is clear that nothing essentially new occurred in relation to the scientific evidence. The shortcomings now recognized were the same shortcomings that had been raised by the defence in the first place. But things had now changed to the point that an objective view could be taken regarding the validity of the evidence, and this objective view made it evident that the Maguires had been convicted on the flimsiest of grounds. *The Times* thundered in an editorial on 13 July 1990: "Yesterday's report by Sir John May, a lord justice of appeal, is a fundamental challenge to the integrity of the criminal justice system, which now bears the hallmarks of a criminal injustice system." Heavy words for a British public that had, with much right behind it, considered British justice to be a guide and example for the whole world.

Subsequently, while May's inquiry was still proceeding toward a final report, a Court of Appeal heard the case of the Maguire Seven. It would have been reasonable to expect that they would be declared innocent and receive compensation for all that they had gone through. But only on 26 June 1991 were their convictions quashed, and even then the decision rested on the possibility that they may have been "innocently contaminated," leaving room for doubt in the minds of those who wanted to doubt – another example of the constant reluctance of the "establishment" to fully admit to error. In the words of Anne Maguire: "We were disappointed because that could still leave room for doubt and, as we feared, it has allowed a 'whispering campaign' where some people still say 'Oh yes, they have been found innocent after all, but no smoke without fire; how could they have been "innocently contaminated" with nitro-glycerine?'"

Sir John May's final report was issued in December 1992. He made no secret that he was surprised at the weak decision made by the Court of Appeal. But the court had spoken. The report was overshadowed by another bombing, this time in the town of Warrington. Two young children were killed. The fear and anger against the IRA were not unfounded.

When the Guildford Four got out of prison, they arrived in a world that had changed substantially since they went in: all kinds of gadgetry had been invented, the pace of life had quickened, the noise of traffic had increased. And they were provided no counselling, nor did they have any money or backgrounds to get jobs. But the worst effects were psychological. All four later received monetary compensation. In June

2000 Prime Minister Tony Blair released an apology to the Guildford Four in a letter to Courtney Kennedy Hill, Paul Hill's wife, in which he said, among other things: "There were miscarriages of justice in your husband's case, and the cases of those convicted with him. I am very sorry that this should have happened."

On 10 February 2005 Prime Minister Blair at last issued a public apology to the eleven people who comprised the Guildford Four and the Maguire Seven, stating: "I recognise the trauma that the conviction has caused the Conlon and the Maguire families and the stigma that wrongly attaches to them to this day. I am very sorry that they were subject to such an ordeal and such an injustice. That's why I'm making this apology today. They deserve to be completely and publicly exonerated."

13

Power, Secrecy, and the Witch Hunt

Witch hunting is a natural human reaction when society is under great threat. It is the result of great fear and hatred that erupts when a group is seen to threaten the state or a significant section of society. Under such threat, people will give up many historic individual protections to protect the common good. At such times, there is an impulse within governments to centralize and exercise unusual powers through the police, the judiciary, and sometimes the military. And given the threat, this is an impulse supported by the media and the public.

The first reaction to a terrible event is fear. The next is to demand action. Action can be initiated and focused only by a central authority. To act quickly and forcefully the central authority requires special powers. These powers increase the authority and might of the state and decrease the rights of the individual. In combating the threat posed by the enemy, errors will occur – these are inevitable. The state cannot admit to error in these circumstances lest the public lose confidence in the authorities. The result is cover-ups, secrecy, restrictions on dissent and criticism, sometimes illegal actions, all hidden and justified by the need to protect society.

The more that power is centralized in the state, the less the state becomes answerable to the people. In times of great crisis, this is what the people want: it seems better to them that mistakes be made or that injustices should occur if this is what it costs to protect society as a whole. Yet, ironically, society wasn't safer in the IRA cases because the guitly were left to continue their bombings while the police focused resources on prosecuting the innocent. We saw this in Bamberg, in Salem, in the Dreyfus Affair, in the case of the Maguire Seven.

At the time of the Salem witch hunts, Increase Mather said: "It were better that ten suspected witches should escape, than that one innocent person should be condemned." But this was at the end of the crisis when the disease had run its course. The opposite holds true while the crisis is at its height. At these times society accepts that it is better that great errors be made than that one suspected guilty and dangerous person should escape.

The appeal to national security, to the protection of society, or to the good of the state by all powerful central authorities means not only secrecy, but also the removal of one's effective right to appeal. It was years in the cases of the Dreyfus Affair, the Guildford Four, and the Maguire Seven before appeals were heard objectively. Until then the state did everything that it could to prevent any entreaty for justice.

There is one final danger in granting special powers to the central authorities: powerful men and women crave more power. They may crave it with good intentions, but once they have it, they will not easily see it torn away. By then, great damage may be done, as seen with the dead of Bamberg.

PART THREE

14

America after 9/11

Awake! For Morning in the Bowl of Night
Has flung the Stone that puts the Stars to Flight
Rubaiyat of Omar Khayyam, trans. Edward Fitzgerald

It was indeed a rude awakening on that September morning. The Western world, which had long dreamed in deep sleep and safety, was thunderstruck to wakefulness. As the stone was flung, the still waters in the bowl turned into shock waves; peace and tranquillity were things of the past. Now there was a looming sense of fear and a loss of certainty – the end of assurance.

The world was changed on 11 September 2001. One of the almost immediate results was the preparation and passage of Prevention of Terrorism Acts in many countries, including Britain, Canada, Australia, and the United States. The American bill was titled Provide Appropriate Tools Required to Intercept and Obstruct Terrorism, or in acronym, the PATRIOT Act. On 26 October 2001, six weeks after the attacks, President George W. Bush signed the Act into law, bringing about massive changes in civil rights and protections.[1]

Like similar Acts in other countries, the passage of such a law met with popular approval. Indeed, if any of the threatened countries had not taken such action, their governments would have suffered a massive loss of support. There was such shock, anger, and fear that the vast majority of people were more than prepared to give up centuries-old rights and protections in order to build defences against terrorists and terrorism.

In the United States the preparedness to give up rights was propelled not only by the fact that the attacks had taken place there, but also by the fear and expectation that further attacks of equal or even greater evil and consequence were possible at any moment – hence the speed of preparation and passage of the PATRIOT Act. The law that resulted was passed with only minor changes and almost without opposition in the House and the Senate, even though the effects upon freedoms were seen by some as being beyond what was essential – to the point of being a serious threat to individual rights and legal protections.

These fears were not purely theoretical; many people had not forgotten the McCarthy years and were concerned that such times might return as a result of some of the provisions of the Act. Still, those who objected most strongly were ignored, largely because they were recognized as not reflecting the views of the vast majority. The general American population had no hesitation about giving great powers to the administration. This readiness to permit special actions against terrorists was strengthened by the fact that, in the minds of most people, the powers were directed against foreigners – foreign terrorists. They would not, perhaps could not, be used against ordinary Americans.

The great mass of American people, guided and led by President Bush, strongly supported the PATRIOT Act. His reactions immediately after 11 September were exactly what the majority of Americans looked for: forceful, direct, and without delay. As their leader, he demanded that powers be given to the legal and defence authorities that were commensurate with the threats that newly faced the United States. Due to their positions in the administration, Vice President Dick Cheney, Secretary of Defense Donald Rumsfeld, and Attorney General John Ashcroft were most immediately responsible for defending the homeland, and by nature, all found centralization of authority under their control to be consistent with their own views.

The bill itself was very substantial in size, at 342 pages, and was introduced in great haste, within weeks of the attacks. In the eyes of the few active critics at the time, it did not contain checks, balances, and oversights to safeguard traditional liberties – and it was prepared and introduced with such speed that some suspected that much of it had been ready before 9/11 and that it contained virtually every power that organizations like the FBI, police, and the prosecuting system would like to have – an investigator's cornucopia. There was some limited objection also to the enormous pressure by the attorney general to get the Act approved with immediacy by both Houses, so there was little debate or time for serious thought by legislators. The attorney general warned that further terrorist acts were imminent and that Congress could be to blame for such attacks if it failed to pass the bill immediately. Few disagreed.

The House passed the monumental bill by a vote of 357 to 66. The Senate approved it by a vote of 98 to 1. The Act was signed into law on 26 October 2001, forty-five days after the attack of 9/11. Those who expressed concerns about the bill were but voices crying in the wilderness.

In the very early days, only one man of real stature spoke out against the bill with both general and specific criticisms, Senator Russ Feingold. He was in an authoritative position to speak out, and he could hardly be ignored. He was a member of the Constitution Subcommittee of the Judiciary Committee of the Senate. He spoke in the Senate on 25 October 2001 and subsequently published his arguments against the bill in the document "Why I Opposed the Anti-Terrorism Bill." Here was a man who, given his Senate position and personal history, had both the right and the knowledge to speak out. The points that he raised are still the central criticisms of the Act:

There have been periods in our nation's history when civil liberties have taken a back seat to what appeared at the time to be the legitimate exigencies of war. Our national consciousness still bears the stain and the scars of those events: The Alien and Sedition Acts, the suspension of habeas corpus during the Civil War, the internment of Japanese-Americans, German-Americans, and Italian-Americans during World War II, the blacklisting of supposed communist sympathizers during the McCarthy era, and the surveillance and harassment of antiwar protesters, including Dr. Martin Luther King Jr., during the Vietnam War. We must not allow these pieces of our past to become prologue.[2]

With these words, Senator Feingold called upon the past to raise alarms in this debate about the present and the future. The removal of civil liberties to protect the national interest, particularly in time of war, had resulted in terrible injustices, not just in theory but in fact. Not only could bad things happen, but they had already taken place in this same freedom-loving society. The past had proved that actions taken in "what appeared at the time to be the legitimate exigencies of war" might in retrospect be viewed as too instantaneous, having been acted upon too speedily and without the sober second thought that American history had proved desirable in the forum that he was addressing. "We must maintain our vigilance to preserve our laws and our basic rights," he said. "We in this body have a duty to analyze, to test, to weigh new laws that the zealous and often sincere advocates of security would suggest to us."

He accepted that massive police powers to investigate and eavesdrop, to have access to private letters and private lives, and to apprehend upon suspicion without proof would "no doubt discover and arrest more terrorists." But the real question raised was how to achieve some balance between the need to grant new centralized powers without reducing individual rights and freedoms more than was absolutely essential.

While Feingold was the only senator brave enough, or foolish enough, to separate himself from all his peers and vote against the Act, others who voted for it also had their concerns. Some other senators no doubt felt like the Senate Judiciary Committee's chairman, Senator Patrick Leahy, an important and respected man, who said after the vote: "Despite my misgivings, I have acquiesced in some of the administrations' proposals because it is important to preserve national unity in this time of crisis and to move the legislative process forward." Two good men, therefore, Feingold and Leahy, were concerned, but they came to different decisions on what to do.

As he spoke, Senator Feingold expanded on his concerns, starting with the dangers and injustices of racial profiling (a danger still expressed by many Muslims in Western societies). He warned "against the mistreatment of Arab Americans, Muslim Americans, South Asians or others in this country. Already, one day after the attacks, we were hearing news reports that misguided anger against people of these backgrounds had led to harassment, violence, and even death." He warned again "under the pressing exigencies of crisis ... there is the greatest temptation to dispense with fundamental constitutional guarantees which, it is feared, will inhibit governmental action ... We must redouble our vigilance to ensure our security and to prevent further acts of terror. But we must also redouble our vigilance to preserve our values and basic rights that make us who we are."

When he moved to the specifics of the PATRIOT Act, he raised a number of issues. Since 9/11, government agents had arrested hundreds of people, usually on immigration charges, but they were continuing to hold them without specific charges being brought against the overwhelming majority of the detainees. He was concerned about provisions in the bill that "would greatly expand the circumstances in which law enforcement agencies can search homes and offices without notifying the owner prior to the search." He raised the issue of infringements on personal privacy related to computers. The bill, in his opinion, gave the authorities far too much power to access information about what e-mails were being sent and received under certain circumstances as well as about library users and Internet users, particularly when school, university, and other public facilities were used. And he was concerned that with one provision, "protections are potentially eliminated for a broad spectrum of electronic communications."

He also raised the concern that, under the bill, information could now be exchanged between law enforcement and intelligence officers. On the surface this seemed sensible enough – but intelligence officers could, for example, record and pass on rumours about individuals, unsubstantiated statements that would be added to police records on individuals and groups. This opened up what he foresaw as a dangerous infringement on personal rights and protections. This was exactly what had happened in the McCarthy years, with disastrous effects for many innocent people. The past proved that the possible effects were not simply theoretical.

He raised other issues, notably that businesses could be compelled to produce records about anybody if there was a connection with terrorism – anybody with even the most remote connection could have their records opened, "perhaps someone who worked with or lived next door, or went to school with, or sat on an airplane with, or has been seen in the company of, or whose phone number was called by – the target of the investigation." And then there were the dangers to individuals regarding deportation: "This language creates a very real risk that truly innocent individuals could be deported for innocent associations with humanitarian or political groups that the government later chooses to regard as terrorist organizations. Groups that might fit this definition could include Operation Rescue, Greenpeace, and even the Northern Alliance fighting the Taliban in northern Afghanistan. This provision amounts to 'guilt by association,' which I believe violates the First Amendment."

The passage of time and subsequent events would bring about wider criticism about elements of the PATRIOT Act, but when Senator Feingold made his speech, he covered the ground well – the most common and significant criticisms still concentrate on the same issues. At the time, Senator Feingold's criticisms of the PATRIOT Act were, in effect, ignored. The Senate voted 98 to 1 for the Act with some minor amendments. In 2006 a few more amendments were effected. One in particular that freed libraries from excessive intrusions was favourably received by liberal critics. But the PATRIOT Act remained essentially unchanged.

The American public in general and the great majority of legislators did not see the Act as excessive at all. They viewed the PATRIOT Act as

giving powers to all the various law enforcement agencies that were
necessary to protect American society against terrorists. There was general belief that the provisions would be used only against terrorists and
that they would be used wisely. And there was another factor at play,
an unspoken one: this was an antiterrorist bill. In the public mind, terrorists were foreigners. The provisions of the bill that worried critics
did not really apply to Americans in the eyes of many. Feingold's warn-
ings that some provisions could apply to everyone were discounted.

Still, at the time, one group in particular was at risk: since the 9/11
terrorists had been Muslims and Middle Eastern, in practice every person of Middle Eastern background became, in the public mind, a potential suspect, whether American or not. Perhaps, in light of the events of
9/11, this was inevitable, but the bill in effect gave these attitudes a kind
of legal authority. On this particular issue, Feingold said:

Now here's where my cautions in the aftermath of the terrorist attacks and
my concern over the reach of the anti-terrorism bill come together ... To
the extent that the expansive new immigration powers that the bill grants
to the Attorney General are subject to abuse, who do we think is most
likely to bear the brunt of that abuse? It won't be immigrants from Ireland, it won't be immigrants from El Salvador or Nicaragua, it won't even
be immigrants from Haiti or Africa. It will be immigrants from Arab,
Muslim, and South Asian countries. In the wake of these terrible events,
our government has been given vast new powers and they may fall most
heavily on a minority of our population who already feel particularly
acutely the pain of this disaster.

After the PATRIOT Act was passed in 2001, there continued a public
assumption, feeling, instinct, satisfaction – call it what you will – that
the powers granted would be exercised only to the degree necessary.
Americans in general did not feel that their rights and freedoms were
at risk by virtue of the Act. There was a general assumption not only
that the powers would be exercised wisely, but also that they would be
exercised against foreigners, not against Americans. So while the legal
changes were very wide, most people felt that there was little that
anybody really needed to worry about in practice. But there was an
additional unspoken, unwritten assumption: to most Americans of the
time, "foreigners" included American Muslims. The lives of Muslim
American citizens really were changed; they were a class apart, a
different caste.

We have seen what can happen to people who are classed in the public mind as the source of a threat. The British Prevention of Terrorism
(Temporary Provisions) Act of 1974, which resulted from the actions of
IRA terrorists, came from the same stable as the PATRIOT Act. It provided the British authorities with the greater powers that were needed
to combat terrorism at the time, but it also made possible the individual
miscarriages of justice in the cases of the Guildford Four, the Maguire
Seven, the Birmingham Six, and others. Thus while antiterrorism acts
were a natural and necessary consequence of 9/11 around the world,
the past teaches that vigilance over antiterrorism acts and how the authorities behave under them is not only justified, but wise.

The PATRIOT Act was essential – but not necessarily essential in all of
its details. We know that in times of national crisis, there is always an increase in governmental powers and a decrease in individual rights. Governments do not create the crisis, but by emphasizing it, they do increase
the sense of crisis. They demand extreme powers – as many as they can
get. They have to defeat this crisis – and worse ones that may follow – so
the only certain way forward is to demand absolute power. The most certain way to success is overkill. It is difficult to argue against this logic.
But, in retrospect, absolute powers require great oversight. We have seen
Feingold's list of America's failures in the past: "The Alien and Sedition
Acts, the suspension of habeas corpus during the Civil War, the internment of Japanese-Americans, German-Americans, and Italian-Americans
during World War II, the blacklisting of supposed communist sympathizers during the McCarthy era, and the surveillance and harassment of antiwar protesters." Other countries have their own lists.

It should not come as any surprise that some of these past events bore
striking similarities to witch hunts. In each of the American cases that
Feingold listed, a perceived crisis produced a demand for immediate
and overwhelming action. In each, there was an "enemy," feared and
hated. In each, the "enemy" was viewed as a "foreigner," not one of us,
not truly American – as was seen in that famous body the House
Committee on Un-American Activities. In each, the "foreigner," per-
ceivedly not imbued with true loyalty, was at best a second-class citizen,
if not despised.

The PATRIOT Act was one source of the powers created to defeat terrorism, but it was not the only one. Some of the most significant decisions and actions that have taken place with respect to the threats
against the United States were performed not within the powers granted

by the PATRIOT Act but by presidential decisions that had nothing to do with this antiterrorism Act. This does not mean that the threats presented by the PATRIOT Act that concerned Senator Feingold were exaggerated or unreal, but it does mean that the PATRIOT Act is only part of the story of the centralization of power following 9/11.

Shortly after 9/11, the president, within his own legal authority, signed into being a number of decisions that would have considerable effect. He created a specific category of prisoners, sometimes referred to as "illegal enemy combatants" or just as "enemy combatants." To try them, "military tribunals" were authorized. The prisoners could be tried in secret, and the death sentence could be applied. Enemy combatants could be held in prisons outside the United States, and if they were so held, they would have no appeal to the American justice system. New methods of treatment were authorized by the administration under the powers of the executive, and within these were measures that did not meet the provisions of the Geneva Conventions and that permitted actions against prisoners that much of the world considered to be "torture." To be classified as an enemy combatant, a person had only to be a foreigner and to be accused by the administration or its functionaries.

Apparent here is that the combination of the PATRIOT Act and the presidential decisions has provided powers that might protect Americans if used wisely but that could be extremely dangerous if employed without restraint, without transparency, or without oversight by independent bodies. The question of concern is whether the newly created powers to deal with terrorism have in fact been used responsibly. Has the legislative branch, for example, exercised due diligence over the actions of the executive branch to ensure that the rights of Americans are protected by Congress? Has the executive branch made available to the legislative branch the information that it requires to exercise reasonable oversight, or has it operated in excessive secrecy? Has the executive branch in carrying out its powers exceeded its constitutional powers according to decisions by the judicial branch? If the responses to these questions are negative, we will know that the conditions now exist in which witch hunts can arise.

Is there a serious threat of a modern witch hunt arising in our society today? From all that has been said about witch hunts so far, we do know what to look for. Western society is under a condition of great fear and anxiety. So one of the preconditions for witch hunts exists.

To defeat terrorism, laws have been passed that substantially reduce individual legal protections and that centralize special powers. Another precondition that we saw in earlier witch hunts has been fulfilled.

We shall see evidence that authorities are exercising powers in such a way that miscarriages of justice could be occurring through lack of adequate oversight. This is typical in witch hunts.

We shall see evidence of an excessive veil of secrecy through an appeal to "national security" – just as there was in the Dreyfus case, for example. As a result, the activities of witch hunters could also be hidden.

Many countries are now acting under special laws as the result of terrorism. Their special laws are similar enough that to examine one country is in large part to speak of them all. But one of these countries, the United States, is the most powerful in the world. It is the recognized leader of the Western world. It was the first to suffer an attack large enough to shock the whole world. It has a history of personal freedom and pride in personal liberty. If an examination of America gives cause for worry about the possibility of witch hunts, then everybody has cause to worry.

Witch hunts, when they do occur, are led in great part by men of honour who are trying to defend the people. But when they occur, they grow out of control like forest fires. The innocent get swept up with the guilty. Torture becomes accepted as a tool of protection for society and of attack against the "evil ones," accusation becomes the same as guilt, and secrecy and darkness hide misdeeds.

All these precedents have to be avoided.

15

The President

The proper and primary concern of President George W. Bush and his immediate subordinates is the national security of the United States. He and his immediate cabinet members have publicly stated and restated their position on this point. There are many in the United States who would agree and who support all the powers that their leaders claim to need. On the other hand, there are those who argue that some of the powers go too far. The trouble is that nothing exists as a touchstone. There is no absolute standard that can be used to judge whether they seek too much power. One can say only that the leaders of the United States are the sole people who will be held responsible if there are further attacks that could have been avoided if only further powers had been asked for and provided. We must recognize the overwhelming duty of the president to protect his nation's people.

We know that a society living in fear of a hidden enemy tends toward a witch-hunt mentality. It tends, naturally, to centralize powers and reduce individual rights. Experience shows that if this goes too far, particularly if the crisis continues or a trigger event occurs, these powers may be used beyond their intent. The McCarthy years are an example. Thus it is now reasonable to ask, more than five years after 9/11, whether the statements and actions of the president, his cabinet members, and his administration are consistent with the threat that now exists or whether they create an excess of centralized power and an excessive reduction in individual protections.

When witch hunts occur, they result from a state of mind within a society – a state of mind that is based on fear. One thing that we should therefore consider is whether the leadership of the country calms, contributes to, or even makes these fears fiercer and more frightening.

Perhaps the most brilliant coined term of the new millennium has been "Axis of Evil." George W. Bush used it four months after the destruction of the World Trade Centre. He chose the president's annual State of the Union Address, certain to be heard worldwide. North Korea, Iran, and Iraq were his Axis of Evil, along with the terrorists whom they supported: "States like these, and their terrorist allies, constitute an axis of evil, arming to threaten the peace of the world."[1]

It was a wonderful phrase comprising but three words – two of them overwhelming in meaning, full of emotional content. The Axis of Evil denoted the centre of an empire of evil, allies of sin and the Devil, inheritors of the evil of the Axis Powers of Europe, which had destroyed sixty million people. And if the enemy were evil, then we were good. This was light against darkness, God against the Devil and his acolytes – the terrorists.

It was a wonderful phrase, but a terrible one, conveying threats of great dangers and perils. There were yet more implications to the words. The three evil states were linked to "their terrorist allies," whom they supported. There were two unspoken conclusions: that these three countries, and their terrorists, were directly connected and that any war against one of these states would be part of the war against terrorists. Given the context of the time, these terrorists in two of the states were Muslims; moreover, by tying them together in this three-word phrase, they became "The Muslims," a designation never spoken but understood by all. The world was now divided into two – the good and the evil, us and them – and whoever was not with us was against us.

The Axis of Evil carried yet more implications. Those who supported evil could not be trusted, had no honour, had given up all values, and therefore had no value to us. By supporting evil and rejecting good, they were despicable. By choosing evil they rejected truth and goodness. There could be no compromise between good and evil, for the phrase implied a battle that would brook no compromise, no negotiation, no quarter. It was not just us against them; it was a holy war. And a peculiar enemy had been identified. Three countries were labelled "state sponsors" of terrorists in the speech – even though there was no proven connection at all between these states and terrorist groups. From this point on, those who sided with the Devil somehow became less than human to us. And being less than human, they could be treated inhumanely: they had to be either converted or destroyed. Their imprisonment, torture, and even death became acceptable, sometimes necessary. These were shadows of the Crusades, which Muslim countries did not fail to recognize.

These three words – Axis of Evil – contained one enormous overall significance: they implied that it was all right to hate an evil enemy!

Hate was not the only emotion implied: fear was called upon as well. Condoleeza Rice was the national security adviser at the time, later to become the secretary of state. It was she who first used the "smoking gun" metaphor, on Sunday, 2 September 2002, in connection with the first anniversary of 9/11. "The problem here," she said, "is that there will always be some uncertainty about how quickly he [Sadaam Hussein] can acquire nuclear weapons. But we don't want the smoking gun to be a mushroom cloud."²

The president soon followed the same line when talking about Iraq on 7 October 2002: "We have experienced the horror of September 11. We have seen that those who hate America are willing to crash airplanes into buildings full of innocent people. Our enemies would be no less willing – in fact they would be eager – to use a biological, or chemical, or a nuclear weapon. Knowing those realities, America must not ignore the threat gathering against us. Facing clear evidence of peril, we cannot wait for the final proof – the smoking gun – that could come in the form of a mushroom cloud."³

He was talking about Iraq, but he subliminally tied this to September 11 and to terrorists by his phrase "We have experienced the horror of September 11."

It is true that the mushroom cloud and the smoking gun were real and potential threats. But this had been true for nearly fifty years from a much more dangerous and powerful source. Americans had lived with this reality and prospered. But now it was being raised again with a heightened urgency. Of course, there was a reality behind the fear; new attacks on America were likely, almost certain over time. But somehow this level of fear was unnatural to a great and powerful people. This was not the president who had said "We have nothing to Fear except Fear Itself"!

The great former Democratic senator Daniel Patrick Moynihan in a speech on 2 February 2003 talked of the days when "we were engaged, across the world, in a fateful struggle with Communist forces" and how "much as in that earlier time, we begin to suspect one another." "Now we confront terrorism. Worldwide sinister, secretive. Much as was that earlier threat." To get into the building where he was speaking, he said, "you have to go by armed guards. Put your briefcase or pocketbook through an X-ray machine. Raise your arms; empty your pockets." Senator Moynihan drew his own conclusions: "There are indeed buildings that need to be secured. And not a few. But there are places in the public square that do not need that. Might something go wrong? Yes. Nothing new. But the stability of the American National Government is not served by an intimidated citizenry."[4]

"An intimidated citizenry"! The term "Axis of Evil" and the references to a potential "mushroom cloud" contributed to producing exactly this outcome. These were phrases that created a climate of fear. The same message of excessive fear was still being spread four years after 9/11. In a speech on 6 October 2005, President George W. Bush argued that the insurgency that was tearing Iraq apart at the time was part of a wider strategy by al-Qaeda and other Islamic militants to wage "war against humanity." He warned that "the militants believe that controlling one country will rally the Muslim masses, enabling them to overthrow all moderate governments in the region, and establish a radical Islamic empire that spans from Spain to Indonesia. With greater economic and military and political power, the terrorists would be able to advance their stated agenda: to develop weapons of mass destruction, to destroy Israel, to intimidate Europe, to assault the American people, and to blackmail our government into isolation."[5]

In an interview in the Oval Office on 8 February 2004 with Tim Russert on NBC's *Meet the Press*, President Bush said:

[It's] very important for, I think, the people to understand where I'm coming from to know that this is a dangerous world. I wish it wasn't.

I'm a war president. I make decisions here in the Oval Office in foreign-policy matters with war on my mind. Again, I wish it wasn't true, but it is true. And the American people need to know they got a president who sees the world the way it is. And I see dangers that exist, and it's important for us to deal with them.[6]

Certainly, it was "a dangerous world" but far less dangerous than it had been at times. Yet here was the president of the most powerful country in the world talking again in terms intended to emphasize danger and to incite fear.

It is interesting to note remarks made a few months earlier by the well-known journalist and author Thomas L. Friedman (probably no great friend to the administration), who said on 16 October 2003: "Every other word out of this administration's mouth now is 'terror' and 'terrorism.' We have stopped exporting hope, the most important commodity America has. We now export only fear, so we end up importing everyone else's fears right back."

As terrible as the events of 9/11 had been and as startling, did they really justify this level of fear creation? Somehow one cannot picture Roosevelt, Eisenhower, Truman, Kennedy, or Johnson speaking in this way – providing this kind of leadership.

There was another marked element in the president's statements after 9/11: his concentration on being a "war president." Now, this was a perfectly legitimate claim for him to make, for on 14 September 2001 Congress passed a joint resolution stating: "The President is authorized to use all necessary and appropriate force against those nations, organizations, or persons he determines planned, authorized, committed, or aided the terrorist attacks that occurred on September 11, 2001, or harbored such organizations or persons, in order to prevent any future acts of international terrorism against the United States by such nations, organizations or persons." This gave the president the authority to use his full powers as commander in chief of the Armed Forces of the United States. And the preamble to the resolution was in warlike terms, talking of "treacherous acts of violence ... committed against the United States" and of "the threat to national security and foreign policy of the United States posed by these grave acts of violence."[7] In the view of Congress, the attacks were clearly acts of war and, at the time, acts that bore similarities to the attacks on Pearl Harbor, which had likewise been sudden and shocking. But in retrospect, these acts were not devastating in the way that the Pearl Harbor attacks had been; this was not a war like the war against Japan. President George W. Bush was not a "war president" in the same sense that President Roosevelt was. But he made good use of the term and the powers that it gave him, both in image and in fact.

Perhaps the best-known image took place in May 2003 when President Bush made a landing aboard the aircraft carrier USS *Abraham Lincoln*. He flew in the co-pilot's seat of a Navy S-3B Viking and circled the carrier twice before landing. The plane was marked with "Navy 1" in the back and "George W. Bush Commander-in-Chief" just below the cockpit window. The president, wearing a military flight suit and holding his white flying helmet, vigorously jumped down in front of the hundreds of assembled sailors and airmen. He saluted those on the flight deck and shook hands with those surrounding him. Above him, the tower was adorned with a huge sign that read, "Mission Accomplished."[8]

This event attracted worldwide attention, as was intended. It was designed to mark the end of the second Gulf War, which unfortunately went on and on after this declared end with ever-increasing casualties. But what was seen on that day in May was a president in the panoply of war speaking of war, danger, threats, terror, and terrorists.

The use of the terms "war," "war president," and "mission accomplished" produced a level of objection from critics of the president and his administration. Franklin D. Roosevelt's grandson, for example, assessed George W. Bush's performance in an article in *Newsweek* on 29 October 2004 titled "What Is a War President?" "A War President isn't self-proclaimed," he said. "A president becomes a true War President by leadership that inspires followers at home and abroad," he added, citing such instances as his own grandfather, Churchill, Stalin, and de Gaulle. Other critics have argued that Afghanistan, Iraq, and the "war on terror" are really not "wars" in the conventional sense: in terms of the history of a great power, they might at best be campaigns.

Of importance in all this is not whether the president perhaps seemed bombastic at times but that his context was a consistent talk of war, of danger, of threats, of anxiety. Consciously or not, his use of these terms following 9/11 created and continued a psychosis of danger marked by fear and hatred of a diabolical hidden enemy. In these conditions, witch hunts can be sparked by an unplanned trigger event – just as they were in Bamberg.

The use by the president and cabinet members of emotional terms – "war," "danger," "mushroom cloud," "peril" – in conjunction with words like "evil" created (perhaps unintentionally, perhaps not) a condition of mind where it was all right for the enemy to be viewed as less than human. There was another underlying message, never quite stated but certainly conveyed: the danger was so great and the enemy so evil that any action was justified. The old rules of behaviour toward an enemy no longer could be applied.

Who was the enemy? Terrorists of any stripe, yes. But in effect, fundamentalist Muslims. But to the common mind any Muslim could be a fundamentalist – and a potential terrorist. Of course, all the appropriate words were said about good Muslims and bad Muslims, both abroad and in America. But the practical effect of the expressions invoking fear, anxiety, danger, and evil was to include American Muslims as at least a source of danger: they too could be the enemy, just as in earlier times it had been Japanese Americans during the Second World War or left-wing American Communists during the McCarthy witch hunts. The world had now been divided into the good and the evil, between those who are with us and all others.

So we have the potential for witch hunts, and we have potential witches.

Shortly after 9/11 the question arose within the administration about what measures could be taken within the law in the treatment of prisoners – at the time, the prisoners taken in Afghanistan. Within the White House a group of activist lawyers was determined to find interpretations of the law that would permit the administration to remove from terrorists and suspected terrorists as many legal protections as possible. It was an aggressive response to the aggressive acts of 9/11.

On 13 November 2001 the president, using the authority granted to him as commander in chief by the joint resolution of Congress of 14 September 2001, issued a Military Order authorizing the detention and retention of any foreigners who might pose a terrorist threat to the United States. They were to be placed under the control of the secretary of defense and hence to be military prisoners. They were to be subject to military tribunals, with punishment up to and including death. They would have no access to American courts or to the justice system. In the words of the Order, "With respect to any individual subject to this order – military tribunals shall have exclusive jurisdiction with respect to offenses by the individual; and the individual shall not be privileged to seek any remedy or maintain any proceeding, directly or indirectly, or to have any such remedy or proceeding sought on the individual's behalf, in (i) any court of the United States, or any State thereof, (ii) any court of any foreign nation, or (iii) any international tribunal."[9] In effect, this meant that any foreigner could be captured and imprisoned anywhere but would not be a prisoner of war. He or she could be tried and punished by a military tribunal (not a court martial), sentenced to death or lifelong imprisonment, and would have no access to any court and would not therefore even be covered by the Geneva Conventions – to which America was a signatory.

It is doubtful if anybody but a few people in the administration foresaw the consequences. The prisoners became known as "enemy

combatants" or sometimes as "illegal enemy combatants." The term
was never defined and thus could cover a multitude of sins. The Order
specifically authorized places of detention "outside or within the United
States." So special prisons were set up: in Cuba at Guantanamo; in
Iraq, where the most famous (or infamous) was called Abu Ghraib; and
in Afghanistan at Bagram. Beyond these, there were the secret prisons
created in secret places. In all these prisons, interrogations took place.
The president's Military Order specifically required that the prisoners
be treated "humanely." But it is well established that the treatment
was, in fact, harsh at times, to the point that bodies like the International Red Cross and reputable organs of both the international and the
national press used the word "inhumane" and "torture." Indeed, by the
summer of 2005 publications like the *Washington Post*, the *New York
Times*, and *Time Magazine* were calling for Guantanamo to be closed
down in the national interest. Similar calls were coming even from both
Republican and Democratic senators in Congress. Guantanamo and
Abu Ghraib had become international scandals.

What concerns us here is that where a climate conducive to witch hunts
occurred in the past (as we have seen), there was fear and hatred, the
witch was made evil and despicable, and torture became permissible to
protect society. These elements are certainly present in American society
today. This does not imply that a witch hunt is in progress now, but it
does mean that a trigger event – perhaps another terrorist attack – would
find a climate conducive to a witch hunt in today's American society.

In creating or eliminating a witch-hunt climate, top-down leadership
can play a significant part – by its nature, the leadership tends to create
the climate, for better or worse. The functionaries below respond to
what they think the leaders want, rightly or wrongly. The point is that
witch hunts are performed by functionaries, agents of the powers-that-
be, men and women who believe that they are carrying out the wishes
of their leaders. To have a witch hunt, a climate has to exist where the
functionaries believe that their leaders are prepared to turn a blind eye
to actions that skirt the law, perhaps even ignore the law, whether national or international. Their view must be that the danger is so great
and the enemies so evil that any action to defeat them is justified. Further, they must believe that their leaders hold these views as well. It is
true that the functionaries can misread the leaders' intentions but not
for long. Leaders who are greatly worried by actions that skirt the law
will quickly put an end to them. Conversely, it soon becomes apparent
to their followers whether the leadership attitude is one of accepting,

condoning, and even encouraging doubtful activities and whether the leaders are prepared to support their functionaries, even to cover up actions that in normal times would not be acceptable.

There is no question that there was mistreatment of prisoners at Abu Ghraib, at Guantanamo, in Afghanistan. Junior soldiers have been charged and tried, but the most senior officer to be found culpable of any responsibility was the brigadier general in charge of prisons in Iraq, including Abu Ghraib. And she was a woman and a reserve officer – not one of the club. None of the officers in the line of command up to and including the general in charge in Iraq or in the Pentagon were held accountable – even though military officers in all armies are held to be responsible for whatever happens in their chains of command. On the contrary, protection and promotion prevailed. The general who was originally in charge of Guantanamo was appointed to take over the prisons in Iraq after the female brigadier was charged.[10] There was considerable criticism of his appointment since the forms of prisoner treatment at Guantanamo had been transferred to Abu Ghraib in the first place. Other appointments and promotions sent a message that severe treatment was acceptable. For example, one of the principal lawyers involved in the development of the White House policies around enemy combatants and "military tribunals" was Alberto Gonzales. In 2004 he was appointed attorney general of the United States against substantial opposition. The vote in the Senate for his confirmation was 60 to 36 – an extraordinarily low level of support for a presidential nominee. Many argued that he was an unsuitable choice for attorney general because of his involvement in developing the rules that resulted in abuse of prisoners. Secretary of Defense Donald Rumsfeld, who had held his position since 9/11, under whose watch Guantanamo and Abu Ghraib had occurred, and who had strong connections with the policies on prisoner treatment, was retained in this position for President Bush's second term. In short, the message conveyed by these actions of the president was that while some reprehensible actions had been taken by individuals, nobody would be held responsible unless they were personally involved in a crime. It was an approach that said "full ahead and damn the torpedoes."

The policies set by the president, the vice president, the secretary of defense, and the former attorney general were designed to prevent new terrorism and to imprison and punish those already in American hands. While never saying so explicitly, they resulted in a level of harsh and unusual treatment of people who internationally would be regarded as prisoners of war. In practice, the exposures of torture and extreme actions showed that the policies were excessively interpreted down the line and on the ground. All the right words were said at the top about torture being unacceptable, but complaints against the prisoner treatment still continued in 2006, close to five years after 9/11.

The actions of the administration sent another significant message, for in two cases American citizens were classed as "enemy combatants." This ultimately brought about a battle between the executive and the judicial branches of the government. The result was a Supreme Court decision that Americans could be classed as enemy combatants but that they had to have access to American courts. A part of this battle was a position taken by the White House that the determination of who was an enemy combatant and how they could be treated was a matter solely for the commander in chief. The Supreme Court, they held, had no right to become involved. The administration suffered a defeat, for the Supreme Court did hear the case and made a decision.[11] All of this sent messages that cannot have been lost on functionaries of the government who were dealing with prisoners. The first was that the president considered everything involving prisoners to be a military matter and only a military matter – nobody had any right to interfere. The Supreme Court may have temporarily denied and overruled this position, but the position and the views of the president, supported by his cabinet, were clear. Even though they might lose on some issues in the Supreme Court, the administration policy was firm treatment and maximum coverage. The second lesson to all was that Americans could be enemy combatants. And since the two Americans who were declared to be enemy combatants were Muslims, it was also clear that American Muslims were at risk. Of course, there was yet another message that largely went unread: all Americans were at risk, for the president only had to declare them to be enemy combatants.

Every initiative that the president has undertaken has been quite legal. So the issue is not legality. At issue here is the climate that he and his most significant cabinet members have established. The concentration in public statements has been on the threats to the United States, the fears, a state of war, a "war president" who will exercise every power to find and defeat the enemy – a message that it is better to be sorry for overkill than to err in adopting underkill. This climate is one of fear. In light of the history of great powers, is the threat really so great as to justify the level of fear that has been encouraged? This is a valid question. Bad things can happen when a society lives for too long in a state of fear.

In the early days after 9/11, those who were worried about the increased centralization of power in the executive branch focused on the PATRIOT Act. In fact and in practice, the powers that the president and his administration used to create "enemy combatants," Guantanamo, military tribunals, "ghost prisoners," and secret prisons and that others have used to justify torture were the powers given to him by Congress on 14 September 2001. This resolution gave the president the authority to use his full powers as commander in chief of the Armed Forces of the United States to combat terrorists and terrorism. He has consistently argued that the existence of a state of war gives him the duty as commander in chief to take any action that he deems necessary to act against terrorists. Further, he holds that having been given these powers by a resolution in Congress, nobody and no other authority has the right to interfere. From time to time, arguments have been put forward by other individuals and groups (by Democratic Senators, for instance, and even on occasion by Republican ones) that the powers granted to him by the resolution are in fact limited by other laws. But the president has his own legal advisers, on whose advice he acts.

So what exists are two groups. One says that he has the powers to do what he has done and to do more if, as commander in chief, he considers this necessary to win the "war." The other says that his lawyers have given him bad advice and that other laws can override these powers. Because two competing legal positions have been put forward on matters so complicated, it will be months or years before any firm decisions are handed down. In the meantime, the president will continue what he has been doing ever since the beginning of this controversy – exercising the "wartime" powers of the commander in chief.

We have seen some of the consequences of the president's increased powers, but at least one more consequence presents a dangerous threat to Americans: domestic spying.[12] In late 2005 it became public that the National Security Administration was monitoring both incoming and outgoing overseas telephone calls and electronic mail traffic. This meant that American citizens, too, were being spied on. There was nothing wrong with this, for a system had long existed that permitted such monitoring to be performed under warrants applied for and granted by a secret federal court, the Foreign Intelligence Surveillance Court. Of concern was that this "eavesdropping" was being carried out without warrants. The court was not being involved at all. The president and his staff held that taking this action was authorized by the powers given to him in order to protect the nation at war. "National security" prevented any release of information about who was being listened in on or about how many people were involved; the administration said that this spying had been limited to cases connected to terrorists in the United States and overseas.

The initial political and press reaction by those concerned about expansion of presidential powers was one of surprise and shock. The Foreign Intelligence Surveillance Court and its secret warrants had been created after the Nixon "abuse" specifically to prevent any possible repetition of domestic eavesdropping without precise approval by the court set up to grant such warrants. Now that this oversight body had been ignored, there was no oversight. The crux of the matter was not whether the administration was acting legally; the real problem was the potential consequences of domestic spying without oversight and approval by the courts. The administration said that its domestic spying only applied to terrorists and to overseas communications. But anybody could see how it could be expanded given the right (or wrong) circumstances. On 7 February 2006, testifying before the Senate Judiciary Committee, Attorney General Gonzales suggested that the administration had considered targeting domestic telephone conversations and e-mails as well, but a possible public backlash had deterred them.[13] Do not let this statement pass too quickly. It means that the administration must have already thought that it might have the legal *right* to spy on Americans in their homes. What stopped them appears to have been not a lack of authority (in their minds) but concerns about the possibility of a hostile public reaction.

The potential dangers are obvious. The administration says that the president has powers to capture conversations to and from foreign sources that have terrorist connections. And the administration says that it can decide by itself what constitutes a terrorist connection. And nobody is allowed to know what conversations are being overheard and recorded or whose conversations. It follows, then, that the spying could be extended to any and all *internal* communications, in addition to foreign ones, if the public were to deem this acceptable. And when would this be? In the current climate of fear, after the next attack!

Everybody accepts that electronic spying is necessary. But spying without warrants is spying without oversight. This endangers the privacy and rights of every American.

On 9 February 2006 Vice President Cheney suggested that the debate on spying on overseas communications involving terrorist suspects ought to become a political issue in the November 2006 midterm elections.[14] The statement was a recognition that whatever objections politicians may put forward, the vice president believes that a very significant number of Americans, probably the majority, are prepared to support the position of the administration.

Fewer than nine weeks before the midterm elections in November 2006, the president put this theory to the test. He made it evident that the November battle would be fought on maintaining and increasing his freedom to act against suspected terrorists without constraint. He publicly confirmed the existence of secret prisons and justified them. He demanded the freedom to continue with warrantless domestic spying. And he demanded that Congress bless military tribunals permitting hearsay evidence. These powers, he argued, were necessary to continuing his task as the protector of American freedoms.

16

Muslim Fears

After 11 September 2001 there was an early round-up of men, with the focus on illegal immigrants. In early June 2003 the Justice Department's inspector general, Glenn A. Fine, issued a report showing that while 762 illegal immigrants were arrested after 9/11, only a few had clear ties to terrorism. But many were imprisoned for months under harsh conditions, often without access to lawyers; inmates in Brooklyn were particularly badly treated. His report noted that:

In conducting our review, we were mindful of the circumstances confronting the department and the country as a result of the Sept. 11 attacks, including the massive disruptions they caused. The department was faced with monumental challenges, and department employees worked tirelessly and with enormous dedication over an extended period to meet these challenges.

It is also important to note that nearly all of the 762 aliens we examined violated immigration laws, either by overstaying their visas, by entering the country illegally or some other immigration violation. In other times, many of these aliens might not have been arrested or detained for these violations.[1]

There was concern in the report both about the length of time that the detainees were held and about their treatment:

Our review also raised various concerns about the treatment of these detainees at the M.D.C. [Some of the detainees were held at the Metropolitan

Detention Center in Brooklyn, New York.] For example, we found that
M.D.C. staff frequently, and mistakenly, told people who inquired about a
specific Sept. 11 detainee that the detainee was not held at the facility
when, in fact, the opposite was true. In addition, the M.D.C.'s restrictive
and inconsistent policies on telephone access for detainees prevented them
from obtaining legal counsel in a timely manner.

With regard to allegations of abuse, the evidence indicates a pattern of
physical and verbal abuse by some correctional officers at the M.D.C.
against some Sept. 11 detainees, particularly during the first months after
the attacks. Although most correctional officers denied any such physical
or verbal abuse, our interviews and investigation of specific complaints developed evidence that abuse had occurred.

We also concluded that, particularly at the M.D.C., certain conditions of
confinement were unduly harsh, such as illuminating the detainees' cells
for 24 hours a day. Further, we found that M.D.C. staff failed to inform
M.D.C. detainees in a timely manner about the process for filing complaints about their treatment.

The immediate cause for arrest, particularly in New York, was largely a
detainee's standing as an illegal immigrant rather than any real connection with terrorist activities. The report suggested that "the authorities
arrested many illegal immigrants – most of them Middle Eastern – who
became entangled in the terrorism investigation by chance through traffic stops, anonymous tips and other means. Investigators found that
many suspects were simply grouped into categories 'of interest' to the
terrorism investigations and subjected to restrictive and sometimes abusive conditions of confinement as a result of that classification."

Given the size of the problems faced by authorities in the United
States after 9/11, it would be unreasonable to dwell too much on this
one set of circumstances. Still, it can be seen that there was great suspicion about illegal Muslim immigrants that lasted well beyond the immediate tensions of late 2001 and that their treatment in some cases was
harsh. Another feature of these arrests was that the government refused
to release the names of those who were imprisoned on the grounds that
this information would aid al-Qaeda.

Of the 762 arrested, 500 were expelled from the United States. These
500 were not the only expulsions. In response to a call from the immigration authorities in early 2003 for Arab and Muslim men to come
forward and register, some 82,000 complied. Of these, some 13,000
were found to be living in the country illegally and therefore subject to

deportation. Many of these had come forward in the hope that their cooperation would save them from deportation, although none were promised any special treatment. It is difficult to fault the authorities for their
strict application of the law in dealing with illegal immigrants. Nevertheless, a particular aspect of this event caused great concern to the community from which these men came. The call to register was directed at
Arabs and Muslims; they were now a special type of immigrant, whether
legal or illegal. "What the government is doing is very aggressively targeting particular nationalities for enforcement of immigration law," said
Lucas Guttentag, director of the immigrants' rights project at the American Civil Liberties Union. "The identical violation committed by, say, a
Mexican immigrant is not enforced in the same way."[2]

This matter of being singled out for special treatment has been of
great concern to Muslim communities in many Western countries since
9/11. There is a fear that racial profiling will be used in many ways to
the detriment of innocent people. In Canada, for instance, Ziyaad Mia,
a director of the Muslim Lawyers Association, commented on provisions of the Canadian Public Safety Act (Bill C-17), saying, in part:
"This could lend more power to racial profiling. We are all quite aware
Muslims are the poster boys for terrorism. Profiling suggests you don't
really have a reasonable suspicion to look at people, only their race
or religion."[3]

Occasionally, a case will come to light that has elements of a witch-
hunt mentality. In the early summer of 2003 four men, all of them immigrants from the Middle East, were tried for forming a terrorist cell
and planning a variety of plots; they had been arrested in 2002 in Detroit.
Federal prosecutors at the time claimed to have eliminated a "sleeper
operational combat cell." The case received wide publicity as one of the
first real successes against internal terrorism. Two of the men were convicted on terror and document-fraud charges, one was convicted on
document-fraud charges, and one was acquitted. Even though it was
only a partial victory for the prosecutors, the attorney general at the
time, John Ashcroft, proclaimed this to be a major success in the war on
terror. These terrorist trials were commonly referred to in the press as
the "Detroit Terror Cases." Nevertheless, sentences were never handed
out because from the time of conviction, there were increasing concerns
in legal circles about how the case had been handled.

The great reversal came in September 2004. Since the 2003 trial, a
mass of information had been collected that totally undermined the case
that had been put forward. Further, it was now apparent that evidence

held by the prosecution in 2003 that should have been provided to the defence had been withheld, thus undermining the defence case. The three men would still be accused of document fraud and would face deportation hearings, but it was evident that a climate of fear in America had been used by the initial prosecution to make terrorists of men whose worst crime was illegal immigration and possible document fraud.

Another, quite different kind of case involved a Muslim chaplain at Guantanamo. Captain James Yee was a West Point graduate who had left the military for four years to study Islam and Arabic, later rejoining the military to become a Muslim chaplain. He was appointed as chaplain at Guantanamo, counselling prisoners in the camp. In September 2003 he was arrested on suspicion of having classified material in his possession; there was suspicion of espionage activities. Pentagon officials trumpeted the event as being part of a major espionage affair. In fact, by the time the military case against him came to court, the charge against him bore no relation to espionage but concerned an extramarital affair that was contrary to military discipline and a number of minor infractions.

It is difficult to sort the wheat from the chaff in a case like this, but it would appear that Captain Yee's real fault was having been too sympathetic to some of the prisoners at Guantanamo. The army initially linked the chaplain to a possible espionage ring, later charging him with mishandling classified material, failing to obey an order, making a false official statement, adultery, and conduct unbecoming an officer. All criminal charges were dropped in March 2004. He was reprimanded for adultery and downloading pornography, but the reviewing general threw out this punishment a month later. He was subsequently notified that his request for an honourable discharge would be approved and effective in January 2005.

Many Muslim American citizens, by virtue of appearance and sometimes of dress, are easily identifiable. There is a public sense that since a good Muslim cannot be distinguished from a fundamentalist, all are potentially suspect. Many Muslims complain of experiencing profiling, particularly when travelling by air. They claim to be picked out for extra questioning and greater suspicion. The complaints are too widespread to be simply paranoia.

Take for example an event in December 2004. Five American Muslims were returning from a conference in Canada. It was a large, respected annual conference organized in Canada with the subject "Reviving the Islamic Spirit." The event is attended each year by thousands of Muslims from Canada, the United States, and elsewhere and is centred on lectures and discussions by Islamic scholars and on music and cultural events.

On their return through Buffalo, these five people, three men and two women – including a hotel manager, a graduate student, an orthodontist, and a teacher – were stopped, held for hours, interrogated, photographed, and fingerprinted. Their cars were searched, and some of their cell phones were removed when they wanted to call their lawyers. Apparently, these were not the only conference members affected on returning to the United Sates: at least thirty-four were stopped at various entry points. The five at Buffalo subsequently complained and filed a lawsuit alleging that their constitutional rights had been violated. A spokeswoman for Customs and Border Protection said that Muslims attending the conference had been stopped because of ongoing credible information that Islamic conferences might be used in connection with terrorist activities and fundraising. While this was but one incident, it is a good example of the basis of Muslim fears.

Events overseas in 2005 and 2006 did not make the situation of Muslim Americans any easier. The war in Iraq, with the rise of insurgency; pacification and resettlement in Afghanistan; American support of Israel; and increasing American concern with Iranian nuclear plans: all led to an increase in anti-American feeling and activity, however much any or all of these might have been justified. Muslim extremists took every opportunity to harness these emotions and to direct them against the United States. In the American public mind, American Muslim citizens were more and more placed in a special "no-man's-land" where they were citizens but not the same as other citizens – suspect or at least liable to suspicion. There was no overt discrimination, but they were not the same as other more recently arrived immigrant groups.

Of course, Muslims in America feel themselves to be the objects of suspicion. Muslim fears are justified. They feel themselves to be second-class citizens. They are not the subject of witch hunts, except perhaps in individual cases. But they are certainly potential sitting targets. They are part of a group separate from most Americans, belonging to a culture and a religion that seem alien to many Americans and that are neither respected nor understood by most fellow citizens. And apart from occasional soothing words of comfort from administration officials, little has been done to make Muslims feel at home or to increase understanding of their values and contributions.

17

Guantanamo Bay

The idea that people can be held by the United States of America, in prison and isolated, without trial or right to appeal, does not sit comfortably with Americans nor, for that matter, with the rest of the civilized world. Yet this is what happened at Guantanamo Bay in Cuba. By the summer of 2003, nearly 700 prisoners were being held in the camp, but their names were unknown; the United States administration argued that releasing their identities would provide useful information to al-Qaeda. The prisoners were believed to come from forty countries and included more than one child under the age of sixteen. At the time, all of the prisoners were believed to be members of the Taliban or al-Qaeda, captured in Afghanistan and transferred in early 2002 to Guantanamo Bay to a specially prepared camp. For the first months, the men were kept in wire-mesh cells about 6 1/2 feet by 8 feet, arranged in blocks of ten or twenty. The cells were covered by a wooden roof but open at the sides to the elements. The prisoners were taken out only once a week for a one-minute shower.[1]

Later, conditions improved somewhat as the prisoners were moved into newly built cells. But they were still very small, and exercise was restricted to two fifteen-minute periods in a week, including a shower period. Interrogations took place sporadically. The prisoners were properly fed and led in prayer by a Muslim chaplain. In general, from what we know, the conditions of incarceration were, at best, marginally acceptable by Western standards, although perhaps more suited to animal husbandry than to respecting human dignity. For a long time the prisoners had no connection with relatives other than by heavily censored mail. Their names had not been released, so no one knew who was there. They had no legal protections. These facts worried many Americans.

Adding to the extreme physical restraints was that the prisoners had no idea what the future held for them. They could be (and were) held for years in these conditions. What is known is that in the first eighteen months of the detention camp, there were twenty-eight suicide attempts on the part of eighteen prisoners, which indicates an extraordinary level of stress. By 2006 only four of the prisoners had been charged with crimes. None had ever been able to defend himself in court. Nor was there any early prospect of such trials.

The prisoners were held under the control of the American Department of Defense. The plan was that they would be brought before military tribunals, courts rather like court martials, where they would be tried in a substantial degree of secrecy and where sentences could be delivered and carried out, even death sentences. In practice, at least until 2006 the American courts up to and including the Supreme Court had delayed these plans from being carried out.

How could this have come about? How could it be that prisoners were being held in the name of the United States without Americans, or anybody else, knowing about their conditions and their legal status? To many, this was almost unthinkable in the land that truly was the home of liberty and freedom. And why was this American activity, staffed and run by Americans, taking place at a prison that was not in the United States? This was seriously beginning to worry some Americans in the summer of 2003. By 2006 some of these questions could be answered, although by no means all, and the answers failed to satisfy the consciences of many Americans.

We need to go back to 2001 when the initial mass of prisoners was captured in Afghanistan. Their American captors believed them to be fanatical al-Qaeda or Taliban fighters (although, subsequently, some were found to be innocent men caught in the wrong place at the wrong time). Under international law, these prisoners, caught in the confused battle conditions of Afghanistan, would normally have been classified as "prisoners of war" (POWs). And there the trouble started, for in the view of the American authorities, they were not prisoners of war; they were supporters of the Taliban and al-Qaeda – and hence terrorists.

The problem was that prisoners of war are governed by the Geneva Conventions, signed by the United States as well as by nearly every other country. Under these conventions the prisoners would have specific legal rights overseen by international bodies like the Red Cross. But the Bush administration considered it a national need that these men be imprisoned and held in prison indefinitely: in their view, to release them was to release terrorists to continue their activities. Further, they had to be held in conditions where they could be interrogated so that investigators could discover information about al-Qaeda and other terrorists. And we must presume from what we have seen that these conditions had to be sufficiently unpleasant that cooperation could be repaid by increasingly better treatment and rewards. How to accomplish all this was the question.

The American government resolved one problem by declaring that these men were not prisoners of war at all. In the eyes of the Bush administration, Taliban and al-Qaeda forces did not qualify as prisoners of war because they did not meet the criteria for recognition as POWs, such as being under a responsible command, having a fixed distinctive sign recognizable at a distance, carrying arms openly, and conducting their operations in accordance with the laws and customs of war. (Of course, the war in Afghanistan was fought with many of the Afghans not having uniforms – on either side of the battles.) So a new and different classification was created and applied to these prisoners by the administration: the "enemy combatant." This specially labelled class of prisoners had, by lack of a definition of rights, no rights. If they were not prisoners of war, then the usual protections for such detainees did not apply, the administration argued.

Who or what determined who was an enemy combatant? Not the Geneva Conventions. It was the functionaries of the government of the United States who declared that a prisoner was or was not an enemy combatant. Once a prisoner was classified as an enemy combatant, the Department of Defense, under the direction of Donald Rumsfeld, had the legal responsibility for him. The idea behind all this was to keep these men as prisoners, forever if necessary, and to put to death those who were the greatest threats. Thus this designation of an enemy combatant provided the Bush administration with a means of (effectively) permanent imprisonment, to be carried out beyond international oversight – the International Red Cross would not have the normal rights to inspect and oversee the prison camps and their conditions, as they would have had for prisoners of war under the Geneva Conventions.

The other big problem for the administration was how to prevent the American courts from becoming involved with these prisoners, whom the administration wanted to keep subject only to military justice and control. This was achieved by two measures: placing the prisoners outside the United States and declaring that the president, as commander in chief, had sole control over them. (In constitutional terms, the executive branch took the position that the judicial branch had no part to play with regard to these enemy combatants.) The administration (under advice from its own lawyers) said that the joint resolution passed by Congress on 14 September 2001 gave the president, as commander in chief, sole authority to take any action against these prisoners.

If these "enemy combatants" had been held as prisoners within the United States, they would have had certain legal rights under American laws. Sooner or later they would have had to be charged with a crime and would have had some rights to a trial with defence lawyers. This is why they were sent to Cuba. Guantanamo Bay is indisputably a part of Cuban territory. But the base there has been administered by the United States since 1903 under a lease that grants America many of the attributes of sovereignty – the treaty uses the phrase "complete jurisdiction and control."[2] Thus Guantanamo is an important American military base in Cuba that is owned and operated by the United States. It is effectively American. However, where the "enemy combatant" prisoners were concerned, the administration held that Guantanamo is only an American base in a foreign country. The prisoners were being held in a foreign country, they said. The laws of the United States, they argued, did not and could not apply there because the prisoners were being held on Cuban, not American, soil. Thus, they proclaimed, the prisoners had no right of access to the American justice system.

Because they were classed by the administration as military prisoners, not prisoners of war, they came under the control of the secretary of defense, Donald Rumsfeld. And since they were in Guantanamo to be interrogated, lists of techniques were issued that could be applied leading up to and during interrogation procedures. Some of these processes gradually became publicly known and grew into a subject of considerable concern both nationally and internationally. The word "torture" began to appear in the world press. The revelations of ill-treatment and torture at Abu Ghraib in Iraq in May 2004 shocked the world. It also became public knowledge around this same time that certain interrogation techniques had migrated to Iraq and Afghanistan from Guantanamo. Critics of the administration pointed out that the general in

charge of Guantanamo had been sent to Iraq to take over the prisons
there and that with him had gone the "spirit" of harsh treatment to
cope with the enormous number of Iraqi prisoners.[3]

So what did go on at Guantanamo? The administration has always
been very secretive about the prison and the prisoners, so what is
known is largely the result of investigative journalism. But by the middle of 2005, some things had become certain: hundreds of men were being held without any recourse to charges, trial, or defence and could be
held for years to come; further, there were grave suspicions that they
had been subjected to harsh, perhaps inhuman, treatment and possibly
torture. Released prisoners had bitterly complained about their treatment, noting extreme pressure and forced false confessions. Without independent confirmation, there must always be reasonable doubt about
such accusations from former prisoners who could be expected to hold
a grudge against their former captors. But the volume of evidence from
press reports and known complaints from bodies like the International
Red Cross amounted to virtual confirmation that unacceptable treatment had been used on prisoners at Guantanamo as a part of official
practices and that it went well beyond unauthorized mistreatment on
the part of individual guards. It is extraordinary that the secrecy sur-
roundeding everything going on at Guantanamo forces us to rely on reports in leaked documents and on unconfirmed statements of people
like former guards.

There are reliable reports of prisoners having been kept in the equivalent of animal cages, of prisoners having been shackled like slaves and
left to soil themselves with their own urine and feces, of prisoners being
kicked, punched, beaten, and kept for long periods in isolation. Other
reports talk of prisoners being forced to strip from the waist down and
of female interrogators taunting prisoners, touching them sexually,
while dressed in miniskirts and tight, revealing clothing and acting pro-
vocatively – behaviours that would all be shameful and humiliating in
the extreme to a devout Muslim. There are further reports of temperatures of extreme heat and prolonged cold having been applied, persis-
tent noise and music, and forced enemas. Some of these were applied
together, with prisoners being stripped to their underwear and shackled
by hand and foot to the floor, the air conditioning turned to maximum,
while strobe lights flashed and very loud music was played close to the
ear. About one in six prisoners was reported to have been treated in
extreme ways. Still, the administration continued to argue that the prisoners were treated "humanely" and in a manner "consistent with legal

obligations prohibiting torture."4 But then one has to ask, who in this case was defining "torture"? And how were they defining it?

The critics of George W. Bush said that his administration had a history of playing with words, of redefining them to mean quite different things. Prisoners of war were no longer prisoners of war, it said, even though the rest of the world still said they were. "Enemy combatants" became a term used to remove all protections and to provide the administration with the power to do anything to these prisoners that it wanted. Secrecy became "national security," designed to hide all facts, including not only human errors that were clearly embarrassing, but also criminal acts. Trials were replaced by "military tribunals," to be conducted in secrecy, whose rules would be made up by the administration. Torture was stated to be unacceptable, but orders were given that treatment of prisoners should be responsive to "military necessity." Of course, if torture is defined too generally as a practice that "must inflict pain that is difficult to endure," then virtually any brutal actions could be interpreted as not overly difficult to endure and thus permissible. A Justice Department definition in the year 2002 used exactly these words.5

But Guantanamo did not work out as it was supposed to. The term "enemy combatants," and the treatment of those so labelled, became the subject of a great deal of intense international concern. In America itself there was considerable legal argument up to and including the United States Supreme Court. By 2006 these arguments had been going back and forth for more than four years, having been about as positively resolved as the subject of how many angels can dance on the head of a pin. In general, however, the decisions of the courts supported the position that, despite the contrary claims of the administration, the prisoners did have some legal rights of appeal to American courts. Similarly, the military tribunals that were going to judge the prisoners were equally tied up in legal argument. By 2006 not a single trial had taken place. And all this time, Guantanamo was cause for international and national criticism.

Guantanamo was, in fact, a running sore for the administration. There were too many public concerns over prisoners being held by America without appeal to the American justice system, too many concerns over the conditions and treatment of the prisoners, too many rumours, gradually substantiated and fleshed out, of inhumane treatment, improper behaviour, even torture – all met by international condemnation. There was increasing American public concern that their country's reputation was being severely damaged, that American soldiers who were captured might be similarly mistreated, that information obtained under ill-treatment was often unreliable (having been offered up only to satisfy the interrogator), that after four years there surely could not be much more to be learned, and that Guantanamo was creating more anti-American terrorists by virtue of the fury that was being engendered in the Muslim world as more and more information about treatment of prisoners bled out, particularly rumours of mistreatment of the Qur'an.

For a long time the administration largely ignored all of this reaction, maintaining that the prisoners were dangerous men who had to be held long term and that they were well treated.

The matter came to a head in late May 2005. Amnesty International released a stinging report, stigmatizing Guantanamo as "the gulag of our time." It was a phrase that reverberated around the world. In America, at least, the description was widely held to be excessive. The secretary of defense, Donald Rumsfeld, termed it "reprehensible." But it certainly got notice. It was as though somebody had finally shouted out: "Look! The emperor has no clothes." Dozens of articles had said the same things before, but this one was carried in on the crest of the wave. The events that followed were probably not caused directly by the Amnesty statements – senators and journalists must have been preparing action already to be able to come out so quickly. Still the Amnesty characterization was certainly a trigger event for what followed.

In the *New York Times* of 27 May 2005, Thomas L. Friedman published an article whose brief but no-nonsense title said it all: "Just Shut It Down." He argued that any of the 500 detainees who were guilty of crimes should be tried and convicted and that the remainder should be released because Guantanamo was doing so much damage to America's international standing. Senator Joseph Biden, the top Democrat on the Senate Foreign Relations Committee, added his voice to those calling for the prison to be closed down. Within a few days a leading Republican senator, Arlen Specter, who was chairman of the Senate Judiciary Committee, said that he planned to hold a hearing with a view to developing a set of clear rules for handling terrorist prisoners who were in American custody, including Guantanamo. Other well-known and respected public figures, including both Democratic and Republican senators, called for the creation of a bipartisan investigative panel to look into the allegations of abuse. Former presidents Jimmy Carter and Bill Clinton added their voices: Clinton said it should "be closed down or cleaned up"; Carter termed it "a disgrace."[6]

The initial response of the administration showed confusion. On 8 June 2005 Donald Rumsfeld said that nobody in the administration was thinking of closing the base down. On 15 June Attorney General Alberto Gonzales said, according to Agence-France-Presse: "We have been thinking about and continue to think about whether or not this is the right approach; is this the right place, is this the right manner in which to deal with unlawful combatants."[7] Two days earlier Vice President Dick Cheney had said that Guantanamo was essential to the administration's efforts to combat terrorism and that the prisoners there had been treated better than "by virtually any other government on the face of the earth." He brushed aside the critics, saying "they probably don't agree with our policies anyway."[8] The last statement was no doubt correct but not completely so: Republicans who supported the administration were among the critics concerned about the damage that Guantanamo was doing. The world press was also actively arguing that it was time for something to be done.

Cheney's statement about the favourable treatment of prisoners was not well received by many. In the *New York Times* of 21 June 2005, Anthony Lewis raised reports of detainees "chained hand and foot in a fetal position to the floor, with no chair, food or water. Most times they had urinated or defecated on themselves and had been left there for 18, 24 hours or more." On 12 June 2005 *Time Magazine* had reported that one prisoner was given 3 1/2 bags of intravenous fluid. When he asked to urinate, he was told that he had to answer questions first. When his answers were not satisfactory to the interrogator, he was told to urinate in his pants, which he did. Earlier, a dog had apparently been used "in an aggressive manner to intimidate him." He was told that he had to learn to show respect like a dog. The log read: "Began teaching detainee lessons such as to stay, come and bark to elevate his social status to that of a dog. Detainee became very agitated." Mr Lewis noted: "In the view of the administration, then, it is 'humane' to give a detainee 3 1/2 bags of I.V. fluid and then make him urinate on himself, force him to bark like a dog, or chain him to the floor for 18 hours."

Here was the nub of the issue. How should a man who was suspected of having been an intended 9/11 hijacker be treated? Should Guantanamo be retained as it was under a blanket of secrecy? Should it be closed? Should it be investigated? Or should open, acceptable rules of imprisonment and interrogation be established for terrorists?

All the debate had some effect. At Guantanamo as of June 2005, the number of prisoners had been reduced from the original 700 to about 500 to 550. Over the past year or two, most released prisoners had been returned to the countries from which they had come. The American authorities never stated why they were released after so long, but in those few cases where the press was able to investigate, the conclusion seems to be that in the beginning they had been swept up in the aftermath of battles and were later found to really be of little or no interest to their captors.

By January 2005 there was talk of another 350 about to be sent back to their countries of origin. By August 2005 the status of the 350 was solidifying; negotiations were taking place with Afghanistan, Yemen, and Saudi Arabia to take back their nationals on the conditions that the recipients would prevent these enemy combatants from undertaking future hostile action and would treat them humanely – whatever this meant in these countries. The administration gave no specifics concerning why these 350, held for four years as great dangers, were enemy combatants one day but not the next. Reading between the lines, which is all that can be done with much relating to Guantanamo, these prisoners, who were too low-level to be a threat and some of whom were even innocent, had now become an embarrassment to the administration. They could not be kept at Guantanamo forever; the criticism was too great. But if they were sent back to their countries of origin, they would become somebody else's problem. "We think a more prudent course is to shift that burden onto our coalition partners" was the administration's view.[9] This decision, once completed, would leave in Guantanamo about 150 prisoners considered to be hardcore and dangerous if released.

It might have been expected that all the public criticism, worldwide and American, would lead to at least more circumspect treatment of the remaining prisoners in Guantanamo. But by September 2005 there were reports of 89 prisoners on hunger strikes to protest their treatment, with 13 being force-fed by tubes. The figures on hunger strikes rose to 131 by mid September out of a total of about 500 prisoners. By February the number was down to 4 as a result of forced feeding.

The fact of hunger strikes was in itself not particularly surprising. The prisoners at Guantanamo had used hunger strikes as a means of protest since 2002. By late 2005 and early 2006, it had clearly become a mass movement, with some prisoners apparently prepared to accept death as a means of protesting their never-ending captivity. The forced feeding was a recognized practice in the domestic American prison system when faced with hunger strikes that threatened life. But by February 2006 it was being reported in the American press that the methods used in Guantanamo went substantially beyond "normal" practice. Once more, terms like "abusive treatment" were being used to describe what was happening: prisoners were being strapped into "restraint chairs," sometimes for hours, to be fed through thick tubes. There were suggestions in the press that the determination to break the hunger strike was based in part on fear that a death from starvation would have dramatic effects in the world press. At the same time, strict measures to stamp out the strike became possible as the result of a measure in Congress that restricted any possibility of access by prisoners to American courts. In other words, harsher treatment in Guantanamo would not appear in a court case in America.

A United Nations report in February 2006 called for closing Guantanamo, saying that the ill-treatment of prisoners "amounted to torture." The administration rejected the findings, arguing that the investigators had not even visited Guantanamo Bay. The independent investigators appointed by the Human Rights Commission, on the other hand, made it clear that they had declined offers to visit on the grounds that they would be denied access to individual prisoners. So the arguments went on as they had over the past years. But such arguments back and forth could not hide that Guantanamo was still a grave concern in the eyes of the whole world and was badly damaging perceptions of America.

What will come of all this is uncertain. But one thing strikes a note: Guantanamo sounds too much like the witches' prisons, the Hexenhausen, that the bishops of Bamberg and Wurzburg constructed for the imprisonment and interrogations of suspected witches.

All the things associated with Guantanamo constitute significant steps toward the real-life practices of witch hunts:

1 a prison specially constructed for the "witches" – and only for these prisoners;
2 prisoners who are assumed to be guilty upon apprehension – no proof required;
3 secret interrogations under extreme pressure;
4 long-term incarceration without charges;
5 planned secret trials, with secret charges and secret testimony;
6 no appeals or normal legal defence assistance.[10]

Guantanamo has all the elements necessary for a future full-scale development of a witch-hunting process in America. And perhaps even more frightening is that the great mass of American people are not concerned. Some are worried about the effects of Guantanamo on the international good name of America. But few seem to be conscious of the dangers to America itself in creating the first "witches' prison" since Salem.

18

Torture, Rendition, and "Ghost Prisoners"

"Is Torture Ever Justified?" This was the startling title of an article in the highly respected *Economist* of 9 January 2003. It startled thinking people. Fifteen, ten, even five years earlier, such a question would have been regarded as ridiculous. To most readers, the idea was almost unthinkable in the nations of the West, with their long history of individual rights and freedoms. The article stated the problem in a nutshell: "How can democratic governments best fight an enemy like al-Qaeda, whose operatives are encouraged to outdo each other in the barbarity of their attacks? In ways that uphold the values democracies stand for, is the answer one would like to give. Yet faced with the sort of threat al-Qaeda poses, this line is not always so easy to draw."[1]

Although we did not know it at the time, or at worst had only suspicions, the American government was already deeply involved in activities that other countries classed as torture. Prisoners at Guantanamo in Cuba were ill-treated, and some, by international standards, were tortured. Clandestine bases in foreign countries were being run by the United States or its allies where torture was almost certainly proceeding. In Iraq and Afghanistan prisoners were being tortured, even to death. Rendition was common, the practice of sending prisoners to foreign countries where torture is used. All were secret activities at the time, and all were the work of Americans with official connections. Some of the activities were official government programs, like

Guantanamo and rendition to foreign countries. Some were unwarranted activities of US soldiers or contracted employees, as in Iraq's Abu Ghraib prison.

Of course, much depends on what is meant by "torture." Barbara Tuchman, in her book *A Distant Mirror*, lists some of the tortures applied by authorities in the fourteenth century: cutting off hands and ears, racking, burning, flaying, pulling apart people's bodies, flogging with a knotted rope, flogging chained upright in an iron collar, strappado, the wheel, gouging of eyes, cutting off facial features one by one. The world today does not accuse America of this sort of torture. What goes on when prisoners are rendered to other countries with a current record of torture is another matter.

There are more modern physical tortures that depend on electrical shock treatments. There are plenty of reports from released rendition prisoners that these have been used against them in the countries to which they were sent. There are well-founded accusations of the use of the water torture (known as "water-boarding") by Americans. What goes on in secret American prisons, of course, is largely unknown. But in general, heavily physical torture is not the major accusation against American functionaries.

What has caused such worldwide concern is not torture of the types above but harsh treatment coupled with threats, humiliation, sexual intimidation and embarrassment, shame, the use of trained dogs to terrify prisoners, psychological pressures of various kinds and degrees, extreme physical conditions of heat, cold, noise, and isolation, and indefinite imprisonment without hope of release or prospect of appeal. These are conditions that by any civilized standards would be termed inhumane and unacceptable treatment of prisoners. By the standards of the Geneva Conventions, they are torture.

Abu Ghraib is perhaps the best known case of totally unacceptable behaviour, but in large part the torture "program" started with Guantanamo. It became a national and international scandal only with Abu Ghraib. In late April 2004 several photographs were broadcast on CBS's *60 Minutes II* that shocked the world. They showed American soldiers of both sexes humiliating Iraqi prisoners in the prison at Abu Ghraib. There was a picture of naked Iraqi prisoners piled on one another in an untidy pyramid with two grinning soldiers giving a thumbs up signal – one a man and the other a woman. There was another picture of a similar pyramid pile of naked Iraqis and yet another of a naked man with his head turned, posed as though he were giving oral sex to another naked prisoner who had his head covered by a sack. These were only some of the pictures revealed then and in increasing quantities later as the dam broke. They were terrible enough in themselves, but even more so to the Arab world, where homosexual activities are against Islamic law and where to be naked in front of other men, and especially in front of women, is so humiliating that these prisoners and all associated with them could be forever rejected.

America was horrified to find out what had been going on. The revelations about Abu Ghraib shocked the world. For weeks the American press and American journalists pursued the subject, finding new facts, revealing new horrors. Something was very far wrong at Abu Ghraib; the army and the administration admitted this quickly. The prison was badly run, they acknowledged. But the perpetrators, they insisted, were rogue soldiers acting on their own and without any authority. They would be tried and punished appropriately.

In fact, the army authorities knew that something was seriously wrong at Abu Ghraib months before the photographs became public. Under the commanding general in Iraq, an inquiry had been carried out by a Major General Taguba. His report was not meant for public release but was leaked at the time of the Abu Ghraib public disaster. He itemized the repugnant events that he had unearthed:

Punching, slapping, and kicking detainees; jumping on their naked feet;
Videotaping and photographing naked male and female detainees;
Forcibly arranging detainees in various sexually explicit positions for photographing;
Forcing detainees to remove their clothing and keeping them naked for several days at a time;
Forcing naked male detainees to wear women's underwear;
Forcing groups of male detainees to masturbate themselves while being photographed and videotaped;
Arranging naked male detainees in a pile and then jumping on them;
Positioning a naked detainee on a MRE Box, with a sandbag on his head, and attaching wires to his fingers, toes, and penis to simulate electric torture;
Writing "I am a Rapest" [sic] on the leg of a detainee alleged to have forcibly raped a 15-year-old fellow detainee, and then photographing him naked;
Placing a dog chain or strap around a naked detainee's neck and having a female Soldier pose for a picture;

A male MP [military police] guard having sex with a female detainee;

Using military working dogs [without muzzles] to intimidate and frighten detainees, and in at least one case biting and severely injuring a detainee;

Taking photographs of dead Iraqi detainees;

Breaking chemical lights and pouring the phosphoric liquid on detainees;

Threatening detainees with a charged 9mm pistol;

Pouring cold water on naked detainees;

Beating detainees with a broom handle and a chair;

Threatening male detainees with rape;

Allowing a military police guard to stitch the wound of a detainee who was injured after being slammed against the wall in his cell;

Sodomizing a detainee with a chemical light and perhaps a broom stick.[2]

Subsequently, nobody in the chain of command above the brigadier general who ran the prisons in Iraq suffered for what went on at Abu Ghraib. The administration failed to hold senior officers responsible for the actions of those under their command. Some were promoted. Those in charge when Guantanamo and Abu Ghraib occurred, from the defense secretary down, have never been held responsible, as they should have been in the opinion of the world at large.

Abu Ghraib and Guantanamo are not the only examples of un-American activities. There is a network of secret prisons and secret prisoners – even though secrecy does not sit well with democracy or with justice. Of course, secret prisons are, by their nature, secret, but there are repeated reports of al-Qaeda suspects being held in isolated prisons outside the jurisdiction of US law – too many references for them to be ignored as mere speculation. Some of them are certain: the prison at the American base at Bagram in Afghanistan, another at a base on the Island of Diego Garcia in the Indian Ocean, another in Qatar, and yet another at a special location in Iraq. Press reports in November 2005 increased the list and added prisons in Poland, Romania, and other eastern European countries. Some of the prisons are small and others very large. It is not known who is being held, but the prisoners are generally believed to be senior al-Qaeda operatives or suspects, most likely the former. How they are treated is similarly unknown. The captives are commonly referred to in the press as "ghost prisoners." The Nazis had a similar deviant system – they called it "nacht und webel" (night and fog). It was used against captured resistance fighters – they simply disappeared into the darkness, their present and future unknown to anyone. The existence of "ghost prisoners" is well reported in the

American press, but relatively few people seem to care. The average American accepts that terrorism must be defeated, and however regrettable it may be that ghost prisoners are part of what is required, their secretive treatment is seen as essential. This view is understandable – but dangerous.

Ill-treatment, humiliation, pain, sexual abuse, and subjection to extreme temperatures are treatments that have been used in various of the prisons where suspected terrorists are held. Near drowning is another and particularly revolting torture; the prisoner's head is held under water until he nearly drowns, then he is allowed to take enough breath to recover: this is water-boarding. The near drowning is repeated until the "proper" response is given. That all of these inhumane treatments have been employed is now too well established by the American press to be in question.

Deaths, too, are part of the litany. Of course, if thousands are captured, there will be deaths by accident and natural causes. But if there is a climate that accepts some level of ill-treatment in order to get valuable information or names of accomplices (as used to be the case in witch interrogations and torture), then excesses of zeal or brutality will occur. This is especially true if the soldiers or other agents involved are reasonably sure that they will be protected from severe punishment by their superiors. There are reports that over 100 prisoners have died in US custody, some no doubt of natural causes. But too many deaths are known to be criminal, and more are suspected to be. There are examples.

The *New York Times* of 16 March 2005 published an article by Douglas Jehl and Eric Schmitt revealing that army and navy internal investigations showed that as many as twenty-six prisoners had died in custody due to acts that were suspected to be criminal homicides.[3] Until this event such deaths had been largely only rumoured. There was the case of an Iraqi general who had been put headfirst into a sleeping bag that was bound with electrical wire, and then soldiers stood on him and sat on him. He died of suffocation.[4] Then in May 2005 the *New York Times* published articles that reported in detail the deaths of two prisoners at the American-run prison at Bagram, Afghanistan.[5] It reported that in December 2002, two men were taken into custody. One of them, named Dilawar, was a taxi driver who was arrested after a rocket attack on an American base. For most of the four days prior to his final interrogation, Dilawar was chained to the top of his cell by his wrists. He was repeatedly kicked at the knees in a manner known as the "common peroneal strike," which causes the legs to buckle, and was tormented in violent and inhumane ways. This twenty-two-year-old man, who weighed 122 pounds and stood 5 feet 9 inches, died in his cell unnoticed. His interrogators were pretty sure by then that he had had nothing to do with the attack – he had just been passing by when it took place. Coroners' reports showed that both Dilawar and the other dead prisoner had been mistreated and subjected to "blunt force trauma" to the legs. Although further evidence showed that they had been repeatedly struck this way while shackled, the investigators advised that they could not determine who was responsible for the injuries. Senior authorities subsequently rejected the recommendations to close the case. But real action to investigate what happened took place only in 2003 after a press report brought the case to public attention. The result was 2,000 pages of testimony and charges against those responsible. The initial reaction to suspicious deaths has been to hush them up and not to lay charges until some external source forces action to be taken. The administration's general response has been to say that these events were carried out by low-level rogue soldiers without the knowledge of senior officers.[6]

Before 9/11 practically nobody had heard the term "rendition." Today, any regular news reader or listener knows the word, associates it with American policy and practice, and is aware that it involves sending suspected terrorists to countries where they can be tortured.

The American administration has repeatedly proclaimed that it considers torture to be unacceptable. The CIA says that it requires verbal assurance from every country to which detainees are sent that they will be treated humanely. The president has confirmed that such assurances are required before prisoners are sent to these countries: "Torture is never acceptable," he has said, "nor do we hand over people to countries that do torture."[7] All the right words are spoken. Yet it is well established that detainees are sent to countries that have terrible reputations regarding torture and that torture is applied: Syria, Egypt, Pakistan, Uzbekistan, Jordan, and Saudi Arabia are only some of the destinations.

Rendition happens only to foreigners. American citizens have their own protection under the law and their own right to appeal to the courts. They should not take too much comfort from this fact. In a future crisis, the administration of the day will undoubtedly use the earlier written words of the now attorney general, Alberto Gonzales, placing a high premium on "the ability to quickly obtain information from captured terrorists and their sponsors in order to avoid further atrocities against American civilians."[8] In a crisis, there can be little doubt that the administration will seek new processes to obtain such information – and extending rendition is an obvious one.

The rendition of American citizens is a risk created by the rendition of foreigners. Two American citizens have been held by the administration as "enemy combatants." One was captured abroad and one in the United States.[9] If there is another major terrorist attack, there is little doubt that there will be more cases of American citizens being classed as "enemy combatants." If urgent interrogation is deemed necessary, rendition of American citizens could and probably will become acceptable to any administration that acts first and only later asks the legal questions – a true witch-hunt mentality.

What is important in our context is that rendition and torture are viewed as necessary steps by some honourable people whose duty it is to protect the community. But by their nature, rendition and torture have to be carried out in secrecy. Excesses will occur. Innocent people will be mistakenly accused. False accusations will sometimes be made. Increased powers will be demanded with every new crisis. And ultimately, those who are to be protected – the citizens of the nation – will come to be equally at risk. This is what a witch hunt is all about.

Kidnapping is an increasing matter of concern. The CIA is known to have a private air fleet to fly rendition prisoners throughout the world. And it is not only prisoners who are rendered. It is sometimes targeted individuals – they are abducted in foreign countries and shipped for torture. In one case, an innocent man was even arrested in the United States and shipped abroad to be tortured. One can see the arguments in favour of capturing proven terrorists, but what happens when mistakes are made and the innocent are caught instead? In the next chapter we will see exactly such a case – marked by false accusations, false arrest, secret rendition to a country that uses torture, the actual use of torture, secrecy, cover-up, and the rationale that national security prevents revealing information. There are always suggestions that if only all that was known could be revealed, guilt would be proved, but the need to ensure security prevents full disclosure. Further, there is usually a continuing fight to prevent innocence being established and a refusal to cooperate with the investigation of what went wrong. All of these elements can be seen in the case of Maher Arar, an innocent Canadian citizen. His story proves how dangerous to innocents a modern witch hunt can be.

Then there is the American response to un-American activities. The public response in the United Sates to Abu Ghraib, Guantanmo, ghost prisoners, secret prisons, kidnapping, rendition, inhumane treatment, and torture has been muted at best. It seems that America and Americans have come to accept that torture is a necessary evil in the face of terrorism. They have come to accept that excesses will occur. They are prepared to punish those immediately responsible for excesses, but they are also prepared to forgive their leaders who created the conditions that permitted excesses.

In the presidential election of 2004, Abu Ghraib and Guantanamo and the torture that had shocked the world were hardly mentioned. And the activities at these two prisons were not the only ones to be largely ignored. By the time of the American elections, readers of the newspapers knew about reports of secret prisons, of "ghost prisoners" held in such secrecy that their existence was kept secret, of "rendition," and of deaths of prisoners in American hands. All these revelations and the accompanying deviations in national behaviour seem to have been accepted as part of the price of defeating terrorism – just part of the price of exterminating the witches.

19

The Case of Maher Arar

This is the case of Maher Arar, a man who was the victim of a witch hunt.

At the age of seventeen Maher Arar emigrated from Syria to Canada, where he grew up, went to university, was married, and had children. In the meantime he had become a naturalized Canadian holding and travelling on a Canadian passport. He had graduated with a master's degree in telecommunications from McGill University in Montreal, and in 1997 he had moved to Ottawa for work. Then in 1999 he took a job with a Boston firm named The MathWorks that involved extensive travelling in the United States. In 2001 he started his own consulting company in Ottawa.

In September 2002 he went on holiday with his family to visit his wife's relatives in Tunisia. While he was there he received an e-mail from The MathWorks saying that they might need him. So, leaving his family in Tunis to complete their visit, he left for Canada, ready to work. His return journey took him via New York, where he was to change aircrafts to continue on to Ottawa. He arrived in New York at 2:00 P.M. on 26 September 2002 with a few hours to wait for his connecting flight. "This is when my nightmare began," he says. "I was pulled aside at immigration and taken to another area. Two hours later some officials came and took my fingerprints and photographs. Then some police came ... and searched my bags and copied my Canadian passport. I asked what was going on and they would not answer. I asked to make a phone call, and they would not let me."[1]

In New York, he was questioned for hours without benefit of a lawyer. The Immigration and Naturalization Service authorities did not inform the Canadian authorities of anything about this although international agreements required them to do so. He was accused of having links to al-Qaeda and questioned about contacts with different people – one individual in particular, Abdullah Almalki, of whom he says:

I told them that I worked with his brother in Ottawa, and that the Almalki family had come from Syria about the same time as mine. I told them I did not know Abdullah well but had seen him a few times ... Then they pulled a copy of my rental lease from 1997. I was completely shocked. They pointed out that Abdullah had signed the lease as a witness. I had completely forgotten that he had signed it for me. When we moved to Ottawa in 1997, we needed somebody to witness our lease, and I phoned Abdullah's brother, and he could not come so he sent Abdullah.

This part of the interrogation would later give clues about why Maher Arar was to be put through his terrible experiences. After hours of questioning, they "put me in chains, on my wrists and ankles, and took me in a van to a place where many people were being held."

During the next few days, he was clearly treated as a suspect: they did not allow him any opportunity to find a lawyer, or to contact the Canadian authorities, or to phone anybody; they just ignored his requests. Finally, after five days they allowed him to call his mother-in-law in Ottawa, and he was able to ask her to find him a lawyer. The Canadian consul finally saw him on 4 October. Arar was scared that the Americans would send him to Syria, as they had been saying that they might do, but the consul assured him that this would not happen – an assurance that proved hollow:

On Sunday night the guards started questioning me again. They said they wanted to know why I did not want to go back to Syria. I told them I would be tortured there. I told them I had not done my military service [the Syrians do not recognize a change in citizenship]. I am a Sunni Muslim; my mother's cousin had been accused of being a member of the Muslim Brotherhood and was put in prison for nine years.

At 3 a.m., 8 October, a prison guard woke me up and told me I was leaving. Based on classified information that they could not reveal to me, I would be deported to Syria.

Chained and shackled, accompanied by a new team of guards, he was taken to a small private jet. The plane landed at Amman, Jordan, at 3 A.M. "There were six or seven Jordanian men waiting for us. They blindfolded and chained me and put me in a van. They made me bend down my head in the back seat. Then these men started beating me. Every time I tried to talk they beat me."

Eventually, he was delivered to the Syrian border and handed over to Syrian authorities. "Three men came in and took me into a room. I was very very scared." If he did not answer questions quickly enough, one of the men would point to a metal chair in the corner and ask "Do you want me to use this?" Arar continues:

I did not know then what that chair was for – to torture people ... I asked him what he wanted to hear. I would say anything to avoid torture. There was no violence, only threats. About 1 a.m. the guards came to take me to my cell downstairs.

We went into the basement, and they opened a door, and I looked in. I could not believe what I saw. It was like a grave. It had no light. It was three feet wide, six deep, seven feet high. A metal door, with a small opening, did not let in light because there was a piece of metal on the outside for sliding things into the cell. There was a small opening in the ceiling, about one foot by two feet with iron bars. Over that was another ceiling, so only a little light came through this. There were cats and rats up there, and from time to time the cats peed through the opening into the cell. There were two blankets, two dishes, and two bottles, one for water and the other one for urinating during the night.

Nothing else. No light. I spent 10 months, 10 days inside that grave.

The next day the beatings started. The second and third days were the worst. I could hear other prisoners being tortured, and screaming and screaming. One tactic they use is to question prisoners for two hours, and then put them in a waiting room, so they can hear others screaming, and then bring them back to continue the interrogation.

He was beaten with two-inch-thick electrical cable mainly on his hands. "They mostly beat me with their hands, hitting me in the stomach and on the back of my neck, and slapping me on the face." They threatened him with even more severe torture, namely the metal chair, the tire, and electric shocks. "They kept beating me so I had to falsely confess and told them I did go to Afghanistan. I was ready

to confess to anything if it would stop the torture." (Shades of
Johannes Junius in Bamberg?) "They wanted me to say I went to a
training camp. I was so scared I urinated on myself twice." His first
consular visit was about two weeks after his incarceration (there were
seven in all):

I was told not to tell anything about the beating [to the consul] ... The
colonel was there, and three other Syrian officials including an interpreter. I
cried a lot at that meeting. I could not say anything about the torture ...
Other visits followed, including one from members of Parliament ... After
the visits I would bang my head and my fist on the wall in frustration. I
needed the visits but I could not say anything ...

I was not exposed to sunlight for six months. The only times I left the
grave were for interrogation and for the visits. Daily life was hell.

On Aug. 19 I was taken upstairs to see the investigator, and I was given a
piece of paper and asked to write what he dictated. If I protested, he kicked
me. I was forced to write that I went to a training camp in Afghanistan.
They made me sign and put my thumb-print on the last page.

He was taken to another prison the next day, where conditions were
somewhat better – he was only beaten once.

Around Sept. 20, I heard the other prisoners stating that another Canadian
had arrived. I saw a man, but I did not recognize him. His head was shaved,
and he was very thin, pale and very weak. When I looked closer, I recognized him: Abdullah Almalki ... He told me he had been severely tortured –
with the tire, the cable, and hanging upside down.

On 5 October 2003 Maher Arar was told that he was going back
to Canada.

I was driven to a court and put into a room with a prosecutor. He read
from my confession. I tried to argue that I was beaten and did not go to
Afghanistan but he did not listen. He told me to stamp my fingerprint and
sign on a document he would not let me see. Then he said I would
be released.

The past year has been a nightmare. I know that the only way I will ever
be able to move on in my life and have a future is if I can find out why this
happened to me.

It was Maher Arar's amazing wife who fought for his release and finally obtained it. She would not stop demanding that the Canadian
government take action to obtain her husband's release. At first she was
almost alone, but over the months public support for her efforts grew.
She had an argument that Canadians could not ignore: the Americans
should never have deported her husband to Syria because he was a Canadian citizen. Under international agreements, the Canadian authorities should have been immediately informed as soon as he was detained
in New York. If there had been anything to charge him with, he should
have been sent back to Canada for further investigation and due process under Canadian law. The actions of the American government infuriated many Canadians and gave them serious cause for concern.
Canada is a country built on immigrants and immigration. Suddenly,
anybody who visited the United States who had emigrated to Canada
might be subject to deportation to his or her country of birth – perhaps
even without any explanation being given to Canadian authorities. Ultimately, the public pressure grew, and the fact that US authorities would
release no information to Canada on the reasons for detaining and de-
porting Maher Arar gradually (and painfully) forced the Foreign Affairs
Department in Canada to try to put some pressure on Syria to release
the prisoner.

Upon his release, Maher Arar stated that he could not get on with his
life until he had been formally cleared of having any terrorist connections. While he has never been charged with any offense under either
American or Canadian law, neither has he ever been proved innocent or
proclaimed innocent. He therefore demanded a public inquiry – which
was refused by the Canadian government. (The witch-hunt mentality in
this case is evident; he had to prove his own innocence even though
charged with no crime.) A public inquiry in Canada is a formal process
that has to be instituted by the government – it requires one or more
commissioners and entails the right to subpoena witnesses. That Arar
demanded a public inquiry proved nothing about his innocence, but it
was certainly an action more likely to be pursued by an innocent man
than by a guilty one.

After Maher Arar's return to Canada and the public shock at his revelations, a number of questions began to be raised, some by him and his
lawyer and others by individuals and the press. Why did the Americans
deport him to Syria in the first place? Had United States authorities
been given information about Arar even before he was detained in New

York, and if so, what information? Had Canadian agencies, particularly the Royal Canadian Mounted Police (RCMP) or the Canadian Security Intelligence Services (CSIS), told the Americans that Canada did not want him returned after he was first detained? Did the United States authorities send him to Syria to be tortured because it was more efficient as a means of getting information – had rendition, in fact, taken place? How did the American authorities have in their hands a copy of Arar's five- or six-year-old lease signed by Mr Almalki unless it had come to them from the RCMP? Further, if the RCMP was, indeed, innocent of deliberately sending an innocent man for torture, were rogue elements within the RCMP or CSIS in league with the FBI or other agencies? Why did the Canadian Foreign Service fail to take more aggressive action with both the United States and Syria once Arar's illegal deportation had taken place? Why did consular officials tell the Canadian Foreign Minister that Arar was being well treated after hearing during their last visit with him that he had been tortured? Why had somebody leaked the fact to the press that Arar had signed a confession – was somebody in the RCMP or some other Canadian agency attempting to paint him as guilty? And how had this source gotten hold of the signed confession if not through direct contact with the Syrians or from United States authorities? These are some of the questions that were raised, and increasingly they worried the Canadian public. This worry only increased when the Americans refused to give any answers or to cooperate in finding the truth.

The Canadian government, too, was unresponsive to increasing demands for answers. It refused a public inquiry and instituted an inquiry only into the RCMP – just one of the agencies involved – and this inquiry was not public. The suspicion quickly grew that the government had too much to hide. Certainly, nobody knew for sure why Arar had come to the attention of the RCMP in the first place. But there were suspicions about this detail. The suggestion was that the RCMP were investigating a suspected al-Qaeda logistical support group in Ottawa. In the process of this investigation, they saw Arar talking to Abdullah Almalki outside in the pouring rain. Almalki was presumably the man in whom they were interested at the time. It appears that the RCMP assumed this conversation to have been held in the rain to avoid any possibility of being overheard, and they considered this action very suspicious. After Arar's return to Canada, journalists piecing snippets of information together arrived at the conclusion that the RCMP considered this contact with Almalki suspicious because the latter was suspected of selling computers that might end up in the hands of terrorists. All very hypothetical! Apparently, the RCMP thus considered Arar to be part of a chain – Arar has always claimed that his contact with Almalki was coincidental and innocent.

American authorities were virtually silent on the case. The *Washington Post* of 5 November 2003 reported that Arar was deported because he had been put on a terrorist watch list. His name appeared on the list, according to American officials, because information from "multiple international intelligence agencies" linked him to terrorist groups. This last statement and subsequent Canadian and American assertions by "officials" were to become typical in the Arar case. And unsupported accusations, such as those based on the claim that information had come from "multiple intelligence agencies," implied guilt without any evidence. By this time it was becoming evident that the Arar case was one of "extraordinary rendition"; he had been handed over to the Syrians to obtain information under torture. (In fact, months later in the press the CIA was identified to be running a small clandestine air fleet for rendition and similar secret activities, and evidence was provided that one of these aircraft had been used for Arar's journey to Jordan on his way to Syria.) By the end of 2003 the whole affair was causing severe embarrassment to the Americans in their relationship with Canadians, who were increasingly upset. Yet so far, at least, it had hardly been mentioned in the American press. Of immediate concern to the American administration was not Maher Arar but his public revelations about the rendition program. And there was cause to be concerned. The Maher Arar case would gradually lead to more and wider revelations in the American press about the "extraordinary rendition" program. By early 2004 both the American and the Canadian agencies involved were forced to recognize that the whole affair was a public-relations disaster. Maher Arar was becoming a living example of rendition and, more and more Canadians believed, a railroaded innocent.

The Canadian public was fully angered by this time. And the source of its ire was not only the United States, but also the fact that there were altogether too many unanswered questions about what part Canadian authorities had played. Had CSIS, the RCMP, or the Foreign Affairs Department acted in some way in concert with the United States and Syrian authorities during Arar's imprisonment there? There were still far too many questions and far too few answers. Maher Arar's vigorous demands for a public inquiry were met with stalling and delays as the Canadian government still dragged its feet in responding to an increasing

demand for a formal and independent public inquiry. People wanted to
know why a supposedly guilty man would be pushing for an official
public investigation. This is how things stood toward the end of January 2004. Nearly three months had passed since Mr Arar had been returned to Canada.

Then suddenly, on 21 January 2004, a totally surprising and unexpected move on the part of the RCMP kick-started action. At eight
o'clock that morning, ten RCMP officers appeared at the house of an
Ottawa resident, Juliet O'Neill, a well-known journalist and a newspaper reporter for the *Ottawa Citizen*. For five hours they carefully went
through everything in the house, all the cupboards, all the drawers.
They left with files, computer records, and materials. Outside, officers
kept the area clear, explaining that a "criminal investigation" was being
conducted. While this was going on at her home, an equivalent invasion
was taking place at her office at the *Ottawa Citizen*, and more material
and items were removed. There were subsequent statements that a defendant charged under the Security of Information Act could be subject
to up to fourteen years in prison, and the implication was that Juliet
O'Neill might be this defendant. Ms O'Neill had been reporting on the
Maher Arar case as an investigative journalist and had been passed a
secret document by a source. She had written an article based on the
information, which may have been secret but which was certainly not
earth-shattering. What did shake the public were pictures of a group of
policemen and women carrying items from O'Neill's home, juxtaposed
with the image of a stressed, upset, and much smaller journalist. This
was not good press for the RCMP.

The fury against the action in Parliament, in the press, and in the
public was extraordinary. The RCMP raid was carried out with such a
degree of overkill that it immediately raised the obvious questions
about whether this was really a reprisal raid on Juliet O'Neill in particular and on the press in Canada as a whole. It heightened all the questions that had already been raised about how much the RCMP had
really been involved in and responsible for the rendition of Maher Arar.
But worst of all, from the viewpoint of the federal police, this was seen
by the whole of the Canadian media as a totally unacceptable attack on
the freedom of the press in Canada. This was a battle that the RCMP
should never have taken on and one that they could not win. "A Black,
Black Day," thundered a headline in the *Ottawa Citizen* the next day,
above the subheading "RCMP Raid the Home and Office of a Citizen
Reporter over the Maher Arar Case and Unleash a Storm of Anger."[2]

Results were swift. On 23 January 2004 a headline in the *Citizen* read: "O'Neill Clearly No Criminal: PM; 'We Are Not a Police State,' Martin Insists; Charges Now Unlikely."[3] Paul Martin was the prime minister of Canada, and it was extraordinary that a prime minister would admit publicly that the actions taken two days earlier by the police were in effect excessive and unacceptable. The statement reflected the public shock and anger. It certainly raised the issue of freedom of the press and pretty much settled it, but it also put the Arar case in bold letters nationally and internationally. The following day, the *Citizen* headlines left no doubt that leading members of the Liberal Party (the governing party at the time) were pressing the prime minister to establish a public inquiry. It was by now seen as inevitable. Further delay was unacceptable to public, press, and Parliament. Soon, on 28 January 2004, Prime Minister Martin announced the creation of a judicial inquiry into the whole Arar case; the mandate was to include determining the roles that different government agencies like the RCMP, CSIS, and the Department of Foreign Affairs had played. An experienced and highly respected judge, Dennis O'Connor, would lead the inquiry and would have the power to require witnesses to appear and give testimony. There were plenty of questions to be answered: How did Arar's name get onto a terrorist watch list in the first place? Who put it there – the RCMP, CSIS, or somebody else – and why? When were the Canadian authorities told of Arar's detention in New York by the Americans? When did the Canadians learn that he was to be deported to Syria, and what, if anything, did they do to try to prevent it? What did the Canadian consular authorities in New York do to secure his release, particularly after they had told him that the Americans would not send him to Syria, as he had feared? And who leaked Arar's so-called "confession" under torture that he had been trained in an al-Qaeda camp? This supposed "confession" took place in Syria – how did it get back to the Americans (and presumably to the Canadians)? Who had leaked this and other unsubstantiated "facts" that had then been fed to the media without attribution to "justify" all that had been done to him?

The inquiry was met with approval, but many also wondered why it had taken so long to get there. As the months went by and 2004 passed into 2005, it became more and more evident that Mr Arar was, in fact, an innocent man. He had never been connected in any way with al-Qaeda, despite the leaked accusations against him. It gradually became apparent that the RCMP had some kind of file on him, probably from observing him talking to his friend Almalki in Ottawa in a rainstorm.

This information, perhaps a full file, was passed on to the American authorities in a normal exchange of security information about suspected terrorists and supporters. How strong the language was that implicated Arar is not known. Information like this was routinely passed between the agencies, but apparently there was normally a proviso that it would not be acted upon without specific agreement from the provider. This was not done, or something went wrong, a procedural slip-up, but we do not know and probably will never know since this was in the American sphere of action. Whatever the case, Arar's name appeared on a list of suspects that led to his being pulled out of transit in New York and then to all that followed.

There have been suggestions that the Americans had offered to send Arar to Canada but only if Canada would undertake to arrest him, charge him with a crime, find him guilty, and imprison him. If this offer was ever made, the Canadians refused on the grounds that it would be unconstitutional. So Arar was sent to Syria. It would appear that for months, the Foreign Affairs Department and the RCMP were at odds: the former, in general, wanted to take firmer action to get Arar back from Syria; the RCMP were, as far as one can see, not only adamantly opposed, but somebody, or some people, may have been telling the Americans and the Syrians that Canada did not want him back.

This all seems very vague, but the truth is that without information from the American authorities, important parts of the puzzle are missing. Moreover, it became clear that within the Canadian public services, there had been infighting within government agencies and between them during the time of Maher Arar's detention. In his evidence before the commission, the Canadian ambassador during the time that Arar was in Syrian hands claimed not to know that Syria used torture in its prisons or that Arar was being mistreated – an extraordinary claim, for it was well documented that Syria used torture. Both press and public were amazed. So there were errors, carelessness, assumptions of guilt, leaks of false information, and ultimately, insufficient action. A sorry mess!

During the life of the inquiry commission, the government always enforced a climate of secrecy. This did not help to clarify the case. In December 2004, for instance, Judge O'Connor produced a twelve-page summary of evidence heard to that date. This judge is a man of great probity, experience, and judgment. Nevertheless, the government released only a heavily edited version with long sections cut out, even including one quotation out of a newspaper article that the whole country had already seen. It is not surprising that the chief legal counsel to the commission complained that the public had commissioned a public inquiry, not a private investigation. Maher Arar, although present in theory, had been excluded from so much of the ivestigation that he still had little certainty regarding what had been said about him at the inquiry and before his arrest and by whom.

New questions are now surfacing in the middle of all the confusion. Was he, in fact, the only case involved here? His acquaintance/friend Almalki, whom he had met in the rain in Ottawa, was arrested, imprisoned, and tortured on a visit to Syria while Arar was there – Arar met him in prison. Almalki was also later released and returned to Canada. He has not spoken publicly since he returned. Two others have also made similar claims and charges about arrest and torture in Syria. They have also returned and have given evidence before the commission. According to newspaper reports, none of the three had contact with American authorities, but all claim that they were asked questions by the Syrians based on information that could have come only from Canadian authorities.

The whole truth about the travesty of justice that is the Maher Arar case may never be known. His innocence is accepted by the Canadian public and the press. Some lessons have certainly been learned that can have useful results in the future. Only the appearance of Judge O'Connor's final report will tell all that we are going to know. But certainly, this case had all the classic characteristics of a witch hunt. Arar was seen by the authorities as "different" from "other" Canadians – more easily suspected, more easily assumed guilty. The hunters accepted evidence that they wanted to believe, and they refused to believe evidence in favour of the accused. They applied torture and maintained that what was obtained could be believed. They avoided performing a review once serious questions had been raised. Their constant argument was that the truth could not be told for reasons of "national security," and connected to this was a constant implication that if only the truth *could* be revealed, all their actions would be shown to be justified.

More important, although the Maher Arar case unfolded in two countries that place great value on the freedom of the individual and the rule of law, this case met all the characteristics of a witch hunt. If it could happen to Maher Arar, it could happen to you and me – and we would have no greater protection from it all than he had.

20

The Shape of Things to Come

What's past is prologue; what to come,
  In yours and my discharge.
                William Shakespeare, *The Tempest*, I.ii

What's past is prologue! The events in America since 9/11 – all the reactions to terrorism of American government and American society – serve only as an introduction to the future. But they have set patterns that will tend to continue – if we allow them to.

And what have these patterns been?

(1) The president has created a climate of fear. Whether fear is real or contrived for political purposes is beside the point. Fear has been established in the American psyche.

(2) Fear! Hatred! Anger! and Righteousness! These are the products of the term "Axis of Evil." The perceived enemies of America are on the side of the Devil. "We" are on the side of good. They are evil – to be despised, to be hated, to be destroyed.

(3) The president has emphasized war and has created a psychosis of war. He has invoked the spectre of the "mushroom cloud," likening it to a "smoking gun." In his own mind, he is a "war president." He has promoted wartime, absolute powers.

(4) The administration has emphasized how serious the dangers are. It has created a feeling in a great civilization that the barbarians are at the gates. Danger has been used to justify the removal of rights and protections.

(5) The president has used his powers to create the category of "enemy combatants." Without definition, this term means whatever the administration wants it to mean. Anybody can be declared an "enemy combatant."

(6) Foreign "enemy combatants" have been held in specially created prisons outside the United States. They have had no appeal to the American justice system. They have been denied the protections of the Geneva Conventions and have been subjected to actions that much of the world considers to be cruel, inhumane, and degrading to the point of torture. Excesses on the part of guards have not been severely punished.

(7) "Enemy combatants" are to be subject to military tribunals, with punishment up to and including death. They have no access to American courts or to the justice system. The Military Order of 13 November 2001 states this clearly: "With respect to any individual subject to this order – military tribunals shall have exclusive jurisdiction with respect to offenses by the individual; and the individual shall not be privileged to seek any remedy or maintain any proceeding, directly or indirectly, or to have any such remedy or proceeding sought on the individual's behalf, in (i) any court of the United States, or any State thereof, (ii) any court of any foreign nation, or (iii) any international tribunal."[1]

(8) American Muslims are citizens but, in practice, are separate and unequal. Since a good Muslim cannot be distinguished from a fundamentalist, all are potentially suspect. Muslims complain of experiencing profiling and of being picked out for extra questioning and greater suspicion.

(9) "Every other word out of this administration's mouth now is 'terror' and 'terrorism.'"[2]

(10) Guantanamo.

> A dungeon horrible, on all sides round
> As one great furnace flam'd; yet from those flames
> No light, but rather darkness visible
> serv'd only to discover sights of woe,
> Regions of sorrow, doleful shades, where peace

And rest can never dwell, hope never comes
That comes to all.

John Milton, Paradise Lost, bk 1, line 60

The prisoners have been isolated since capture – without trial or access to courts. They have endured inhumane treatment by international standards. There is good evidence of torture in about one in five cases. All is cloaked in great secrecy: the prisoners names are secret, and they have no contact with families. Guantanamo is a specially created prison – similar to the specially constructed witches' prisons, the Hexen-hausen, of Bamberg and Wurzburg. Prisoners are classified and held in a way that gives them no rights.

(11) Secrecy.

And you all know security
Is mortal's chiefest enemy

William Shakespeare, Macbeth, act 3, scene 5

"National security" has hidden much of what is going on. In a nation with a powerful and free press, it is remarkable how little we actually know either about those who have been imprisoned in Guantanamo and in secret prisons overseas or about rendition.

(12) Kidnapping, rendition, secret prisons, ghost prisoners, torture, and prisoner deaths.

All hope abandon, ye who enter here.

Dante, Divine Comedy, Inferno, canto 3, line 9

The extraordinary means by which prisoners have been apprehended and their ill-treatment during incarceration have been well documented in the mainline American press. Humiliation, pain, sexual abuse, extreme temperatures, extreme noise, and near drownings are but some of the treatments that have been used in various of the prisons where suspected terrorists are held.

(13) Nobody in the senior chain of command has been punished for the excesses and illegalities at Abu Ghraib and Guantanamo. Leaders appear to be prepared to turn a blind eye to actions that skirt and perhaps

even ignore the law, whether national or international law. The terrorist "industry" is permitted freedom of action for the "common good."

(14) *Americans have shown that they are willing to sacrifice their civil liberties.* They do not really care that laws have been passed that substantially reduce individual legal protections and that centralize special powers in the executive, legal, police, and judicial authorities. There has been muted public outcry over torture, rendition, and other crimes that have taken place.

(15) *"I spy with my little eye."* The administration has authorized domestic spying without warrants or oversight. To date, this has been restricted to listening in on calls to and from other countries by persons suspected of terrorism connections. The president has claimed that he is acting within the law in doing this. If he is correct, some have argued, he could extend the spying to anybody within the Unites States who might be suspected of terrorist connections. Based on past actions, he would not have to say on whom the government was spying or on what grounds any individual had been classed as a suspect. A new terrorist attack in the United States (and everyone regards one as certain) would likely be the trigger. George Orwell's predictions in *1984* were but twenty years too early!

(16) *The draft* PATRIOT II *Act would allow American citizens to be stripped of their citizenship.* We do not hear much about the PATRIOT II Act these days, but it has already been prepared.

In early 2003 the attorney general of the United States, John Ashcroft, circulated for comment the draft of an Act titled "The Domestic Security Enhancement Act of 2003."[3] It was an eighty-seven-page document. Among its proposals:

- American citizens could be stripped of citizenship if they associate with an organization deemed unilaterally by the Justice Department to be related to terrorism. (Presumably, they could be deported, or if there was no place to which they could be sent, making deportation impossible, they could be imprisoned.)
- Any individual could be wiretapped for fifteen days if the government declared a national emergency – without a judge being involved. (The legal protections of hundreds of years will have gone by the board. Functionaries, not judges, will rule.)

- Genetic sampling and cataloguing could take place – without consent or judicial order. (Shades again of George Orwell's *1984*.)
- Federal, state, and local law enforcement officials could freely exchange highly confidential information about individuals, including credit card data and educational records. (Unrestricted exchange of information between law enforcement agencies was prohibited after the McCarthy witch hunts.)
- Both spying on neighbours and terrorism tips would be encouraged by giving businesses blanket immunity even if the tips were false and had no basis. (Secret accusations were part of a system used in the thirteenth century by the Inquisition and again in the seventeenth century by witch hunters.)
- Release of information about people detained, even if not charged, could be prohibited. (This would permit secret arrests – for the first time in American history.)[4]

These are only a few examples. This draft Act, popularly called PATRIOT II, never got very far. There was, at the time, a feeling among lawmakers that PATRIOT I had gone far enough and that the administration was asking for too much more. The administration's draft plainly did not resonate with the legislators. When PATRIOT I came up for review in 2005, PATRIOT II was simply not an issue.

But remember, PATRIOT I was a 342–page document, written, passed, and signed into law in seven weeks. It must have been drafted and ready for tabling when the events of 9/11 occurred. PATRIOT II is likewise now ready for tabling. When the next big attack happens, PATRIOT II will be on the table in twenty-four hours. Given the experience of the passage of PATRIOT I at rush speed, who can doubt that the eighty-seven page PATRIOT II will pass as quickly?

In PATRIOT II, sitting on the sidelines for the future, there are the provisions for secret accusations and for people to be arrested and held in secrecy with names or charges withheld. Any supporter of a suspect can themselves become under suspicion if the organization involved is declared, unilaterally by the Justice Department, to be a terrorist organization, even retroactively. The loss of American citizenship would be a threat that could be applied to extract confessions or to obtain accusations against others, falsely or otherwise. These are all processes typical of a witch hunt, as we have seen in past cases.

We live in dangerous times, but the threat is not as grave as during the Second World War. Nor is life as dangerous as during the Cold War, when there was the risk of atomic attack. The possibilities of a dirty bomb, a nuclear bomb within a city, and a biological attack are all real and dangerous, but they are far less dangerous than some dangers of the past.

The attacks of 9/11 were terrible. Thousands died in New York City amid frightful scenes of burning and crumbling buildings as people in the streets fled. But the physical damage done was nothing compared to the effects of the September 2005 hurricane in New Orleans. The casualties were less than a day's losses in single battles on American soil in the Civil War and less than a single day's losses during the great influenza pandemic that followed the First World War. We have to retain, or regain, a sense of proportion in the West.

In this light, look again at the sixteen items detailing the pattern of the American administration's reactions to 9/11. They are consistent with the characteristics that can lead to a witch hunt. The key elements of fear, hatred, and a despised group – an evil group that wants to destroy a Godly society – are all present. And how has this society protected itself? It has given extraordinary powers to its leaders. It has permitted the creation of special prisons, of secret prisoners, of incarceration without trial, of torture, of secrecy. The witch hunters are already in operation. But so far – and only so far – the hunt has not spread to the rest of us. In the early days of Salem, the innocent, no doubt, felt that they were safe as well.

We must not forget that witch hunting is not only an activity but a state of mind. A climate conducive to witch hunting exists today: there is excessive fear, excessive hatred, excessive centralization of power, excessive loss of individual protections, excessive secrecy. The "Axis of Evil," the "smoking gun," the "mushroom cloud," the draft of PATRIOT II, the fear of Muslims, the prison at Guantanamo, secret prisons, torture, ghost prisoners, rendition: all are consistent with the witch hunter's state of mind. But it is not too late to learn from this prologue. Not yet.

In Shakespeare's *Macbeth*, three witches gather around a cauldron, chanting as they prepare their spells: "Double, double, toil and trouble; Fire burn and caldron bubble." This is an apt quotation for us at this point: this book is about witch hunts, and the final section is about the potential for witch hunts in our own time and in our own societies. The situation is like the witches' cauldron with the fire lit beneath it. As it heats up, bubbles form on the bottom and begin to rise, causing the still waters to move within the cauldron in little swirls. As this movement becomes stronger, steam begins to appear on the water's surface, and the surrounding air begins to heat and moisten. Then the swirls become widespread motion, producing the first signs of boiling – a popping bubble of air that is quickly followed by two at once and then three until the whole surface is roiling. The full cauldron boils over. If the heat has been turned high, all this happens very quickly. If it is turned down before the water boils, the boiling is slowed down, or suspended, or never even happens. If the heat is turned off, the water slowly cools.

Today, the climate of fear, hatred, and anger, combined with the continuing interpretation of everything as terror, has heated up the water in our society cauldron. How much? The water has begun to move, there is steam, there is even a popping bubble now and then. We see the bubbles: reports of another rendition, of torture, of long-term "terrorist" prisoners released who suddenly pose no threat at all, of Muslims being picked out for special treatment at borders, of secret prisons and secret prisoners, of the Maher Arar case, of domestic spying. And we have seen society's relative unconcern about the excesses that have occurred. The water is hot but not yet at a boil. Nor is it getting hotter at the moment – nor cooler. If nothing more happens to threaten us directly, things will probably stay about where they are: hot enough to bubble here and there but not to boil. The social and cultural climate that holds our society together will not permit too many excesses to take hold. We have, in short, the potential for witch hunts but not a society that will permit them – as things stand.

But in the event of a new attack of serious proportions against the United States, everything will change.

All the provisions of PATRIOT I will come into effect. All of the sudden arrests, incarcerations, and interrogations will happen as they did after 9/11. Everybody will be suspect, but some more than others, depending on when, where, and how the attack takes place. There will be general suspicion. Anybody accused will be swept up and held – forever if deemed necessary and without trial if necessary. Everybody's lives will be open to domestic spies. Privacy will be a thing of the past. Innocence will never be assumed.

By day two or three or four – but no later, PATRIOT II will be before the House and Senate. No time will be given, or demanded, for thought or reservation. Delaying passage of the "essential" protections within the Act will be labelled an act of treason. Citizenship will disappear as a protection. Being labelled an "enemy combatant" or some equivalent will take precedence over citizenship. New prisons will be set up, some perhaps abroad. Secrecy will abound in everything that the government

does – all in the name of "national security." The agents of the government will believe that their leaders are prepared to turn a blind eye to
actions that skirt the law, perhaps even ignore the law, whether the law
be national or international. Innocent organizations will unilaterally be
declared terrorist operations on the say-so of the Justice Department
under PATRIOT II. There will be kidnapping, rendition, and torture of
selected foreign suspects.

These are not just wild imaginings: most of these things are happening now, as the last few chapters have well illustrated. And the remainder of these measures are provided for in PATRIOT II. The difference
between now and the future is one of degree, not one of kind. What is
now happening here and there that causes concern to a few will become
universal. The witch hunters will be upon us all. They will once more be
striving for the "Godly state" on our behalf.

We have seen the prologue and its effects above. We cannot change
what has transpired to date. But what is to come is "in yours and my
discharge." The prologue does not have to set the pattern for the future
if we are able to recognize that the dangers of excess can be as great as
the dangers of terrorism. We can choose to let the past control the future, or we can use the past as a means to change the future.

There are no easy ways to break with the recent past, nor can one
prescribe a simple way to avoid all that has been forecast. There are no
magic solutions, no quick resolutions. Still, there are things that can be
done to avert the worst, mainly by the legislators, and all the more
quickly if the public makes demands. PATRIOT II is the key. PATRIOT I
is well established, and nobody is going to be able to reverse its effects.
The new and present danger is PATRIOT II. We know what it looks like
in draft. The final bill that will be tabled after an attack will contain at
least the provisions laid out above. There will be no time allowed for discussion, no delays permitted. So now is the time for discussion in the
committees of the House and the Senate. There is presently time for the
legislative arm of government to let the executive know how PATRIOT II
looks to them in draft. The time for sober second thought is now, while
there is still time for any thought at all. It is ridiculous that even though
the bill has been drafted and its proposals are known, legislators should
ignore the dangers that it presents because it has not been tabled, only
to rush it through in a crisis.

There is another whole area that legislators need to address. Terrorism
on a modern scale is going to be with us for a long time. We have rules of
war, but we have no rules of terrorism. We need to step back and take a

very long-term view. So far Western governments have taken a very short-term, almost day-to-day view of how to deal with terrorists or suspected terrorists, resulting in the preconditions of witch hunts. In the absence of rules, new categories and norms have been created, such as "rendition," "enemy combatants," and "military tribunals" that are neither trials nor court martials and that have no established parameters. These norms have been created in response to questions that we have not openly asked, such as: What should we do with terrorists who are captured but are clearly not prisoners of war? How do we distinguish who should fall into each category? What do we do with somebody who is clearly a terrorist if we do not have proof? What do we do with somebody for whom we have insufficient evidence for trial but who is too dangerous to release? What legal processes need to be put in place to ensure some kind of public justice in all cases and to avoid unilateral, or arbitrary, or secret decisions on the part of government agents? What should we do with citizens who are believed to be terrorists? What should be the conditions in prisons created for terrorists or suspects? What oversight provisions should be made for prisons and prisoners. What interrogation processes should we permit? How should we treat a prisoner believed to have information about a planned attack. What level and type of interrogation and what urgent judicial procedures to authorize intensive interrogation should we permit? (We are back to the "Is Torture Ever Justified?" question.)

So far, we have acted on a "business as usual" basis. And where we cannot, we have cobbled together solutions that are dangerous to all. Instead, we must recognize that a new world is upon us. We need new rules. We need open rules and processes. And where there cannot be open processes, we need oversight and an assurance that there is justice. This applies not just to the United States, but equally to Canada, Britain, Australia, and to other countries faced with terrorism that have roots going back to Magna Carta.

The American Senate and House need to take on these issues, which are neither partisan nor political. They must recognize the need for long-term solutions to the problem of how to deal with a world that is different. They must make decisions about how to cope with terrorism without creating a witch-hunt mentality that will threaten the lives and liberties of free men and women. These are issues that need wide discussion if the legislators are to get it right. The universities, the press, the churches, and social and legal activists need to raise and talk about these issues so that the legislators and administrators are made aware of the possible and acceptable solutions.

The first hint of a new dawning occurred in early October 2005. The Senate voted to bring America's prison camps under strict control. Ninety senators voted on a measure that would make illegal "cruel, inhumane and degrading" treatment of military prisoners.[5] This was no casual act. The measure was passed against the opposition of the White House and despite a threat from the president to veto the offending bill. Nonetheless, among the ninety senators were forty-six Republicans, members of the president's own party. The bill was endorsed by other important supporters, including two former chairmen of the Joint Chiefs of Staff, one of whom was Colin Powell, who had also held the position of secretary of state under George W. Bush in his first administration. In one sense, it was a small step, for the measure did little more than enforce existing American laws and international treaties. But in another respect, it was a first solid recognition that the executive could no longer just make up its own rules for dealing with the impacts of terrorism.

This small measure is significant for what it has done, but it marks only a beginning. If actions like this are not pursued further, the next attack will bring about a world that we will not recognize – a world of witch hunts.

Notes

CHAPTER ONE

1 A first-class book that I would recommend to any reader is Robin Briggs, *Witches and Neighbours*. Another excellent source of information is Richard M. Golden, ed., *Encyclopedia of Witches and Witchcraft*.

CHAPTER TWO

1 Particularly valuable on the subject of Bamberg are R.S. Walinski-Kiehl, "'Godly States'"; and Hans Sebald, "Witches' Confessions."
   For the Junius records and the letter of the chancellor of the prince-bishop of Wurzburg, I have gratefully, and with permission, used the records of the Hanover Historical Texts Project, scanned by Mike Anderson, May 1998, proofread and pages added by Jonathan Perry, March 2001, http://www.history.hanover.edu/texts/bamberg.html and http://www.history.hanover.edu/texts/wurz.html. The written source is George L. Burr, ed., "The Witch Persecution at Bamberg."
2 Martin Del Rio, *Martin Del Rio*, ed. and trans. P.G. Maxwell-Stuart, 92–3.
3 An incubus: a demon in male form that seeks to have sexual intercourse with sleeping women; the corresponding spirit in female form is called a succubus. In medieval Europe, union with an incubus was supposed by some to result in the birth of witches, demons, and deformed offspring. The series of questions can be found in Roger Hart, *Witchcraft*, 70.

4 These interesting figures come from Walinski-Kiehl, "'Godly States,'" 19.
5 The records of the Junius interrogations, together with Junius's letter to his daughter Veronica and the chancellor's letter on Wurzburg, are on the Hanover Historical Texts Project website, http://www.history.hanover.edu/texts/bamberg.html and http://www.history.hanover.edu/texts/wurz.html.
6 "Otherwise baptized" is the usual phrase for the rite, a parody of baptism, by which the Devil was believed to initiate his followers.
7 The strappado consisted of a rope attached to the hands of the prisoner, which were bound behind his or her back. The rope was then carried over a pulley at the ceiling. The prisoner would be drawn up and left hanging. To increase the pain, weights were attached to his or her feet, or the prisoner was suddenly jerked up and let drop.

CHAPTER THREE

1 I have used as my primary source Professor Douglas O. Linder, University of Missouri, Kansas City Law School, "Famous Trials" – "The McMartin Preschool Abuse Trial," http.www.law.umkc.edu/faculty/project/ftrials/mcmartin/mcmartinaccount.html.
2 McMartin was not the only child sexual abuse case with similar public reactions; see the Cleveland case in England or the Klassen case in Canada, which are both widely covered on the Internet.

CHAPTER FOUR

1 This is only a broad outline of the Loudun case, intended to illustrate how a witch hunt developed in a particular place and at a particular time. In keeping with the broad sweep of this book, I have omitted notes. For a more detailed account and sources see my book *A Case of Witchcraft*.

CHAPTER SIX

1 The quotations from court records and contemporary Puritan ministers that I have used are widely available in books. Thanks to the University of Virginia, they are available under the title "The Salem Witchcraft Papers" at www.etext.virginia.edu/salem/witchcraft/texts. With permission, I have gratefully used the University of Virginia's website as an important source, which contains, among other documents on the Salem witchcraft trials: Paul Boyer and Stephen Nissenbaum, eds, *The Salem Witchcraft Papers*, verbatim transcripts of the legal documents of the Salem witchcraft

outbreak of 1692, with an introduction and index by the editors; Deodat Lawson, *A Brief and True Narrative* (1692); *Letter of Thomas Brattle, F.R.S.* (1692); *Letters of Governor Phips to the Home Government* (1692-93); excerpts from Cotton Mather, *The Wonders of the Invisible World* (1693); excerpts from Robert Calef, *More Wonders of the Invisible World* (1700); John Hale, *A Modest Inquiry into the Nature of Witchcraft* (1702); George Lincoln Burr, *Narratives of Witchcraft Cases* (1992).

2 There is a massive literature on Salem. For my purposes, very useful was Larry Dale Gragg, *The Salem Witch Crisis.*

3 I debated whether to translate the old text into modern English but decided that the original spellings in the records convey more of the feeling of those days in Salem.

4 I have used extracts from the petition of Mary Easty. The full document can be found on the University of Virginia website at http://etext.virginia.edu/salem/witchcraft/texts/BoySal1.html.

CHAPTER EIGHT

1 There are many books and articles on the Dreyfus case. For my purposes, I found most useful Jean Bredin, *The Affair: The Case of Alfred Dreyfus.* I would also recommend Georgetown University's extensive *Chronology of the Dreyfus Affair: May 2000 Version*, http://www.georgetown.edu/faculty/guieuj/DreyfusCase.htm.

2 Only since 11 September 2001 have Western governments made it legal to give a court secret information without the defendant or his lawyer having knowledge of the contents, the source, or even its existence.

CHAPTER NINE

1 There is in fact a continuum that ranges from simple miscarriages of justice to full witch hunts. There is no absolute borderline. There are indeed cases, a few, that might be classified as one or the other. In Canada the treatment of David Milgaard, Donald Marshall, Guy Paul Morin, and Steven Truscott might well be viewed as either extreme cases of miscarriages of justice *or* as witch hunts. I maintain that they are the latter.

CHAPTER TEN

1 Because these events took place over seventy years ago in Alabama, the court testimony that will be quoted used the term "negro." I have quoted

the testimony as given. In my own text, I have tried to use the term African American. Sometimes the context would make doing so incongruous since the term was not used at the time. Where this is the case, I have sometimes employed the term "black" or "blacks" so that I talk of white girls and black men. I employ the term without any sense of disparagement.

2 Law Professor Douglas O. Linder of the University of Missouri, Kansas City Law School, has made a mass of material available on the website "Famous American Trials," specifically "The Scottsboro Boys' Trials 1931–1937," http://www.law.umkc.edu/faculty/projects/FTrials/ scottsboro/scottsb.htm. This material includes Miss Hollace Ransdall's "Report on the Scottsboro Alabama Case"; "Biographies of Key Figures in the Scottsboro Boys' Trials"; and "The 1933 Trial before Judge Horton." With permission, I have gratefully used quotations from the trial records, from the Hollace Ransdall report, and from Justice Horton's "Decisions Overturning Patterson's Conviction," contained in the latter of the above documents.

3 As Roy Wright had been given a life sentence at the first trial because he was so young, he was not tried again.

CHAPTER TWELVE

1 Bob Woffinden, *Miscarriages of Justice* (available at http://www.innocent. org.uk/cases/guildford4/guildford4.pdf) has chapters on the Guildford Four, the Maguire Seven, and the Balcombe Street Four. In conjunction with other sources, these were very helpful. Equally valuable is Gerry Conlon, *In The Name of the Father*.

2 The story of the Maguire Seven that I have used for my primary source is *Miscarriage of Justice: An Irish Family's Story of Wrongful Conviction as IRA Terrorists*, by Anne Maguire, with Jim Gallagher, introduction by Elizabeth Shannon, foreword by Cardinal Basil Hume. This is the personal story of a remarkable woman and her family that I would recommend to anybody as a record of courage and forgiveness in the face of the terrors of a modern witch hunt. Although unfortunately out of print, it is available at http://www.innocent.org.uk/cases/maguire7/moj.pdf.

3 These words come from Cardinal Hume's foreword to Mrs Maguire's *Miscarriage of Justice*.

4 The events related to the Balcombe Street Gang are covered in both Woffinden, *Miscarriages of Justice*, and Conlon, *In The Name of the Father*. See, for example, Woffinden's record at http://www.innocent.org.uk/ cases/guildford4/guildford4.pdf.

CHAPTER FOURTEEN

1 The PATRIOT Act is available at http://fl1.findlaw.com/news.findlaw.com/cnn/docs/terrorism/hr3162.pdf.

2 Senator Russ Feingold, "Why I Opposed the Anti-Terrorism Bill," http://www.counterpunch.org/feingold1.html.

CHAPTER FIFTEEN

1 The State of the Union Address was delivered by President George W. Bush on 29 January 2002. It can be found at http://www.whitehouse.gov/news/releases/2002/01/20020129-11.html.

2 For reference to the "mushroom cloud" speech, see, for example, http://archives.cnn.com/2002/ALLPOLITICS/09/08/iraq.debate.

3 For President Bush's "mushroom cloud" speech, see, for example, http://archives.cnn.com/2002/ALLPOLITICS/10/07/bush/transcript.

4 Senator Daniel Patrick Moynihan, address to a conference marking the fortieth anniversary of the "Guiding Principles for Federal Architecture"; see *Washington Post*, 3 February 2003, A23.

5 The text of President Bush's speech can be found at http://www.whitehouse.gov/news/releases//2005/10/20051006-3.html.

6 For the text of the *Meet the Press* interview, see http://www.msnbc.msn.com/id/4179618.

7 The Congress Joint Resolution of 14 September 2001 can be found at http://www.pbs.org/newshour/bb/military/terroristattack/joint-resolution_9-14.html.

8 President Bush's landing aboard the USS *Abraham Lincoln* is well described in Internet reports of 2 May 2003; see, for instance, http://archives.cnn.com/2002/ALLPOLITICS/05/01/bush.carrier.landing.

9 The Military Order of 14 September 2001 can be found at http://www.fas.org/irp/offdocs/eo/mo-111301.htm.

10 In January 2006 this same general, Major General Goeffrey D. Miller, invoked his rights not to incriminate himself in court-martial proceedings against two soldiers accused of intimidation at Abu Ghraib. This was an action under military law similar to taking the Fifth Amendment; see Josh White, "General Asserts Right on Self-Incrimination in Iraq Abuse Cases," *Washington Post*, 12 January 2006.

11 But the administration did not suffer this defeat for long. The right of American "enemy combatants" to be tried in American courts was later taken away from the prisoners by Congress; see, for instance, Eric

Schmitt, "Senate Approves Limiting Rights of U.S. Detainees," *New York Times*, 11 November 2005.

12 For more detailed information on domestic spying, see newspaper articles in the Bibliography and James Risen, *State of War.*

13 See, for instance, Dan Eggen, "Gonzales Defends Surveillance: Senators from Both Parties Challenge Attorney General on Program," *Washington Post*, 7 February 2006.

14 See, for example, Jim VandeHei, "Cheney Says NSA Spying Should Be an Election Issue," *Washington Post*, 10 February 2006.

CHAPTER SIXTEEN

1 Inspector General Fine's report can be found at http://www.usdoj.gov/oig/special/0306/chapter10.htm.

2 See Rachel L. Swarns, "More than 13,000 May Face Deportation," *New York Times*, 7 June 2003.

3 For full coverage of Muslim concerns regarding the Canadian Public Safety Act (2002), see *Submission of the Coalition of Muslim Organizations*, presented to the Legislative Committee on Bill C-17, 27 February 2003, at http://www.muslimlaw.org/como.c17.final.pdf.

CHAPTER SEVENTEEN

1 There is a section on Guantanamo Bay in the Bibliography listing a selection of newspaper reports in order of their publication dates. Reading the titles alone gives a sense of the development of facts and opinion about Guantanamo. The reports themselves, of course, convey the history in detail.

2 The treaty can be found under US Treaty series No. 426.

3 On Guantanamo's connection with Abu Ghraib, see Seymour M. Hersh, *Chain of Command.*

4 See Maureen Dowd, "Torture Chicks Gone Wild," *New York Times*, 30 January 2005.

5 See http://www.tomjoad.org/bybeeintro.htm.

6 See, for example, "Clinton Urges Guantanamo Closure," http://news.bbc.co.uk/2/hi/americas/4110388.stm; and "Guantanamo a Disgrace Says Carter," http.www.cbc.ca/story/world/national/2005/07/31/carter050731.html?print.

7 See Tom Brune, "Battle of Guantanamo," *Newsday.com*, 16 June 2005.

8 See Ann McFeatters, "Cheney again Defending Guantanamo," *Post Gazette.com*, Pittsburgh, 14 June 2005.

9 See Josh White and Robin Wright, "3 Nations Discuss Shift of Guantanamo Inmates," *Washington Post*, 5 August 2005.

10 For an excellent ninety-minute television documentary on Guantanamo, Abu Ghraib, and torture, see the PBS documentary program *Frontline*, 18 October 2005, "The Torture Question: In Fighting the War on Terror, How Far Should the United States Be Willing to Go to Protect Itself?" written, produced, and directed by Michael Kirk.

CHAPTER EIGHTEEN

1 "Is Torture Ever Justified?" *Economist*, 9 January 2003.

2 Major General Taguba's report on his findings at Abu Ghraib is widely covered on the Internet.

3 Douglas Jehl and Eric Schmitt, "U.S. Military Says 26 Inmate Deaths May Be Homicide." *New York Times*, 16 March 2005.

4 The American soldier in charge, who was originally charged with murder, was convicted of negligent homicide and as punishment received a reprimand from a military jury.

5 See Tim Golden, "In U.S. Report, Brutal Details of 2 Afghan Inmates' Deaths," *New York Times*, 20 May 2005; and Tim Golden, "Abuse Inquiry Bogged Down in Afghanistan," *New York Times*, 22 May 2005.

6 The sorry pursuit of this case is well covered in Tim Golden, "Years after 2 Afghans Died, Abuse Case Falters," *New York Times*, 13 February 2006.

7 See Edward J. Markey, "US Must Stop 'Outsourcing' Torture," *Boston Globe*, 12 March 2005.

8 White House Counsel Gonzales, in a memorandum to the president, 25 January 2002; see Neil A. Lewis, "Justice Memos Explained How to Skip Prisoner Rights," *New York Times*, 21 May 2004.

9 These are the "Padilla" and the "Hamdi" cases.

CHAPTER NINETEEN

1 All quotations by Maher Arar are from the article "I Am Not a Terrorist," *Globe and Mail*, 5 November 2003, A9. This article consists of excerpts from a prepared statement that Maher Arar delivered on 4 November 2003 in Ottawa upon his return from captivity, available at http://www.cbc.ca/news/background/arar/arar_statement.html.

2 Editorial, "A Black, Black Day," *Ottawa Citizen*, 22 January 2004.

3 Mark Kennedy, Mike Blanchfield, and Anne Dawson "O'Neill Clearly No Criminal: 'We Are Not a Police State,' Martin Insists; Charges Now Unlikely," *Ottawa Citizen*, 23 January 2004.

CHAPTER TWENTY

1 The Military Order of 13 November 2001 can be found at http://www.whitehouse.gov/news/releases/2001/11/20011113-27.html.

2 See http://www.theworldaroundyou.com/2003/10/16.

3 The Domestic Security Enhancement Act of 2003 (the draft Act commonly known as PATRIOT II) can be found at multiple websites, including http://www.ratical.org/ratville/CAH/PA2draft.html.

4 For press articles on PATRIOT II, see Rajeev Goyle, "Patriot Act Sequel Worse than Original," *Baltimore Sun*, 21 February 2003; David Cole, "Patriot Act's Big Brother," *The Nation*, 27 February 2003; Matt Welch, "Tell Us How We're Doing: Get Ready for PATRIOT II," *AlterNet*, 2 April 2003; and Eric Lichtblau, "Ashcroft Seeks More Power to Pursue Terror Suspects," *New York Times*, 6 June 2003. For a comprehensive analysis of the Act, see American Civil Liberties Union, "Interested Persons Memo: Section-by-Section Analysis of Justice Department Draft 'Domestic Security Enhancement Act of 2003,' Also Known as 'PATRIOT Act II,'" 14 February 2003, particularly the first few pages, which summarize the analysis.

5 "Binding the Hands of the Torturers," *New York Times*, 8 October 2005. Ninety senators voted to bring America's chain of military prison camps under the rule of law.

Bibliography

GENERAL

Ankarloo, Bengt, and Gustav Henningsen, eds. *European Witchcraft: Centres and Peripheries.* Oxford: Clarendon, 1989.

Barry, J., M. Hester, and C. Jones, eds. *Witchcraft in Early Modern Europe.* Cambridge, UK: Cambridge University Press, 1996.

Brémond, Henri. *Histoire littéraire du sentiment religieux en France, depuis la fin des guerres de religion jusqu'à nos jours.* Vol. 5. Paris: A. Colin, 1967.

Briggs, Robin. *Witches and Neighbours.* London: Harper Collins, 1996.

Clark, Stuart. *Thinking with Demons: The Idea of Witchcraft in Early Modern Europe.* Oxford: Oxford University Press, 1997.

Delumeau, Jean. *La Peur en Occident, XIV-XVIII siècles.* Paris: Fayard, 1978.

Evans, Martha Noel. *Fits and Starts: A Genealogy of Hysteria in Modern France.* Ithaca, NY: Cornell University Press, 1991.

Golden, Richard M., ed. *Encyclopedia of Witches and Witchcraft: The Western Tradition.* 4 vols. Santa Barbara, Denver, and Oxford, UK: ABC-CLIO, 2006.

Klaits, Joseph. *Servants of Satan: The Age of the Witch Hunts.* Bloomington, IN: Indiana University Press, 1985.

Levack, Brian, ed. *Articles on Witchcraft, Magic and Demonology.* 12 vols. New York: Garland, 1992.

– *New Perspectives on Witchcraft, Magic and Demonology.* 6 vols. New York and London: Routledge, 2001.

– *The Witchhunt in Early Modern Europe*. London and New York: Longman, 1995.

Linder, Douglas O. "The McMartin Preschool Abuse Trial, 1987–90: A Commentary." University of Missouri, Kansas City School of Law, 2003. http.www.law.umkc.edu/faculty/project/ftrials/mcmartin/mcmartin.html.

Mandrou, Robert. *Magistrats et Sorciers en France au XVIIᵉ Siècle: Une Analyse de Psychologie Historique*. Paris: Plon, 1968.

Michelet, Jules. *La Sorcière Paris*. 1862. Reprint, revised and with a preface by Paul Viallaneix, Paris: Garnier/Flammarion, 1866.

– *Satanism and Witchcraft*. Translation of *La Sorcière Paris* by A.R. Allinson. New York: Citadel, 1939.

Midelfort H.C. *Witch Hunting in Southwestern Germany, 1562–1684*. Stanford, CA: Stanford University Press, 1972.

Monter E.W. *European Witchcraft*. New York: A. Wiley, 1969.

Muchembled, Robert. *Magie et Sorcellerie en Europe*. Paris: A. Colin, 1994.

Purkiss, Diane. *The Witch in History*. London: Routledge, 1997.

Quaife, G.P. *Godly Zeal and Furious Rage: The Witch in Early Modern Europe*. London: Croom Helm, 1987.

Roper, Lyndal. *Oedipus and the Devil: Witchcraft, Sexuality and Religion in Early Modern Europe*. London: Routledge, 1994.

Thomas, Keith. *Religion and the Decline of Magic*. Markham, ON: Harmondsworth, 1978.

BAMBERG AND WURZBURG

Burr, George L., ed. "The Witch Persecution at Bamberg." In *Translations and Reprints from the Original Sources of European History*, vol. 3, no. 4, 23-8. Philadelphia: University of Pennsylvania History Department, 1898-1912. On-line through the Hanover Historical Texts Project, http://history.hanover.edu/texts/bamberg.html.

Del Rio, Martin. *Martin Del Rio: Investigations into Magic*. Edited translation of *Disquisitiones Magicae* (1608) by P.G. Maxwell-Stuart. Manchester: Manchester University Press, 2000.

Gibbons, Jenny. "Recent Developments in the Study of the Great European Witch Hunt." *The Pomegranate*, no. 5 (1998): http://www.cog.org/witch_hunt.html.

Hart, Roger. *Witchcraft*. London: Wayland; New York: G.R. Putnam and Sons, 1973.

Kors, Alan, and Edward Peters. *Witchcraft in Europe: The Persecutions at Bamberg*. Philadelphia: University of Pennsylvania Press, 1972.

Maple, Eric. "Bamberg Witches." In *Man, Myth and Magic,* vol. 1, 227–8. New York: Marshall Cavendish, 1983.

McDougall, William. *Psychology: The Study of Behaviour.* London: Williams and Norgate, 1912.

Midelfort. *Witch Hunting in Southwestern Germany, 1562–1684: The Social and Intellectual Foundations.* Stanford, CA: Stanford University Press, 1972.

Sebald, Hans. "Witches' Confessions: Stereotypical Structure and Local Colour – The Case of the Prince Bishopric of Bamberg." *Southern Humanities Review* 24 (1990): 301–19.

Walinski-Kiehl, R.S. "Devil's Children: Child Witch-Trials in Early Modern Germany." *Continuity and Change* 11 (1996): 171–89.

– "'Godly States': Confessional Conflict and Witch Hunting in Early Modern Germany." *Mentalities-Mentalités* 5, no. 2 (1988): 13–24.

– "La chasse aux sorcières et le Sabbat dans les évechés de Bamberg et Wurzburg." In *Le Sabbat des Sorciers,* 213–25. Grenoble: Jérome Millon, 1993.

– "Males, 'Masculine Honor' and Witch Hunting in Seventeenth Century Germany." *Men and Masculinities* 6, no. 3 (January 2004): 254–71.

– "Prosecuting Witches in Early Modern Germany, with Special Reference to the Bishopric of Bamberg, 1595–1690." Master's thesis, Portsmouth Polytechnic, 1981.

THE DEVIL IN AIX AND LOUDUN

Aix

Archives Départmentales Bouches-du-Rhone, 83 H 1 (Aix records) and 86 H 1 (Marseille records).

de Feller, Francois Xavier. *Biographie universelle ou Dictionnaire historique.* Lille: Lefort, 1838–39.

de Pommereau, Marie-Augustine. *Chroniques de l'ordre des Ursulines, recueillies pour l'usage des religieuses du mesme ordre.* Paris: N.p., 1673.

Lorédan, Jean. *Un grand procès de sorcellerie au XVIIᵉ siècle, l'abbé Gaufridy et Madeleine de Demandolx, 1608–1670.* Paris: Perrin, 1912.

Mandrou, Robert. *Magistrats et Sorciers en France au XVIIᵉ Siècle: Une Analyse de Psychologie Historique.* Paris: Plon, 1968.

Michaelis, Sebastien O.P. *Histoire admirable de la possession et conversion d'une pénitente, séduite par un magicien la faisant sorcière et princesse des sorciers au pays de Provence.* Paris: Ch. Chastellain, 1613.

Michaud, J.-F., and L.G. Michaud, eds. *Biographie universelle ancienne et moderne*. Paris: Michaud, 1811–62.

Michelet, Jules. *La Sorcière Paris*. 1862. Reprint, revised and with a preface by Paul Viallaneix, Paris: Garnier/Flammarion, 1866.

– *Satanism and Witchcraft*. Translation of *La Sorcière Paris* by A.R. Allinson. New York: Citadel, 1939.

Sarre, Claude-Alain. *Un procès de sorcière*. Le Grand Pin: N.p., 1999.

– *Vivre sa Soumission*. Paris: Publisud, 1997.

Loudun

Aubin, Nicolas. *Histoire des diables de Loudun*. Amsterdam: Abraham Wolfgang, 1693.

Bibliothèque Mazarine, 1209 (collection of spiritual letters of Mère Jeanne des Anges).

Bibliothèque Municipale Tours, Ms. 1197: Jeanne des Anges, Autobiography.

– Ms. 1134: Collected Manuscripts.

Bibliothèque Municipale Poitiers, A2 Ms 303.

Bibliothèque Nationale, 6764 (records of proceedings from 1635).

– 7618–7619 (original records, 1630–38).

– 12017, 14596, 18695, 19869, 24163, 25253, 12047 (original records, 1632–37).

– 17368, 17370–17373 (writings of Laubardemont on the trial at Loudun and interrogations of the nuns).

Bleau, Alphonse. *Précis d'histoire sur la ville et les possédées de Loudun*. Poitiers: H. Oudin frères, 1877.

Brémond, Henri. *Histoire littéraire du sentiment religieux en France, depuis la fin des guerres de religion jusqu'a nos jours*. Vol. 5. Paris: A. Colin, 1967.

Carmona, Michel. *Les Diables de Loudun: Sorcellerie et Politique sous Richelieu*. Paris: Fayard, 1988.

de Certau, Michel. *La Possession de Loudun*. Paris: Archives Gallimard/Julliard, 1970.

de La Menardaye, Abbé Jean-Baptiste. *Examen et Discussion critique de l'Histoire des diables de Loudun, de la possession des religieuses ursulines, et de la condemnation d'Urbain Grandier*. Paris: Debure l'aînè, 1747.

Figuier, Louis. *Histoire du merveilleux dans les temps modernes: Les diables de Loudun*. 2nd ed. Vol. 1. Paris: L. Hachette, 1881.

Grandier, Urbain. "Factum pour Maistre Urbain Grandier." In Bibliothèque Nationale, fonds français, 24163. Also in F. Danjou, *Archives Curieuses de l'Histoire de la France*, series 2, vol. 5, 225–57. Paris: Beauvais, 1838.

Huxley, Aldous. *The Devils of Loudun*. London: Chatto and Windus, 1952.

Legué, Gabriel. *Urbain Grandier et les possédées de Loudun*. Paris: Baschet, 1880.

– and Gilles de la Tourette. *Soeur Jeanne des Anges, supérieure des Ursulines de Loudon (XVIIᵉ siècle): Autobiographie d'une hystérique possédée*. N.p.: Éditions Millon, 1985.

Leriche, Pierre Ambroise. *Etudes sur les possésions en général et sur celle de Loudun en particulier*. Paris: N.p., 1859.

Rapley, Robert. *A Case of Witchcraft: The Trial of Urbain Grandier*. Montreal and Kingston: McGill-Queen's University Press, 1998.

– "Loudun Nuns." In Richard M. Golden, *Encyclopedia of Witches and Witchcraft: The Western Tradition*, vol. 3, 669–72. Santa Barbara, Denver, and Oxford, UK: ABC-CLIO, 2006.

Tranquille, Fr. "Véritable relation des justes procédures observées au fait de la possession des Ursulines de Loudun, et au procès de Grandier." Poitiers: Thoreau et Veuve A. Mesnier, 1634. Reprinted in F. Danjou, *Archives Curieuses de l'Histoire de France*, series 2, vol. 5. Paris: Beauvais, 1838.

Villeneuve, Roland. *La Mystérieuse Affaire Grandier: Le Diable à Loudun*. Paris: Payot, 1980.

THE WITCHES OF SALEM

Books

Booth, Sally Smith. *The Witches of Early America*. New York: Hastings House, 1975.

Boyer, Paul, and Stephen Nissenbaum. *Salem Possessed: The Social Origins of Witchcraft*. Cambridge, MA, Harvard University Press, 1974.

– and Stephen Nissenbaum, eds. *Salem-Village Witchcraft: A Documentary Record of Local Conflict in Colonial New England*. Belmont, CA: Wadsworth, 1972.

– and Stephen Nissenbaum, eds. *The Salem Witchcraft Papers*. 3 vols. New York: De Capo, 1977.

Burr, George Lincoln. *Narratives of the Witchcraft Cases, 1648-1706*. New York: Notable Trials Library, 1992.

Demos, John. "New Directions." In Marc Mappen, ed., *Witches and Historians: Interpretations of Salem*, 399–432. Huntington, NY: R.E. Krieger, 1980.

Franklin, Burt. *Records of Salem Witchcraft* (copied from the original documents). 2 vols. Burt Franklin Research and Source Works Series. New York: B. Franklin, 1972.

Gragg, Larry Dale. *The Salem Witch Crisis*. New York: Praeger, 1992.

Hale, John. "A Modest Enquiry into the Nature of Witchcraft" (1702). In George L. Burr, *Narratives of the Witchcraft Cases, 1648-1706*, 399–432. New York: Notable Trials Library, 1992.

Hall, David D., ed. *Witch Hunting in Seventeenth Century New England: A Documentary History, 1638–1693*. Boston: Northeastern University Press, 1999.

Hansen, Chadwick. *Witchcraft at Salem*. New York: Braziller, 1969.

Hoffer, Peter Charles. *The Salem Witchcraft Cases: A Legal History*. Kansas: University Press of Kansas, 1997.

LeBeau, Bryan. *The Story of the Salem Witch Trials*. Upper Saddle River, NJ: Prentice Hall, 1997.

Levack, Brian P., ed. *Articles on Witchcraft, Magic and Demonology*. 12 vols. New York: Garland, 1992.

– ed. *Witchcraft in Colonial America*. New York: Garland, 1972.

Mappen, Marc, ed. *Witches and Historians: Interpretations of Salem*. Huntington, NY: R.E. Krieger, 1980.

Mather, Cotton. *Memorable Providences Relating to Witchcraft and Possessions*. Boston: Andrew Anderson, 1697.

– *The Wonders of the Invisible World*. Boston: John Dutton, 1693.

Norton, Mary Beth. *In the Devil's Snare: The Salem Witchcraft Crisis of 1692*. New York: Knopf, 2002.

Reis, Elizabeth. *Damned Women: Sinners and Witches in Puritan New England*. Ithaca, NY, and London: Cornell University Press, 1997.

– *Spellbound: Women and Witchcraft in America*. Wilmington, DE: Scholarly Resources, 1998.

Starkey, Marion Lena. *The Devil in Massachusetts: A Modern Inquiry into the Salem Witch Trials*. New York: Knopf, 1950.

Upham, Charles W. *Salem Witchcraft, with an Account of Salem Village and a History of Opinions on Witchcraft and Kindred Subjects*. 2 vols. 1867. Reprint, New York: Frederick Ungar, 1978.

Weisman, Richard. *Witchcraft, Magic, and Religion in 17th Century Massachusetts*. Amherst: University of Massachusetts Press, 1984.

Theatre

Miller, Arthur. *The Crucible*. 1953.

Video

Discovery Channel. *The Salem Witchcraft Trials*. 50 minutes. 1997.

New World Video. *The Witches of Salem: The Horror and the Hope*. 35 minutes. 1972.

Internet

Karson, Anastasia. *Revenge in the Salem Witchcraft Hysteria: The Putnam Family and George Burroughs.* http://www.loyno.edu/history/journal/1998-9/KARSON.htm.

Linder, Douglas O. *An Account of Events in Salem.* http://www.law.ukmc.edu/faculty/projects/ftrials/salem/salem/htm.

– "Salem Witchcraft Trials" (collection of records and commentary). http://www.law.ukmc.edu/faculty/projects/ftrials/salem/salem/htm.

University of Virginia Library. http://etext.lib.virginia.edu/salem/witchcraft/texts; and http://etext.lib.virginia.edu/salem/witchcraft/index.html. Full text of court records and other documents relating to the Salem witchcraft trials, including:

– Boyer, Paul, and Stephen Nissenbaum, eds. *The Salem Witchcraft Papers* (verbatim transcripts of the legal documents of the Salem witchcraft outbreak of 1692).

– Burr, George Lincoln. *Narratives of the Witchcraft Cases, 1648-1706.* 1992.

– Calef, Robert. *More Wonders of the Invisible World.* Excerpts. 1700.

– Hale, John. *A Modest Inquiry into the Nature of Witchcraft.* 1702.

– Lawson, Deodat. *A Brief and True Narrative.* 1692.

– *Letter of Thomas Brattle, F.R.S.* 1692.

– *Letters of Governor Phips to the Home Government.* 1692-93.

– Mather, Cotton. *The Wonders of the Invisible World.* Excerpts. 1693.

THE DREYFUS AFFAIR

Books

Boussel, Patrice. *L'Affaire Dreyfus et la Presse.* Paris: A. Colin, 1960.

Bredin, Jean. *L'Affaire.* Paris: Julliard, 1983.

– *The Affair: The Case of Alfred Dreyfus.* Trans. Jeffrey Mehlman. New York: George Braziller, 1986.

Burns, Michael. *France and the Dreyfus Affair: A Documentary History.* New York: Bedford/St Martin's, 1999.

Busi, Frederick. *The Pope of Anti-Semitism: The Career and Legacy of Edouard Adolphe Drumont.* Lanham: University Press of America, 1986.

Delmaire, Danielle. *Antisémitisme et Catholiques dans le Nord pendant L'Affaire Dreyfus.* Lille: Villeneuve d'Ascq and Presses Universitaire de Lille, 1991.

Derfler, Leslie, ed. *The Dreyfus Affair, Tragedy of Errors?* Boston: Heath, 1963. Contains excerpts from:

– Arendt, Hannah. *The Origins of Totalitarianism*. 1951.
– Bainville, Jacques. *La Troisième République*. 1935.
– Chapman, Guy. *The Dreyfus Case*. 1955.
– Chastenet, Jacques. *Histoire de la Troisième République*. 1955.
– Dutrait-Crozon, Henri. *Précis de l'Affaire Dreyfus*. 1924.
– Goguel, François. *La Politique des Partis sous la IIIe République*. 1946.
– Halasz, Nicholas. *Captain Dreyfus: The Story of a Mass Hysteria*. 1955.
– Kayser, Jacques. *The Dreyfus Affair*. 1931.
– Reinach, Joseph. *Histoire de l'Affaire Dreyfus*. 1901.
– Soltau, Roger. *French Political Thought in the Nineteenth Century*. 1931.
– Thomas, Marcel. *L'Affaire sans Dreyfus*. 1961.
– Zévaès, Alexandre. *L'Affaire Dreyfus*. 1931.
Dreyfus, Alfred. *Five Years of My Life*. Freeport, NY: Books for Libraries Press, 1971.
– and Pierre Dreyfus. *The Dreyfus Case*. Trans. and ed. Donald C. McKay. New York: H. Fertig, 1977.
Johnson, Douglas. *France and the Dreyfus Affair*. London: Blandford: 1966.
Lewis, David L. *Prisoners of Honor: The Dreyfus Affair*. New York: Morrow, 1973.
Manevy, Raymond. *La Presse de la IIIe République*. Paris: J. Foret: 1955.
Zola, Émile. *J'Accuse! La Verité en Marche*. Translated with an introduction by Mark K. Jensen. Soquel, CA: Bay Side Press, 1992.

Internet Sources

Captain Dreyfus and Mr. Zola. http://www.metropoleparis.com/1998/302/zola302.html.
Chronology of the Dreyfus Affair. http://www.georgetown.edu/faculty/guieuj/chronology.htm.
Collection de Petit Journal sur les Affaires Dreyfus et Zola: Degradation d'Alfred Dreyfus. http://www.pro.wanadoo.fr/images.collection/petit_journal.htm.
Dreyfusgate. http://www.jajz_ed.org.il/antisemitism/Dreyfus.

THE SCOTTSBORO BOYS

Books

Carter, Dan T. *Scottsboro: A Tragedy of the American South*. London: Oxford University Press, 1971.

Chalmers, Allan Knight. *They Shall Be Free*. Garden City, NY: Doubleday, 1951.

Goodman, James. *Stories of Scottsboro*. New York: Pantheon Books, 1994.

Hays, Arthur Garfield. *Trial by Prejudice*. New York: Covici, 1933.

Norris, Clarence, and Sybil Washington. *The Last of the Scottsboro Boys: An Autobiography*. New York: Putnam, 1979.

Manuscript Collections

Papers of the American Civil Liberties Union. Seeley Mudd Library, Princeton University.

Scottsboro Cases Legal Document Collection. 10 vols. Cornell University Law Library.

Internet Sources

Biographies of the Scottsboro Boys. http://www.law.umkc.edu/faculty/projects/FTrials/Scottsboro/SB_bPATT.html and http://www.law.umkc.edu/faculty/projects/FTrials/Scottsboro/SB_bSBs.html.

Linder, Douglas O. *The Trials of the Scottsboro Boys*. http://www.law.umkc.edu/faculty/projects/FTrials/scottsboro/SB_acct.html.

– *Without Fear or Favor: Judge James Edwin Horton and the Trial of the Scottsboro Boys*. http://www.law.umkc.edu/faculty/projects/FTrials/trialheroes/essayhorton.html.

Picture of a model of the train where the alleged attacks took place. http://www.law.umkc.edu/faculty/projects/FTrials/Scottsboro/SB_TRRA.jpg.

Ransdall, Hollace. *Report on the Scottsboro, Ala. Case, Made by Miss Hollace Ransdall representing the American Civil Liberties Union. May 27, 1931*. http//www.law.umkc.edu/faculty/projects/ftrials/scottsboro/SB_HRrep. html.

Testimony of Haywood Patterson. Excerpts. http://www.law.umkc.edu/faculty/projects/FTrials/scottsboro/Pattersontestimony.html.

Testimony of Lester Carter. http://www.law.umkc.edu/faculty/projects/FTrials/scottsboro/Cartertestimony.html.

Testimony of Victoria Price. http://www.law.umkc.edu/faculty/projects/FTrials/scottsboro/Pricetestimony.html.

Documentaries

Court TV. *The Scottsboro Boys*. http://www.courttv.com/greatesttrials/scottsboro/index.html.

PBS. *Scottsboro: An American Tragedy.* http://www.pbs.org/amex/scottsboro.

The Scottsboro Boys: A Civil Rights Legacy. http://home.early.com/~amistad/ scotts.htm.

THE GUILDFORD FOUR AND THE MAGUIRE SEVEN

Books

Conlon, Gerry. *In the Name of the Father.* New York: Penguin Books, 1993.

Kee, Robert. *Trial and Error.* London: H. Hamilton, 1986.

Maguire, Anne, with Jim Gallagher. *Miscarriage of Justice: An Irish Family's Story of Wrongful Conviction as IRA Terrorists.* Niwot, CO: Roberts Rinehart, 1994. http://www.innocent.org.uk/cases/maguire7/moj.pdf.

May, John, Rt. Hon. Sir. *Report on the Guildford Four and the Maguire Seven.* London: HMSO, 12 July 1990.

Victory, Patrick. *Justice and Truth: The Guildford Four and the Maguire Seven.* London: Sinclair Stevenson, 2001.

Walker, Clive, and Keir Starmer, ed. *Miscarriages of Justice.* London: Blackstone Press, 1999.

Woffinden, Bob. *Miscarriages of Justice.* London: Hodder and Stoughton, 1987.

– *Miscarriages of Justice: The Guildford and Woolwich Pub-Bomb Case.* http://www.innocent.org.uk/cases/guildford4/index.html.

– *Miscarriages of Justice: The Maguire Family.* http://www.innocent.org.uk/cases/Maguire7/index.html.

Film

Sheridan, Jim, director. *In the Name of the Father.* 1991.

AMERICA AFTER 9/11

The PATRIOT Act

Babington, Charles. "Congress Votes to Renew Patriot Act, With Changes." *Washington Post,* 8 March 2006.

– "Patriot Act Compromise Clears Way for Senate Vote." *Washington Post,* 10 February 2006.

Bronner, Ethan. *New York Times Book Review,* 22 February 2004, eight reviews:

– "Casualty of War: The Bush Adminstration's Assault on a Free Press."

- "Enemy Aliens: Double Standards and Constitutional Freedoms in the War on Terrorism."
- "Lost Liberties: Ashcroft and the Assault on Personal Freedom."
- "The Naked Crowd: Reclaiming Security and Freedom in an Anxious Age."
- "The Soft Cage: Surveillance in America from Slavery to the War on Terror."
- "Terrorism, Freedom and Security: Winning without War."
- "The War on the Bill of Rights and the Gathering Resistance."
- "The War on Our Freedoms: Civil Liberties in an Age of Terrorism."

Feingold, Russ, Senator. "Why I Opposed the Anti-Terrorism Bill." Delivered on the Senate floor, 25 October 2001. http://www.counterpunch.org/feingold1.html.

- and John Sununu. "Deadline for the Patriot Act." *Boston Globe*, 9 November 2005.

Lazarus, Edward. "The Bush Administration and Secrecy: Limiting What We Can Know about the Government, while Expanding What It Can Know about Us." *Findlaw's Legal Commentary*, 27 November 2001.

Lichtblau, Eric. "Congress Nears Deal to Renew Antiterror Law." *New York Times*, 17 November 2005. [Lichtblau characterizes this deal as "a surprising victory for the Bush administration," noting that it "maintains government powers with only minor changes."]

Stout, David. "Supporters of Patriot Act Suffer a Stinging Defeat in Senate." *New York Times*, 16 December 2005.

Uniting and Strengthening America by Providing Appropriate Tools Required to Intercept and Obstruct Terrorism (PATRIOT) Act of 2001. http://www.epic.org/privacy/terrorism/hr3162.html.

Weisman, Jonathan. "Congress Arrives at Deal on Patriot Act." *Washington Post*, 17 November 2005. [Weisman notes that "the administration largely got what it wanted ... on balance the compromise sides with a stronger government hand."]

THE PRESIDENT

Authorization of the Use of Military Force. Joint Resolution of the US Congress, 18 September 2001. http://news.findlaw.com/wp/docs/terrorism/sjres23.es.html.

President Issues Military Order Detention, Treatment, and Trial of Certain Non-Citizens in the War Against Terrorism. White House, Office of the Press Secretary, 13 November 2001. http://www.whitehouse.gov/news/releases/2001/11/20011113-27.html.

Risen, James. *State of War: The Secret History of the CIA and the Bush Administration.* New York: Free Press, 2006.

Articles

20 June 2002. Tom Jackman and Dan Eggen, "'Combatants' Lack Rights, U.S. Argues." *Washington Post.*

23 December 2003. Kenneth Roth, "The Law of War in the War on Terror." *New York Times.*

18 April 2004. Linda Greenhouse, "Detention Cases before Supreme Court Will Test Limits of Presidential Power." *New York Times.*

17 October 2004. Neil A. Lewis, "Broad Use of Harsh Tactics at Base in Cuba." *New York Times.*

18 October 2004. "The Choice on Liberty." *Washington Post.*

24 October 2004. Tim Golden, "After Terror: A Secret Rewriting of Military Law." *New York Times.*

4 February 2005. "The Senate and Mr. Gonzales." Editorial. *New York Times.*

29 April 2005. Bob Herbert, "The Big Shots Walk Free." *International Herald Tribune.*

27 July 2005. Eric Lichtblau, "Justice Nominee Is Questioned on Departmental Torture Policy." *New York Times.*

7 October 2005. Paul Koring "Threat to the West: Bush Likens Islamic Radicals to Hitler, Stalin and Pol Pot." *Globe and Mail.*

8 November 2005. Michael A. Fletcher, "Bush Defends CIA's Clandestine Prisons: 'We Do Not Torture,' President Says." *Washington Post.*

Domestic Spying

22 March 2004. Murray Polner, "FBI Notified Local Police Forces to Keep Close Tabs on People and Groups Opposed to the War and Occupation of Iraq." *Boston Globe.*

2 January 2006. Tabassum Zakaria, "Bush Defends Eavesdropping as Protecting Nation at War." *Globe and Mail.* [Two weeks earlier, the *London Times* reported that Mr Bush had authorized the National Security Agency (NSA) to monitor the international telephone calls and e-mails of US citizens suspected of links to foreign terrorists.]

5 January 2006. Jim VandeHei and Dan Eggen, "Cheney Cites Justifications for Domestic Eavesdropping: Secret Monitoring May Have Averted 9/11 He Says." *Washington Post.*

7 January 2006. Carol D. Leonnig, "Report Rebuts Bush on Spying: Domestic Action's Legality Challenged." *Washington Post.*

19 January 2006. Dan Eggen, "Congressional Agency Questions Legality of Wiretaps." *Washington Post.*

24 January 2006. Dan Eggen and Walter Pincus, "Campaign to Justify Spying Intensifies: NSA Effort Called Legal and Necessary." *Washington Post.*

29 January 2006. "Spies, Lies and Wiretaps." Editorial. *New York Times.* [Useful summary article bringing domestic spying criticisms up to date.]

10 February 2006. Peter Baker and Dan Eggen, "Intelligence Officials Play Down Importance of Case, Attribute Remarks to Politics." *Washington Post.*

29 January 2006. "Spies, Lies and Wiretaps." Editorial. *New York Times.*

7 February 2006. Adam Liptak, "In Limelight at Wiretap Hearings: 2 Laws, but Which Should Rule?" *New York Times.*

7 February 2006. Dan Eggen, "Gonzales Defends Surveillance: Senators from Both Parties Challenge Attorney General on Program." *Washington Post.*

8 February 2006. "Mr. Bush's Wiretaps." Editorial. *Globe and Mail.*

10 February 2006. Jim VandeHei, "Cheney Says NSA Spying Should Be an Election Issue." *Washington Post.*

11 February 2006. Sheryl Gay Stolberg, "Republican Speaks Up, Leading Others to Challenge Wiretaps." *New York Times.*

13 February 2006. Walter Pincus, "Spying Necessary, Democrats Say: But Harman, Daschle Question President's Legal Reach." *Washington Post.*

15 February 2006. Charles Babington, "Congressional Probe of NSA Spying Is in Doubt: White House Sways Some GOP Lawmakers." *Washington Post.*

9 March 2006. "The Death of the Intelligence Panel." Editorial. *New York Times.*

9 March 2006. Dan Eggen and Walter Pincus, "Ex-Justice Lawyer Rips Case for Spying: White House's Legal Justifications Called Weak." *Washington Post.*

12 May 2006. Colin Freeze, "Huge Database of Phone Calls a Hidden Trove of Behaviours." *Globe and Mail.*

12 May 2006. Richard Morin, "Poll: Most Americans Support NSA's Efforts." *Washington Post.*

24 June 2006. Karen De Young, "Officials Defend Financial Searches: Critics Assert Secret Program Invades Privacy." *Washington Post.*

MUSLIM FEARS

24 Dec 2002. "INS Detentions Lead Some Who Admired US to Change Opinion." *ABCNews.com.*

14 Apr 2003. Rachel L. Swarns, "Coalition Says It Will Fight Local Pursuit of Immigrants." *New York Times.*

7 June 2003. Rachel L. Swarns, "More Than 13,000 May Face Deportation." *New York Times.*

2 January 2004. Linda Greenhouse, "Justices Refuse to Review Case on Secrecy and 9/11 Detentions." *New York Times*.

13 January 2004. Linda Greenhouse, "Justices Allow Policy of Silence on 9/11 Detainees." *New York Times*.

29 January 2004. Danny Hakim, "Inquiries Begun into Handling of Detroit Terror Cases." *New York Times*.

3 April 2004. Lloyd Francis, "Caught in the Crossfire of the War on Terror." *Ottawa Citizen*.

30 July 2004. Lynette Clemetson, "Homeland Security Given Data on Arab-Americans." *New York Times*.

1 September 2004. Allan Lengel and Susan Schmidt, "U.S. to Seek Dismissal Of Terrorism Convictions." *Washington Post*.

2 September 2004. Danny Hakim, "Justice Dept. Seeks End to Its Detroit Terror Case." *New York Times*.

15 September 2004. "Capt. Yee to Receive Honorable Discharge." KOMO *Staff & News Services*.

18 December 2004. Juliet O'Neill, "The Enemy Within." *Ottawa Citizen*.

19 December 2004. Tim Golden, "How Dubious Evidence Spurred Relentless Guantanamo Spy Hunt." *New York Times*.

21 April 2005. Andrea Elliott, "5 American Muslims Suing over Detentions." *International Herald Tribune*.

GUANTANAMO

16 January 2004. Anthony Lewis, "The Justices Take on the President." *New York Times*.

16 January 2004. Neil A. Lewis, "Bush's Power to Plan Trial of Detainees is Challenged." *New York Times*.

21 January 2004. D. Mark Jackson, "Detaining the 'Enemy,' Diluting the Law." *Washington Post*.

21 April 2004. Linda Greenhouse, "Supreme Court Hears the Case of Guantanamo." *New York Times*.

22 April 2004. "Detainees' Rights." Editorial. *Boston Globe*.

28 June 2004. David Stout, "In 3 Rulings, Supreme Court Affirms Detainees' Rights to Use Courts." *New York Times*.

19 September 2004. James Risen, "35 Guantanamo Detainees Are Given to Pakistan." *New York Times*.

24 October 2004. Tim Golden, "After Terror, a Secret Rewriting of Military Law." *New York Times*.

8 November 2004. David Stout, "U.S. Judge Halts Military Trial of Qaeda Suspect at Guantanamo." *New York Times.*

17 December 2004. Dana Priest and Scott Higham, "At Guantanamo, a Prison within a Prison." *Washington Post.*

1 January 2005. Neil A. Lewis, "Fresh Details Emerge on Harsh Methods at Guantanamo." *New York Times.*

5 January 2005. Reuters, "Military to Investigate Prison Abuse Charges." *New York Times.*

27 January 2005. Associated Press, "Britain: Police Release Guantanamo Men." *New York Times.*

30 January 2005. Maureen Dowd, "Torture Chicks Gone Wild." *New York Times.*

1 February 2005. Neil A. Lewis, "Judge Extends Legal Rights for Guantanamo Detainees." *New York Times.*

2 February 2005. Associated Press, "Secret Report Questions Guantanamo Tactics." *New York Times.*

4 February 2005. Bob Herbert, "Our Battered Constitution." *New York Times.*

7 February 2005. Bob Herbert, "Stories from the Inside: Piecing Together the Horrors of Guantanamo." *New York Times.*

8 March 2005. Neil A. Lewis, "U.S. Eroding Inmates' Trust at Cuba Base, Lawyers Say." *New York Times.*

12 March 2005. Francis Harris, "U.S. Set to Clear Out up to 360 Captives." *Ottawa Citizen.*

13 March 2005. Scott Shane, "Judge Blocks the Transfer of 13 Detainees from Guantanamo." *New York Times.*

1 April 2005. Bob Herbert, "We Can't Remain Silent." *New York Times.*

2 May 2005. Neil A. Lewis and Eric Schmitt, "U.S. Inquiry Finds Abuses at Guantanamo." *International Herald Tribune.*

27 May 2005. Thomas L. Friedman, "Just Shut It Down." *New York Times.*

29 May 2005. "Further Abuse." *Washington Post.*

31 May 2005. Charlie Savage, "Push on to Clarify Rights for Detainees: Specter Wants Hearing to Establish Legal Order." *Boston Globe.*

5 June 2005. Jesse J. Holland, "Specter Eyes Detainees' Rights: Will Hold Hearings on the Treatment of Terror Suspects." *Boston Globe.*

5 June 2005. "Un-American by Any Name." Editorial. *New York Times.*

6 June 2005. Associated Press, "Biden to Take Steps to Close Prison at Guantanamo." *New York Times.*

7 June 2005. Floyd Abrams, Bob Barr, and Thomas Pickering, "Justice before Politics." *Washington Post.*

8 June 2005. Thom Shanker, "Rumsfeld Says U.S. Won't Shut Base at Guantanamo." *New York Times*.

10 June 2005. "Close Down Guantanamo." Editorial. *Globe and Mail*.

14 June 2005. Elisabeth Bumiller, "Cheney Calls Guantanamo Prison Essential." *New York Times*.

15 June 2005. Associated Press, "Pentagon Officials Defend Practices at Guantanamo Prison." *New York Times*.

15 June 2005. Brian Knowlton, "Future of Guantanamo Camp under Study, Attorney General." *New York Times*.

15 June 2005. Brian Knowlton, "Senators Criticize Practices at Guantanamo." *New York Times*.

16 June 2005. Charlie Savage, "Republican Urges Change in Detainee Rules: Says Congress Should Define Rights of Those Held at Guantanamo." *Boston Globe*.

20 June 2005. Jefferson Morley, "The Guantanamo Debate Comes Home." *Washington Post*.

22 June 2005. Douglas Jehl, "Some Republicans Seek Prison Abuse Panel." *New York Times*.

24 June 2005. Neil A. Lewis, "Interrogators Cite Doctors' Aid at Guantanamo Prison Camp." *New York Times*.

15 July 2005. "The Women of Gitmo." Editorial. *New York Times*.

16 July 2005. Neil A. Lewis, "Ruling Lets U.S. Restart Trials at Guantanamo: Victory for the White House, Court Says Administration Did Not Violate Global Law or Constitution." *New York Times*.

19 July 2005. Neil A. Lewis, "Detainee Trials to Resume Soon, Rumsfeld Says." *New York Times*.

24 July 2005. Eric Schmitt, "Cheney Working to Block Legislation on Detainees." *New York Times*.

31 July 2005. "Guantanamo Prison 'a Disgrace': Carter." *Ottawa Citizen*.

1 August 2005. Neil A. Lewis, "Two Prosecutors Faulted Trials for Detainees." *New York Times*. [Cites claims that planned tribunals were secretly arranged to get convictions.]

2 August 2005. Nick Squires, "Guantanamo Bay Trials 'Rigged' Former U.S. Prosecutors Charge." *Ottawa Citizen*.

5 August 2005. Josh White and Robin White, "Afghanistan Agrees to Accept Detainees." *Washington Post*.

6 August 2005. Tim Reid, "U.S. Plans to Transfer Detainees from Cuba: 70% of Guantanamo Inmates May Be Sent to Jails in Homelands." *Ottawa Citizen*.

10 September 2005. "Hunger Strikers Being Force Fed through Tubes." *Ottawa Citizen*.

7 October 2005. Estanislao Oziewicz, "U.S. Prisoners are Force-Fed, Amnesty Says: Terrorism Suspects Simply Seeking Media Play, Guantanamo Official Counters." *Globe and Mail.*

18 October 2005. Michael Kirk, writer, producer, director, "The Torture Question: In Fighting the War on Terror, How Far Should the United States Be Willing to Go to Protect Itself?" Television documentary. 90 minutes. PBS, *Frontline.*

14 November 2005. M. Gregg Bloche and Jonathan H. Marks, "Doing Unto Others as They Did Unto Us." *New York Times.*

14 November 2005. Shankar Vedantam, "Medical Experts Debate Role in Facilitating Interrogations." *Washington Post.*

14 January 2006. Paul Koring, "The Uneasy Mix Called Guantanamo: Bush's War on Terrorism Has Tripled Population, Turning Sleepy U.S. Base into a Legal Twilight Zone." *Globe and Mail.*

15 January 2006. "A General's Dishonor." Editorial. *Washington Post.*

9 February 2006. Tim Golden, "Tough U.S. Steps in Hunger Strike at Camp in Cuba." *New York Times.*

17 February 2006. Paul Koring, "White House Rejects UN Call to Shut down Guantanamo: Report Called 'Rehash' of Old Allegations and a 'Discredit' to World Organization." *Globe and Mail.*

20 May 2006. Colum Lynch, "Military Prison's Closure Is Urged: U.N. Panel Faults Detention Policies." *Washington Post.*

11 June 2006. James Risen and Tim Golden, "3 Prisoners Commit Suicide at Guantanamo." *New York Times.* [This is an important summary article on Guantanamo.]

12 June 2006. Alan Freeman, "Guantanamo Suicides Stir Fresh Outrage: Critics Demand the Facility Be Shut Down; One U.S. Official Calls the Deaths 'PR Move'." *Globe and Mail.* [This gives interesting figures on Guantanamo.]

22 June 2006. "Close Guantanamo? Yes, But Keep in Mind: It's Not the Main Problem." Editorial. *Washington Post.* [Advocates new rules for terrorism prisoners, arguing that they "should receive Red Cross visits; their detention should be governed by law, with the right of review and appeal to independent judges."]

TORTURE

Books

Danner, Mark. *Torture and Truth: America, Abu Ghraib, and the War on Terror.* New York: New York Review of Books, 2005.

Greenberg, Karen J., and Joshua L. Dratel, eds. *The Torture Papers: The Road to Abu Ghraib*. Introduction by Anthony Lewis. Cambridge, UK: Cambridge University Press, 2005.

Hersh, Seymour M. *Chain of Command: The Road from 9/11 to Abu Ghraib*. New York: Harper Collins, 2004.

Levinson, Sandford, ed. *Torture: A Collection*. Oxford: Oxford University Press, 2005.

Mackey, Chris, with Greg Miller. *The Interrogators: Inside the Secret War Against Al-Qaeda*. London: Murray, 2005.

Risen, James. *State of War: The Secret History of the CIA and The Bush Administration*. New York: Free Press, 2006.

Rose, David. *Guantanamo: The American War on Human Rights*. London: Faber and Faber, 2004.

Strasser, Stephen, ed. *The Abu Ghraib Investigations: The Official Report of the Independent Panel and Pentagon on the Shocking Prisoner Abuse in Iraq*. New York: Public Affairs, 2005.

Articles

12 March 2002. Duncan Campbell, "U.S. Sends Suspects to Face Torture." *The Guardian* (London, UK).

9 January 2003. "Is Torture Ever Justified?" *Economist*.

27 December 2002. "Torture Is Not an Option." Editorial. *Washington Post*.

4 March 2003. Tu Thanh Ha, "Mohammed Faces Tough to Torturous Interrogation." *Globe and Mail*.

24 October 2004. Tim Golden, "After Terror, a Secret Rewriting of Military Law." *New York Times*.

30 December 2004. Andrew Rosenthal, "Legal Breach: The Government's Attorneys and Abu Ghraib." *New York Times*.

16 December 2004. Neil A. Lewis, "Ex-Military Lawyers Object to Bush Cabinet Nominee." *New York Times*.

1 January 2005. Neil A. Lewis, "Justice Dept. Toughens Rule on Torture." *New York Times*.

1 January 2005. R. Jeffrey Smith and Dan Eggen, "US Revises Definition of Torture." *Boston Globe*.

3 January 2005. Neil A. Lewis, "Gonzales Is Likely to Face Hard Questions in Hearings." *New York Times*.

5 January 2005. David Johnston and Neil A. Lewis, "Bush's Counsel Sought Ruling about Torture." *New York Times*.

6 January 2005. Annotated listing of all the memos designed to "avoid constraints against mistreatment and torture of detainees." *New York Times*.

6 January 2005. Mark Danner, "We Are All Torturers Now." *New York Times*.

7 January 2005. Bob Herbert, "Promoting Torture's Promoter." *New York Times*.

7 January 2005. "Mr. Gonzales's Testimony." *Washington Post*.

26 January 2005. "The Wrong Attorney General." Editorial. *New York Times*.

7 May 2005. David Stout, "U.S. Tells U.N. That It Continues to Oppose Torture in Any Situation." *New York Times*.

23 May 2005. "Patterns of Abuse." *New York Times*.

12 June 2005. Joseph Lelyveld, "Interrogating Ourselves." *New York Times Magazine*. [An extensive article on whether torture should be applied and under what restrictions – assesses what works and what doesn't.]

30 July 2005. "The Roots of Prisoner Abuse." *New York Times*.

2 August 2005. Nick Squires, "Guantanamo Bay Trials 'Rigged' Former U.S. Prosecutors Charge." *Ottawa Citizen*.

3 August 2005. Josh White, "Document's Tell of Brutal Improvisation by GIs: Interrogated General's Sleeping Bag Death, CIA's Use of Secret Iraqi Squad Are among Details." *Washington Post*.

8 August 2005. Tim Golden, "Abuse Cases Open Command Issues at Army Prison." *New York Times*.

24 September 2005. Eric Schmitt, "3 in 82nd Airborne Say Beating Iraqi Prisoners Was Routine." *New York Times*.

6 October 2005. Charles Babington and Shailagh Murray, "Senate Supports Interrogation Limits." *Washington Post*.

8 October 2005. "Binding the Hands of the Torturers." *New York Times*. [Ninety senators voted "to bring America's chain of military prison camps under the rule of law."]

18 October 2005. Michael Kirk, writer, producer, director, "The Torture Question: In Fighting the War on Terror, How Far Should the United States Be Willing to Go to Protect Itself?" Television documentary. 90 minutes. PBS, *Frontline*.

25 October 2005. R. Jeffrey Smith and Josh White, "Cheney Plan Exempts CIA from Barring Abuse of Detainees." *Washington Post*. [Counter-proposal to ninety-senator vote of 8 October 2005.]

26 October 2005. "Legalized Torture, Reloaded." Editorial. *New York Times*. [Cheney asked McCain to support mistreatment and torture of prisoners "as long as that behaviour was part of 'counterterrorism operations conducted abroad' and they were not American citizens." Editorial says, "That would

neatly legalize the illegal prisons the C.I.A. is said to be operating around the world and obviate the need for torture outsourcing known as extraordinary rendition."]

26 October 2005. "Vice-President for Torture." Editorial. *Washington Post.*

7 November 2005. Dan Froomkin, "Cheney's Dark Side Is Showing: Vice-President Cheney Is on a Passionate, Mostly Secret and Sometimes Lonely Campaign to Prevent Congress from Approving Prohibitions against Torture." *Washington Post.*

8 November 2005. Michael A. Fletcher, "Bush Defends CIA's Clandestine Prisons: 'We Do Not Torture,' President Says." *Washington Post.*

9 November 2005. Lolita C. Baldor, "New Rules on Detainees Issued: Pentagon Seeks Humane Treatment." *Boston Globe.*

9 December 2005. Sarah Lyall, "Britain's Top Court Rules Information Gotten by Torture Is Never Admissible Evidence." *New York Times.*

19 January 2006. Estanislao Oziewicz, "U.S. Interrogation Tactics Slammed." *Globe and Mail.* [Cites a Human Rights Watch report.]

24 January 2006. Jan Silva, "Investigator: U.S. 'Outsourced' Torture." *Yahoo!News.*

24 January 2006. Josh White, "Army Interrogator Reprimanded in Iraqi's Death." *Washington Post.* [Case of an Iraqi general who died under interrogation. The interrogator was issued a reprimand by a military jury.]

25 January 2006. Estanilao Oziewicz, "Europeans Likely Aware of Torture, Report Says: Swiss Official Says Evidence Suggests That Governments Knew about U.S. 'Outsourcing.'" *Globe and Mail.*

19 March 2006. Eric Schmitt and Carolyn Marshall, "In Secret Unit's 'Black Room,' a Grim Portrait of U.S. Abuse." *New York Times.*

FAILURE TO FIND SENIOR OFFICERS RESPONSIBLE

29 April 2005. Bob Herbert, "The Big Shots Walk Free." *International Herald Tribune.*

3 May 2005. "An Indefensible Outcome." Editorial. *Boston Globe.*

3 May 2005. Eugene Robinson, "Torture Whitewash." *Washington Post.*

12 May 2005. R. Jeffrey Smith, "Abu Ghraib Officer Gets Reprimand: Non-Court-Martial Punishment for Dereliction of Duty Includes Fine." *Washington Post.*

14 July 2005. Josh White, "Abu Ghraib Tactics Were First Used at Guantanamo." *Washington Post.*

28 July 2005. Josh White, "Army General Advised Using Dogs at Abu Ghraib, Officer Testifies." *Washington Post.*

10 September 2005. "Abu Ghraib Unresolved." Editorial. *New York Times.* [Argues that it is "not acceptable that a few low-level reservists go to prison," while seniors are promoted.]

12 January 2006. Josh White, "General Asserts Right on Self-Incrimination in Iraq Abuse Cases." *Washington Post.*

15 January 2006. "A General's Dishonor." Editorial. *Washington Post.*

24 January 2006. Josh White, "Army Interrogator Reprimanded in Iraqi's Death." *Washington Post.* [Case of an Iraqi general who died under interrogation. The interrogator was issued a reprimand by a military jury.]

22 March 2006. Eric Schmitt, "Army Dog Handler Is Convicted in Detainee Abuse at Abu Ghraib." *New York Times.*

23 March 2006. "The Joy of Being Blameless." Editorial. *New York Times.* [Reports that lower ranks were punished and senior officers promoted.]

29 April 2006. Ann Scott Tyson, "No. 2 Abu Ghraib Interrogation Officer Charged." *Washington Post.*

SECRET PRISONS AND GHOST PRISONERS

26 December 2002. Dana Priest and Barton Gellman, "U.S. Decries Abuse but Defends Interrogations: 'Stress and Duress' Tactics Used on Terrorism Suspects Held in Secret Overseas Facilities." *Washington Post.*

8 March 2003. Don Van Natta, "Questioning Terror Suspects in a Dark and Surreal World." *New York Times.*

11 May 2004. Dana Priest and Joe Stephens, "Secret World of U.S. Interrogation." *Washington Post.*

26 October 2004. "The CIA's Disappeared." *Washington Post.*

10 February 2005. Seymour M. Hersh, "The Gray Zone: How a Secret Pentagon Program Came to Abu Ghraib." *New Yorker.*

12 March 2005. Josh White, "2 Died After '02 Beatings by U.S. Soldiers." *Washington Post.*

16 March 2005. Douglas Jehl and Eric Schmitt, "U.S. Military Says 26 Inmate Deaths May Be Homicide." *New York Times.*

3 April 2005. Robert Weller, "Records Shed Light on Alleged Beating: Imprisoned Iraqi Was Abused, Died." *Boston Globe.*

3 May 2005. "An Indefensible Outcome." Editorial. *Boston Globe.*

20 May 2005. Tim Golden, "In U.S. Report, Brutal Details of 2 Afghan Inmates' Deaths." *New York Times.*

22 May 2005. Tim Golden, "Abuse Inquiry Bogged Down in Afghanistan." *New York Times.*

23 May 2005. "Patterns of Abuse." *New York Times.*

2 November 2005. Dana Priest, "CIA Holds Terror Suspects in Secret Prisons: Debate Is Growing within Agency about Legality and Morality of Overseas System Set Up after 9/11." *Washington Post*. [Seminal article revealing existence of secret prisons in eastern Europe, referred to as "black sites."]

3 November 2005. "Rebellion against Abuse." *Washington Post*.

4 November 2005. Alan Freeman, "EU Eyes Alleged CIA Jails." *Globe and Mail*.

7 November 2005. Dan Froomkin, "Cheney's Dark Side Is Showing: Vice-President Cheney Is on a Passionate, Mostly Secret and Sometimes Lonely Campaign to Prevent Congress from Approving Prohibitions against Torture." *Washington Post*.

6 December 2005. Paul Koring, "Rice Talks Tough to Europeans: Allies Knew about Secret Detentions, Other Anti-Terror Measures, U.S. Official Insists." *Globe and Mail*.

7 December 2005. Joel Brinkley, "Rice Is Challenged in Europe over Secret Prisons." *New York Times*.

8 June 2006. Craig Whitlock, "European Probe Finds Signs of CIA-Run Secret Prisons." *Washington Post*.

RENDITION

29 November 2004. Farah Stockman, "Terror Suspects' Torture Claims Have Mass. Link: Secrecy Shrouds Transfer Jet." *Boston Globe*.

14 February 2005. Jane Mayer, "Outsourcing Torture: The Secret History of America's 'Extraordinary Rendition' Program." *New Yorker*.

6 March 2005. Douglas Jehl and David Johnston, "Rule Change Lets C.I.A. Freely Send Suspects Abroad to Jails." *New York Times*.

8 March 2005. "Torture Proxy." Editorial. *New York Times*.

12 March 2005. Edward J. Markey, "US Must Stop 'Outsourcing' Torture." *Boston Globe*.

17 March 2005. Jeff Jacoby, "Where's the Outrage on Torture?" *Boston Globe*.

17 March 2005. Dana Priest, "CIA's Assurances on Transferred Suspects Doubted: Prisoners Say Countries Break No-Torture Pledges." *Washington Post*.

24 March 2005. Farah Stockman, "US Handling of Terror Suspects Questioned: Ex-Envoy Says Dozens Are Sent to Uzbekistan and at Risk of Torture." *Boston Globe*.

31 May 2005. Scott Shane, with Stephen Grey and Margot Wilson, "C.I.A. Expanding Terror Battle under Guise of Charter Flights." *New York Times*.

THE MAHER ARAR CASE

5 November 2003. Maher Arar, "I Am Not a Terrorist." *Globe and Mail*. [Consisting of excerpts from a prepared statement that Arar delivered on 4 November 2003 in Ottawa upon his return from captivity in Syria.] *Globe and Mail*.

5 November 2003. DeNeen L. Brown and Dana Priest, "Deported Terror Suspect Details Torture in Syria." *Washington Post*.

6 November 2003. Jeff Sallot, "At Home, Arar Still Haunted by Anger and Fear." *Globe and Mail*.

6 November 2003. Jeffrey Simpson, "Paul Martin Should Look into the Arar Outrage." *Globe and Mail*.

8 November 2003. Robert Fife, "Canada Had Hand in 'Dirty Work': Arar – Man Jailed and Tortured in Syria Accuses RCMP and CSIS of Playing a Role in His Deportation." *Ottawa Citizen*.

8 November 2003. Julliet O'Neill, "Canada's Dossier on Maher Arar." *Ottawa Citizen*.

15 November 2003. Clifford Krauss, "Qaeda Pawn, U.S. Calls Him. Victim, He Calls Himself." *New York Times*.

30 December 2003. Robert Fife, "Officials Link Arar to Qaeda Camp." *Canada.com news*.

22 January 2004. "A Black, Black Day: RCMP Raid the Home and Office of a Citizen Reporter over the Maher Arar Case and Unleash a Storm of Anger." Editorial. *Ottawa Citizen*.

23 January 2004. Mark Kennedy, Mike Blanchfield, and Anne Dawson, "O'Neill Clearly No Criminal: PM; 'We Are Not a Police State,' Martin Insists; Charges Now Unlikely." *Ottawa Citizen*.

24 January 2004. Bruce Garvey, Mark Blanchfield. and Jack Aubry, "Liberals Call for Arar Inquiry." *Ottawa Citizen*.

27 January 2004. Jack Aubry, "Arar Denied Full Access to Own File." *Ottawa Citizen*.

29 January 2004. Jeff Sallot, "Judicial Inquiry Set into Arar Affair." *Globe and Mail*.

8 July 2004. Colin Freeze, "RCMP in Contact with U.S. as Arar Held, Report Says." *Globe and Mail*.

25 September 2004. Jeff Sallot, "Mounties Bungled Arar File." *Globe and Mail*.

27 November 2004. Colin Freeze, "Mounties Warned against Release of Arar." *Globe and Mail*.

21 December 2004. Sean Gordon, "Censors Black out CSIS Report on Arar." *Ottawa Citizen*.

14 February 2005. Jane Mayer, "Outsourcing Torture: The Secret History of America's 'Extraordinary Rendition' Program." *New Yorker*.

3 April 2005. James Gordon, "All Canadians Could Face Arar's Plight: Law Allows U.S. to Deport Anyone to a Third Country, Not Just Dual Citizens." *Ottawa Citizen*.

31 May 2005. Michael Den Tandt, "Graham Says He Was in Dark: Testifying at Arar Inquiry, Minister Says He Was Often Told Little about the Case." *Globe and Mail*.

31 May 2005. Scott Shane, with Stephen Grey and Margot Wilson, "C.I.A. Expanding Terror Battle under Guise of Charter Flights." *New York Times*.

2 June 2005. Neco Cockburn, "Jail Arar, U.S. Told Canada: Senator – Government Denies U.S. Issued Demand to Canadian Officials." *Ottawa Citizen*.

2 June 2005. Michael Den Tandt, "Ottawa Refused U.S. Appeal to Jail Arar: Canadians Cited Charter Protection in Rejecting Request to Press Charges." *Globe and Mail*.

3 June 2005. Neco Cockburn, "Graham Tells Arar Inquiry He's Sorry – Case Could Have Been Handled 'Differently': Ex-Foreign Affairs Boss." *Ottawa Citizen*.

3 June 2005. Michael Den Tandt, "Graham Expresses Personal Regret over Arar's Ordeal." *Globe and Mail*.

4 June 2005. Neco Cockburn, "CSIS Wanted Arar Kept in Syria: Memo – Letter Reveals 'Paralysis' of Federal Agencies, Lawyer Says." *Ottawa Citizen*.

4 June 2005. Michael Den Tandt and Brian Laghi, "CSIS Wanted Arar Kept in Syria, Memo Showed." *Globe and Mail*.

4 June 2005. James Gordon and Neco Cockburn, "Judge Backs Citizen's Bid to See Names on Secret Warrants." *Ottawa Citizen*.

26 June 2005. Doug Struck, "Inquiry Exposes Canada's Role in 'Renditions.'" *Washington Post*.

30 June 2005. Michael Den Tandt, "9/11 Crisis Led RCMP to Share Its Secrets: Sensitive Details Offered to Other Nations, Including Syria, Mountie Tells Arar Probe." *Globe and Mail*.

16 July 2005. James Gordon, "Terror Suspects Used Spy-Like Methods: RCMP – Counter-Surveillance Described in Newly Released Documents." *Ottawa Citizen*.

28 July 2005. Neco Cockburn, "Arar's File Exchanged during Post-9/11 Police Cooperation: Foreign Affairs Kept Partly out of Loop on Deportation Case." *Ottawa Citizen*.

28 July 2005. Michael Den Tandt, "RCMP Not Told to Jettison Rules, Arar Probe Hears: Retired Mountie Contradicts Earlier Testimony on Information Sharing Policies." *Globe and Mail*.

29 July 2005. Neco Cockburn, "Arar Inquiry Reveals Rift at RCMP: Mounties' Handling of Case Shows 'Staggering Lack of Connection.'" *Ottawa Citizen.*

30 July 2005. Michael Den Tandt, "Ottawa Aware of Torture in Syria, Probe Told: Memo on Another Canadian's Ordeal Circulated before Arar Arrest, Envoy Says." *Globe and Mail.*

2 August 2005. James Gordon, "Hunting Al Qaeda: Inside the RCMP's Search for a Terror Cell – Police Operation Shrouded in Mystery." *Ottawa Citizen.*

10 August 2005. Campbell Clark, "Rifts in RCMP Re-Emerge at Arar Inquiry." *Globe and Mail.*

23 August 2005. Bill Curry, "Mountie Describes Big Trouble on Arar File: Sergeant Cites a Lack of Communication and Professionalism by Investigation Team." *Globe and Mail.*

23 August 2005. James Gordon, "Mounties Kept Bosses 'Out of Loop": Officers Also Failed to Share Info with Foreign Agencies, Arar Inquiry Hears." *Ottawa Citizen.*

24 August 2005. Bill Curry, "Mountie Didn't Believe Arar Would Go to Syria: Inquiry Hears New RCMP Details Leading up to the Oct. 8 Deportation." *Globe and Mail.*

24 August 2005. James Gordon, "Mountie Never Suspected U.S. Planned to Deport Arar: Officer 'Never Thought Syria Was in Play.'" *Ottawa Citizen.*

25 August 2005. Bill Curry, "Official Disputes Testimony over Arar: Statements that CSIS Wanted Arar Kept in Syria Denied Bureaucrat." *Globe and Mail.*

25 August 2005. James Gordon, "CSIS Wanted to Keep Arar in Syria, Inquiry Told: Spy Agency Allegedly Said It Lacked 'Resources to Watch Him in Canada.'" *Ottawa Citizen.*

26 August 2005. Bill Curry, "CSIS Had Concerns over Arar's Release: Spy Agency Felt Case Was a 'Hot Potato' but Denies Wanting to Leave Him in Syria." *Globe and Mail.*

26 August 2005. James Gordon, "Deputy Director Denies CSIS Wanted Arar Kept in Syria: Jack Hooper Rejects Claim Spy Agency Interfered in Bid to Secure Arar's Release." *Ottawa Citizen.*

27 August 2005. Jeff Sallot, "Abdullah Almalki Tells His Story – He Was Thrown in a Syrian Jail on a Family Visit – He Says He Was Tortured and Canada's Complicit – Some Say He's a Terrorist, but is That the Point?" *Globe and Mail.*

29 August 2005. Jeff Sallot, "Road to Damascus began with CSIS." *Globe and Mail.*

29 August 2005. "What Canada Knew about Arar's Treatment." Editorial. *Globe and Mail.*

30 August 2005. Bill Curry, "Arar's Allegations Are Made Up, Consular Official Insists – Motives Unclear, Ex-Envoy Says." *Globe and Mail.*

30 August 2005. Jeff Sallot, "Torture Tactics Indefensible, Cotler Says." *Globe
and Mail.*

31 August 2005. Tim Naumetz, "Former Diplomat Grilled at Arar Inquiry:
Probe Asks Official Who Visited Arar Why He Didn't Flag Prison Mistreatment." *Ottawa Citizen.*

31 August 2005. Alex Neve, "Canada's Syrian Connection." *Globe and Mail.*

1 September 2005. Bill Curry, "Consul Challenged on His Arar Story: Martel,
Who Had Called Civil Suit a 'Big Lie,' Was Last Scheduled Witness." *Globe
and Mail.*

1 September 2005. Tim Naumetz, "Arar Torture Claim Was Censored: Consul
Insists Ottawa Initially Denied Abuse, Says Quote in Report Refers to Someone Else." *Ottawa Citizen.*

2 September 2005. Bill Curry, "Investigate Canadian Link to Syrian Torture,
Groups Say." *Globe and Mail.*

3 September 2005. Bill Curry, "Martin Declines to Comment on Arar: New
Cases of Canadians Detained in Syria Prompt Calls for Broader Investigation." *Globe and Mail.*

8 September 2005. Daniel Leblanc, "Calls Grow for Torture Inquiry." *Globe
and Mail.*

9 September 2005. Jeff Sallot, "Mounties Were Reined in after Arar Claims:
Timing of Directive Coincidence, Easter Claims." *Globe and Mail.*

16 September 2005. Jeff Sallot, "McLellan Contradicts CSIS on Torture Policy." *Globe and Mail.*

19 September 2005. Jim Brown, "No Apology for Arar Deportation, Wilkins
Says: U.S. Ambassador Defends Action." *Globe and Mail.*

20 September 2005. "A Man Is Tortured and the U.S. Shrugs." Editorial.
Globe and Mail.

28 October 2005. Jeff Sallot, "Other Victims Found Credible." *Globe and Mail.*

28 October 2005. Stephen Toope, "If He Could Have Figured out Some Way
to Kill Himself, He Would Have Done It." *Globe and Mail.*

AMERICAN CITIZENS AS "ENEMY COMBATANTS":
PADILLA AND HAMDI

20 June 2002. Tom Jackman and Dan Eggen, "'Combatants' Lack Rights, U.S.
Argues." *Washington Post.*

8 January 2004. Eric Lichtblau, "U.S. Reasserts Right to Declare Citizens to Be
Enemy Combatants." *New York Times.*

10 January 2004. Linda Greenhouse, "Justices to Hear Case of Citizen Held as Enemy." *New York Times*.

21 January 2004. D. Mark Jackson, "Detaining the 'Enemy,' Diluting the Law." *Washington Post*.

11 February 2004. "U.S. to Allow 'Enemy Combatant' to See a Lawyer." *New York Times*.

28 March 2004. "Undermining Due Process." *Boston Globe*.

26 April 2004. "'Enemy Combatants' in Court." *New York Times*.

29 April 2004. Linda Greenhouse, "Court Hears Case on U.S. Detainees." *New York Times*.

23 September 2004. Eric Lichtblau, "U.S., Bowing to Court, to Free 'Enemy Combatant.'" *New York Times*.

1 March 2005. Neil A. Lewis, "Judge Says U.S. Terrorist Can't Be Held as an Enemy Combatant." *New York Times*.

23 November 2005. Paul Koring and Alan Freeman, "U.S. 'Dirty Bomb' Suspect to Face Unrelated Charges." *Globe and Mail*.

2 January 2006. "The 4th Circuit v. Mr. Bush." *Washington Post*.

SECRECY

27 November 2001. Edward Lazarus, "The Bush Administration and Secrecy: Limiting What We Can Know about the Government, while Expanding What It Can Know about Us." *Findlaw's Legal Commentary*.

18 November 2002. Neil A. Lewis, "U.S. Says Revealing Names Would Aid Al Qaeda." *New York Times*.

28 March 2003. "Secrecy: The Bush Byword." Editorial. *New York Times*.

9 July 2003. "Wrestling for the Truth of 9/11." *New York Times*.

17 June 2003. Associated Press, "Names of 9/11 Detainees Can Remain Secret, Court Rules." *New York Times*.

17 June 2003. Paul Krugman, "Dereliction of Duty." *New York Times*.

3 September 2005. "Secrecy in U.S. Government on the Rise, Report Finds." *Globe and Mail*. [Eighty-one per cent more information was classified than in 2001].

THE SHAPE OF THINGS TO COME

14 February 2003. American Civil Liberties Union, "Interested Persons Memo: Section-by-Section Analysis of Justice Department Draft 'Domestic Security Enhancement Act of 2003, Also Known as PATRIOT ACT II.'"

21 February 2003. Rajeev Goyle, "Patriot Act Sequel Worse Than Original." *Baltimore Sun.*

27 February 2003. David Cole, "Patriot Act's Big Brother." *The Nation.*

2 April 2003. Matt Welch, "Tell Us How We're Doing: Get Ready for PATRIOT II." *AlertNet.*

15 January 2005. Glen McGregor, "Using the 'Salvador Option' in Iraq." *Ottawa Citizen.*

25 January 2005. Douglas Jehl and Eric Schmitt, "Reports on Pentagon's New Spy Units Set off Questions in Congress." *New York Times.*

7 May 2005. David Stout, "U.S. Tells U.N. That It Continues to Oppose Torture in Any Situation." *New York Times.*

23 May 2005. "Patterns of Abuse." *New York Times.*

25 May 2005. Paisley Dodds, "Amnesty International Takes Aim at U.S." *Washington Post.*

26 May 2005. Alan Cowell, "U.S. 'Thumbs Its Nose' at Rights, Amnesty Says." *New York Times.*

5 June 2005. "Un-American by Any Name." Editorial. *New York Times.*

5 June 2005. Jesse J. Holland, "Specter Eyes Detainees' Rights: Will Hold Hearings on the Treatment of Terror Suspects." *Boston Globe.*

ABUSE AND LOSS OF CIVIL LIBERTIES

Human Rights First. *Assessing the New Normal: Liberty and Security for the Post-September 11 United States.* 18 September 2003.

– *Assessing the New Normal.* Report, March 2003 to September 2003.

– *Imbalance of Powers.* Report, September 2002 to March 2003.

– *A Year of Loss.* Report, September 2001 to September 2002.

16 November 2001. Helen Thomas, "President Bush and John Ashcroft Trample the Bill of Rights." *Hearst Newspapers.*

9 March 2002. Anthony Lewis, "Taking Our Liberties." *New York Times.*

8 September 2002. "Reflecting on Rights Lost in the Past Year." *Star-Telegram* (Fortworth).

11–17 September 2002. Alisa Solomon, "Things We Lost in the Fire: While the Ruins of the World Trade Center Smoldered, the Bush Administration Launched an Assault on the Constitution." *Village Voice.*

23 November 2002. Eric Lichtblau, "Justice Dept. Acts to Use New Power in Terror Inquiries." *New York Times.*

1 December 2002. Charles Lane, "In Terror War, 2nd Track for Suspects." *Washington Post.*

21 February 2003. Rajeev Goyle, "Patriot Act Sequel Worse Than Original." *Baltimore Sun.*

27 February 2003. David Cole, "Patriot Act's Big Brother." *The Nation.*

6 April 2003. Eric Lichtblau, "Statute Becomes Justice Department's Weapon of Choice." *New York Times.*

23 April 2003. Eric Lichtblau, "'No Fly' List Is Challenged in a Lawsuit." *New York Times.*

2 May 2003. Eric Lichtblau and James Risen, "Broad Domestic Role Asked for C.I.A. and the Pentagon." *New York Times.*

21 May 2003. Eric Lichtblau, "Justice Dept. Lists Use of New Power to Fight Terror." *New York Times.*

25 May 2003. "Power, Ever More Power." Editorial. *Truthout.*

3 June 2003. "The Abusive Detentions of Sept. 11." *New York Times.*

3 June 2003. "Excerpt of Analysis of Detention of Foreigners after 9/11 Attacks." *New York Times.*

3 June 2003. Eric Lichtblau, "U.S. Report Faults the Roundup of Illegal Immigrants after 9/11." *New York Times.*

5 June 2003. Eric Lichtblau, "Ashcroft Defends Detentions as Immigrants Recount Toll." *New York Times.*

6 June 2003. Eric Lichtblau, "Ashcroft Seeks More Power to Pursue Terror Suspects." *New York Times.*

8 June 2003. Adam Liptak, "The Pursuit of Immigrants in America after Sept. 11." *New York Times.*

13 June 2003. Eric Lichtblau, "U.S. Will Tighten Rules on Holding Terror Suspects." *New York Times.*

16 June 2003. Frank J. Murray, "Patriot Act of 2001 Casts a Wide Net." *Truthout.*

19 June 2003. Michael Moss, "False Terrorism Tips to F.B.I. Uproot the Lives of Suspects." *New York Times.*

1 July 2003. Dean Schabner, "Patriot Revolution? Cities from Cambridge to Berkeley Reject Anti-Terror Measure." *ABCNews.com.*

21 July 2003. Philip Shenon, "Report on USA Patriot Act Alleges Civil Rights Violations." *New York Times.*

7 November 2005. Associated Press, "Senators Question Terrorism Inquiries." *Washington Post.* [Expresses concern that the FBI is pushing limits to "retrieve private phone and financial records of ordinary people" – 30,000 alleged cases per year.]